Public Procurement Reforms in Africa

Challenges in Institutions and Governance

Christine Léon de Mariz, Claude Ménard, and
Bernard Abeillé

T0323381

UNIVERSITY PRESS

OXFORD

UNIVERSITY PRESS

Great Clarendon Street, Oxford, OX2 6DP,
United Kingdom

Oxford University Press is a department of the University of Oxford.
It furthers the University's objective of excellence in research, scholarship,
and education by publishing worldwide. Oxford is a registered trade mark of
Oxford University Press in the UK and in certain other countries

First Edition published in 2014
Impression: 2

Published in the United States of America by Oxford University Press
198 Madison Avenue, New York, NY 10016, United States of America

British Library Cataloguing in Publication Data
Data available

Library of Congress Control Number: 2014934194

ISBN 978-0-19-871491-0

Printed and bound by
CPI Group (UK) Ltd, Croydon, CR0 4YY

'In identifying the tax system as the intestines of the state, Joseph Schumpeter seriously neglected the other side of the government budget. Building an effective state requires not just resources, but the ability to spend those resources in the interests of society. This book is a seminal study of what it takes to do that in Africa. An essential for anyone trying to understand how to build modern states.'

James A. Robinson, Harvard University

'This important book deftly analyses African public procurement, where weak public institutions, including ineffectual enforcement and corruption, have defeated the aims and ambitions of countless aid projects. The book's novel approach fills a major gap in our understanding of this thorny problem, and draws actionable insights by comparing the few successful and many failed reforms.'

Mary M. Shirley, President, Ronald Coase Institute

'This important new book is a model study of how to reform public policy-making in developing countries. Most reform efforts spend too little time on engineering the micro-institutional details necessary to give the relevant parties incentives to implement the reform. Focusing on public procurement in sub-Saharan Africa, the authors construct the institutional details necessary for successful reform.'

Barry Weingast, Stanford University

To our families, for their support and their patience

Acknowledgements

Our special thanks go to all the participants to the seminars, workshops, meetings, and discussions, and to the authors of thousands of emails, who provided us with information, documentation, comments, and critiques in relation to our project. We also owe a special debt of gratitude to all the decisionmakers and representatives of governments and international/bilateral organizations who helped us to learn so much about the development of public procurement over the years. They all contributed greatly to the drafting of the book. We would also like to acknowledge and applaud our third author, Christine, for her courage and dedication to continue working on the book after her tragic accident in Haiti in 2011. Lastly, we would like to thank Adam Swallow and Aimee Wright at Oxford University Press for their support and suggestions, and Liisa Roponen, who did much to polish our style; they all contributed to improve the contents of the book.

Contents

Contents

List of Figures

List of Tables

List of Boxes

List of Acronyms

AAA	analytic and advisory activities
AfDB	African Development Bank
CAS	country assistance strategy
COMESA	Common Market of Eastern and Southern Africa
CPAR	country procurement assessment review
CPI	corruption perception index
CPIA	country policy and institutional assessment
CTBs	central tender boards
DAC	Development Assistance Committee of the OECD
EC	European Commission
EU	European Union
ESW	economic and sector work
GDP	gross domestic product
GNI	gross national income
GPA	Government Procurement Agreement
HIPCs	heavily indebted poor countries
ICB	international competitive bidding
ICRG	international country risk guide
IDA	International Development Association
IDS	international debt statistics
IMF	International Monetary Fund
IO	industrial organization
LIB	limited international bidding
NIE	new institutional economics
NCB	national competitive bidding
PFM	public finance management
PPRPI	public procurement reform progress index
PRA	procurement regulatory authorities
PRSC	poverty reduction support credit
PRSP	poverty reduction strategy papers
PUIs	project implementing units
SSA	sub-Saharan Africa
UEMOA	Union Economique et Monétaire Ouest-Africaine

UNCITRAL   United Nations Commission on International Trade Law
WAEMU   West African Economic and Monetary Union
WB   World Bank
WGI   world governance indicators
WTO   World Trade Organization

Introduction

Institutional reforms and their contribution to development and growth have been the subject of numerous studies as well as the source of many challenges over the last two decades.[1] This renewed interest in institutional changes has put intellectually difficult and politically sensitive issues high on the agenda of researchers and policymakers. What forces are pushing towards reform? How much do we know about the conditions that determine the success or failure of reforms? What organizational arrangements are needed to make modifications to the rules of the game sustainable? What are the limits to the transfer of reforms? Are international organizations and foreign institutions of any help in the process of change? What support, if any, can they provide to improve public governance?

This book attempts to address these questions from an economic perspective based on the experience of the public procurement reforms carried out in sub-Saharan Africa (SSA) since the late 1990s. More specifically we carefully examine the measures taken by SSA countries to modernize their existing procurement institutions and the organizations put in place for their implementation. Using an original dataset, we also explore the gap between the expectations and the accomplishment achieved in the difficult process of reform. Through our analysis of reforms implemented within a relatively short period of time in several different countries, each with a distinct institutional background, we hope to shed light on the interaction between institutional and organizational changes. In doing so, we follow the distinction introduced by Douglass North, the Nobel Prize winner: 'Institutions are the rules of the game in a society or, more formally, are the humanly devised constraints that shape human interaction' (North 1993: 3), while organizations are 'the players of the game' (ibid.: 5) and as such develop strategies that make them central to institutional changes.

Taking advantage of an in-depth examination of the institutions that support public procurement reform, our analysis identifies several factors that

---

[1] Influential contributions and challenges can be found in North (1990b; 2005), Engermann et al. (2000), Acemoglu et al. (2001), Rodrik (2004), Laffont (2005), Shirley (2008), and Acemoglu and Robinson (2012), among others.

underlie the difficulties in changing institutions and in creating new modes of governance because of institutional environment constraints. On a more positive side, we also highlight the institutional and organizational conditions that explain why some countries outperform others, thus hopefully indicating the future path for successful reform. From a scientific perspective, we also hope to push the institutional issues at stake in public procurement reform to a more prominent position on the agenda of economists, social scientists, and policymakers.

1 Why Public Procurement?

Public expenditures, of which public procurement is a substantial component, have been at the forefront of economic and political debates over recent decades, due to financial resource constraints and the controversy over the efficiency of government expenses. Public procurement is the governmental purchase of goods and services from the private sector and/or from state-owned enterprises. Because of the significance of these expenses in the GDP, public procurement has become a strategic issue, providing indicators and measures of the quality of resource management and public governance. International organizations and donors have put increasing pressure on developing countries to reform their procurement systems. In that respect, particular attention has been paid to Africa, particularly sub-Saharan Africa, and several countries in the area, facing external as well as internal pressure, have made substantial efforts to reform and improve their public procurement system.

Public procurement represents a substantial part of the economic activities in the countries under review. Our estimate shows that at the global level public expenditure allocated to public procurement (capital expenditure and goods and services) may account for about 15 per cent of GDP in SSA; and during the period covered in this book, public procurement was on average responsible for 50 per cent of government expenditure.[2] Because of its significance and of the problems that plague public procurement, several institutions (the World Bank, the African Development Bank [AfDB], and the European Union [EU], among others) have conducted country procurement assessment reports and supported procurement reforms. There are, however, very few studies that systematically analyse specific country experiences, and even fewer that can propose a comparative approach to examining these experiences.

---

[2] There is, of course, significant variation from one country to the other, depending on the size of the government, the importance of state-owned enterprises, etc. More on this issue in Part I.

Our review of the present literature indicates that only a handful of contributions related to public procurement reforms in SSA exist, and these are dominated by legal perspective analyses. This is particularly true if one focuses on the period when these reforms were initiated. A few African researchers have discussed early public procurement reforms in Kenya, Nigeria, Tanzania, and Uganda, while others have examined capacity-building in case studies relating to reform in South Africa and Guinea. As early as 1999, Kabbaj looked at capacity-building issues in Africa in the context of reform, and Wittig (1999) presents case studies on initial public procurement reforms in South Africa, Uganda, Kenya, and Guinea. Lionjanga (2003) later examines the Public Procurement and Asset Disposal Board (PPAD) in Botswana. Obiri (2003), Ekphenkio (2003), Nkinga (2003), and Agaba (2003) discuss the public procurement reforms in Kenya, Nigeria, Tanzania, and Uganda, respectively. Odhiambo and Kamau (2003) outline some lessons based on the early experience of Kenya, Tanzania, and Uganda. More recently, a paper by Lecat and Sanchez (2008) summarizes the characteristics and lessons learned from reforms aimed at improving the quality of public spending on the continent. Also, Quinot and Arrowsmith (2013) provide a systematic review of the legal frameworks introduced in the context of public procurement regulation in several English-speaking African countries. Their book also offers perspective on some issues, such as corruption or the potential contribution of procurement to social policy, relevant to most procurement systems in their sample. Lastly, a broader review of capacity-building in public procurement has been carried out by the World Bank in 2011 to take stock of what has been accomplished on all continents over the last ten years to improve procurement (Abeillé 2011). But, all in all, if one considers the importance of the topic, the literature on the issue of public procurement in Africa is very limited, particularly from an economic perspective.[3]

Our book intends to partially fill this wide gap between the many actual or partial reforms and the lack of analyses of their nature and of the causes of success or failure. We offer an innovative review of these reforms, providing a cross-country analysis based on a sample of twenty-eight countries to give the reforms a broader perspective. We do so by revisiting and interpreting the public procurement reforms in SSA, with particular emphasis on the beginning of this century, i.e. the period during which reforms were implemented. We focus on the institutional and organizational changes introduced through these reforms, and we explore the impact and consequences these have had.

---

[3] Indeed, the legal perspective prevails in the analysis of public procurement reforms, with many relevant papers published in journals such as the *Public Procurement Law Review*, the *Journal of Public Procurement*, or the *Public Contract Law Journal*.

Many disciplines (e.g. law, management, industrial organization, and more recently business intelligence) have been mobilized to shed light on various aspects of procurement, not only as business opportunities, but also as the foundation for the organization of transactions of public goods and services through what is often identified as the 'supply chain'. Very little, however, is known about the institutional requirements and conditions of public procurement reforms, except for lip-service acknowledging their significance for the success of reform. And there is almost nothing on organizational design, despite the fact that organizations are the vectors of institutional change.

This paucity of information and analysis is particularly striking if we consider the many attempts at reform over the past two decades in various SSA countries. Our book is motivated by the urgent need to fill this gap and to build a coherent analysis of these reform efforts in order to decipher the issues at stake, and to provide a theoretical framework that could help countries set up appropriate institutions and organizations.

In doing so, we are particularly aware of the importance of public procurement from a development point of view. Developing countries, especially those in Africa, are characterized by a scarcity of public resources and private investment, which makes the efficient use of these resources crucial. Weak public institutions, including ineffectual enforcement mechanisms, have negative ramifications on the quality and efficiency of public service delivery. When public institutions are deficient, the risk of delivering goods, utilities, and services of poor quality, in insufficient quantities, and at non-competitive prices is high. For instance, a leak in a poorly maintained distribution system prevents the delivery of safe drinkable water; a newly constructed road suffering damage during the rainy season because of poor quality, exacerbated by the lack of routine maintenance, needs constant repairs; books not delivered to enough schools or distribution delayed long after the beginning of the school year hinders teaching; poor quality drugs are useless against disease; inefficient pesticides are distributed to farmers, etc.

Conversely, an effective institutional system intrinsically promotes a sound environment by protecting individuals and property, promoting the peaceful resolution of disputes, facilitating economic transactions, and providing government accountability for citizens. Institutions 'do matter' for guaranteeing the provision of adequate infrastructure and services (roads, electricity, water, health care, educational facilities), essential for the eradication of poverty.

2 What Goals? With What Tools?

The objective of this book is to review, assess, and explain the institutional and organizational reforms undertaken by central governments in the area of public procurement, using a consistent set of data for the period crucial for these reforms. Even though public procurement reforms have been ongoing in SSA since the 1990s, they reached a peak, at least in number and intensity, at the beginning of this century, the period on which our book focuses. These reforms have led to the development of new formal rules (regulations, procurement codes) and new organizational arrangements for their implementation and oversight. The period under review corresponds to an essential phase in the impulse towards these changes. Our book examines closely not only these developments, but also the rationale behind these changes, their pace, as well as their impact over time.

It does so mainly through the new institutional economics (NIE) lens, drawing from the two branches that developed within that approach.[4] On the one hand, the book deals with background conditions, i.e. the institutional environment defined by Davis and North (1971: 6–7) as being the 'rules of the game' that delineate the context in which economic activity takes place. Political, social, and legal ground-rules establish the basis for production, exchange, and distribution. They determine the general conditions under which transactions are more or less successfully organized and at greater or smaller cost. On the other hand, we also analyse the organizational consequences of the new rules of the game. Ménard (1995) compares the concept of institutions and organizations, and stresses the fact that institutions operate as an overarching structure within which different organizational modes operate. In the following chapters, we look at public governance structures as the institutional matrix in which the integrity of a certain class of transactions is decided and organized (Williamson 1996: 378). We contrast public governance structures with governance alternatives commonly recognized in the commercial sector. In doing so, we underscore some unique properties of the organizations responsible for implementing public procurement, and we refer to these organizations as micro-institutions (Ménard 2009: 40 sq.). By 'micro-institutions', we mean the organizational arm in charge of actually implementing the rules of the game defined at the institutional level, thus framing the actual activities of operators.

---

[4] The generic term summarized in the acronym NIE was introduced by Oliver Williamson in 1975, and it designates attempts to 'incorporate a theory of institutions into economics' (North 1992a). NIE does not assume the institutional framework as given, as it is in the traditional neoclassical approach, but treats it as the object of research. The diverse contributors to this field believe that institutions matter and that the relationship between institutional structures and economic behaviour requires attention. The term 'new institutional economics' is now used generically by different authors in different fields, ranging from economics to political sciences, sociology, management sciences, legal studies, and so on. Four Nobel Prize winners are among its prominent contributors: Roland Coase, Douglass C. North, Elinor Ostrom, and Oliver E. Williamson. In this book, we mostly rely on economic contributions from NIE, although the approach has been and remains very influential beyond economics.

We also quite systematically refer to the key concepts developed within the NIE approach, among which transaction costs, property rights, and contracts are the most prominent. Following Coase (1998), Ménard and Valceschini (2005: 422) observe that

> transaction cost provides the unifying concept of the new institutional approach [because] arranging transactions among parties is decisive for taking advantage of the division of labour and requires complex devices at the micro level (modes of organizing theses transfers) as well as at the macro level (institutions facilitating and enforcing these transfers).

Endorsing this perspective, our analysis examines: *the institutional changes* that have occurred in public procurement, i.e. changes in the rules of the game (laws, rules and regulations, informal rules, and enforcement mechanisms) as well as the context and reasons for these changes; and *the organizational arrangements* that resulted from the institutional changes and that are in charge of the actual implementation of these changes.

On the institutional side, North (1990b) distinguishes two types of rules of equal importance: formal institutions with rules that are socially constructed, and informal constraints derived from cultural behaviour.[5] These informal and often tacit rules that structure social conduct are of utmost importance. 'They range from conventions of neighbourhood conduct to ethical norms defining degrees of honesty in information exchange between the parties involved' (North 1990b: 63). North and other new institutionalists add another important dimension: the elements of enforcement of both the formal and informal constraints. Our analysis offers strong support to this notion: notwithstanding the importance of the quality of existing or ex-ante introduced rules, ultimately it is the way these rules are implemented that makes the difference.

On the organizational side, we find different ways of organizing transactions within the institutional environment, as defined in the previous paragraph (Williamson 1996: chap. 4; Ménard 2005: chap. 12).[6] Each mode of organization has its own costs. Let us illustrate with contracts, another key concept in NIE and a main tool in public procurement. Contracts, whether

---

[5] North's (1990b: 3) full definition of institutions is as follows: '... the rules of the game in a society or, more formally, the humanly devised constraints that shape human interaction [...] they reduce uncertainty by providing a structure to everyday life [...] institutional constraints include both what individuals are prohibited from doing and, sometimes, under what conditions some individuals are permitted to undertake certain activities'.

[6] North (1990b: 5) defines and identifies organizations as follows: 'a group of individuals bound by some common purpose to achieve objectives. Organizations include political bodies (political parties, regulatory agencies), economic bodies (firms, trade unions), social bodies (churches, clubs), and educational bodies (schools, universities). The term "institution" refers to the rules of the game, whereas "organization" refers to players of the game'. Williamson (1996: 378) prefers the term 'governance structure' to identify organizations that he defines as 'the institutional matrix in which the integrity of a transaction is decided'.

6

formal or informal, are typical tools applied to different arrangements for organizing transactions in market economies. Ex-ante, contracts involve the costs of drafting, negotiating, and safeguarding the agreement; ex-post are the costs of monitoring and enforcement, and costs related to maladaptation and adjustment that may arise when contract execution is misaligned as a result of gaps, errors, omissions, and unanticipated disturbances.

Contracts, and more generally the different modes of organization in which contracts are embedded or through which they are supported, relate to the transfer of rights, which is at the core of transactions; hence the importance of property rights, the third concept already mentioned. Property rights are often identified with private property rights. As rightly noted by several authors (for example, Alchian 1965; Libecap 2005/2008; Ostrom 2005/2008), the concept is much more general and concerns the different ways of allocating the 'right to use', whether it is related to private interests, to publicly controlled entities, or to specific groups as in common pool resources.

There are important differences between the institutional environment and the organizational arrangements operating within such environment, the two dimensions discussed previously. The former can be thought of as delineating the domain of action of the latter, while modes of governance (or modes of organization) operate at the level of individual transactions. For instance, outsourcing the purchase of seats to equip cars is an individual transaction that falls under organizational arrangements, while an indicator such as composite economic growth relates directly to the institutional environment. We adapt the following figure (Figure 0.1) from Williamson (1996) and Nee and Sweedberg (2005/2008) to summarize the possible interactions between the institutional environment, the different modes of organizations, and the individual dimension within which beliefs, norms, and behaviours are embedded.

3 Application to Public Procurement Reforms

We interpret public procurement in this book as the succession of transactions or the transfer of rights oriented towards the provision of goods, works, and services to the public sector, with the goal of reaching results expected from such investments; and we examine the cost of these transactions, describing the rationale for institutional and organizational change. These transactions are embedded in and framed by an institutional environment, and they are carried out through arrangements that support the implementation of these transactions. In the study, we introduce a distinction between the operators (public or private entities) in charge of actually delivering goods, works, or services, and the organizational arrangements (identified as

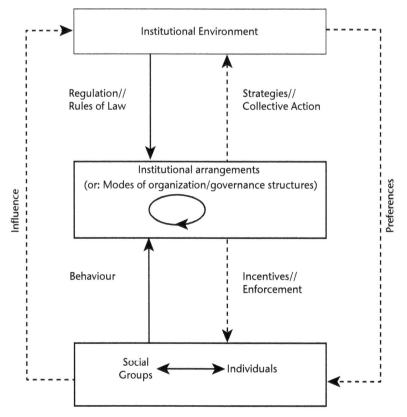

Figure 0.1 Interactions between institutional environment, modes of organization, and actors

Source: Adapted from Williamson (1996: 326), and Nee and Sweedberg (2005: 801).

'micro-institutions') that translate and interpret the general rules articulated at the institutional level into the specific guidelines that frame the actions of operators. Sector regulators illustrate the point.

We shall argue that this intermediate level, that of the micro-institutions, plays a crucial role in the success or failure of reforms. We find the NIE framework particularly appropriate for examining the related issues because it enables us to understand why transaction costs are high under certain conditions, what mechanisms are at work in the transfer of rights in the public procurement process, and how these transactions have been modified over time, leading to new organizational arrangements.

However, we are aware that NIE competes with alternative theories that complement NIE as well. For example, the recent literature on procurement often refers to agency theory, which is particularly useful for understanding the problem of incentives in the relationship between public authorities and contractors.

In the vein of Laffont and Tirole (1993), several contributions have focused on the problem of information, that is, adverse selection and moral hazard, and on their effect on the design of contracts. The principal–agent model has also been used quite extensively to examine the relationship between public procurement and corruption, and the problems it raises for 'good' governance once the reforms under review are initiated.[7] For instance, Tanzi (1997, 1999) and Mauro (1998) discuss corruption in public finances and highlight the categories of public expenditure most affected by corruption, public procurement included. In a somewhat similar perspective, issues of public procurement, and particularly of corruption, have also been studied through the theory of procurement contracts. For instance, Klitgaard (1998) and Rose-Ackerman (2001) examine corruption, the accompanying costs and distortions, as well as policy reform for their control, while Strombom (1998) and Soreide (2002) analyse the cause and consequences of corruption in public procurement.

Trade theory has also been mobilized for understanding the reasons behind the impulse to introduce institutional reform in public procurement. Some of these contributions (Arrowsmith 1998; Rege 2001; Hoekman and Mavroidis 1995; Hunja 1998) will be referred to in the book to enrich our analysis. For example, Arrowsmith (1998), Rege (2001), and Hoekman and Mavroidis (1995) examine the reasons for the reluctance of developing countries to abide by the World Trade Organization (WTO) agreement on government procurement (GPA) and the problems developing countries may face in applying the rule of such an agreement. They focus on procurement, trade, and transparency as part of international cooperation and negotiations. Others such as Hoekman (1998), and Evenett and Hoekman (1999, 2000, and 2004) discuss the WTO-government procurement agreement and its effects on national welfare. They analyse market access and discrimination against foreign suppliers of goods and services, and the non-transparency of procedures used to allocate government contracts to domestic firms. They show that greater domestic competition and transparency in procurement markets improve economic welfare. Other approaches have focused on procurement issues from a legalistic or management position, examining the instruments available for modernizing procurement systems and the ultimate goals of these systems (Hunja 1998; Schooner 2002; Kelman 2002, 2004; Quinot and Arrowsmith 2013).

However, for reasons to be developed and explained here, we find these theories of limited use and some even radically deficient when it comes to providing an adequate economic framework for understanding the key issue of our focus: the strategic question of the appropriate (or inappropriate) matching of institutional and organizational changes in shaping the success

---

[7] For a recent review of different mechanisms of corruption in different countries (although with very little on Africa), see OECD (2010).

(or failure) of public procurement reforms. In this respect, we find a better support in new institutional economics than in alternative paradigms, as we will substantiate later on.[8]

4 Sources

To examine the two dimensions of reform—institutional changes and the related changes in organizational arrangements—we rely mainly on two complementary sources of information. First, we use the 'Country Procurement Assessment Reports' (CPARs) made public by the World Bank. Some of these assessment reports have been prepared by Christine Léon de Mariz and Bernard Abeillé, two co-authors of this book.[9] Second, we also utilize the 'Public Procurement Reform Progress Index', a database created by the World Bank at the initiative and with the contribution of the Bank's Africa Region during the period under review. This later became a monitoring tool which helped the World Bank to support public procurement reforms with intensive advisory services and technical assistance programmes.[10]

In order to generate our diagnosis of public procurement problems in SSA countries, we draw on the assessments and the database produced for a number of francophone African countries (e.g. Côte d'Ivoire, Togo, Cameroon, and Niger), lusophone countries (e.g. Angola and Mozambique), and anglophone countries (e.g. Tanzania, Uganda, Kenya, and Mauritius). Although our sources, particularly the database, are far from being comprehensive, they are the only ones available that can provide us with cross-country information on the institutional reform processes evolving in sub-Saharan Africa during the period under review.

5 Outline of the Book

This book is divided into three parts which address three interrelated questions. First, why were extensive reforms in public procurement undertaken

[8] Let us, however, make it clear that there are some issues (e.g. incentive mechanisms involved in procurement) for which alternative approaches are better suited, and we will not hesitate to refer to these approaches when appropriate.

[9] The partial review of CPARs provided by Lecat and Sanchez (2008) has been complemented recently by a general survey of public procurement reforms (Abeillé 2011).

[10] Identified as 'Analytic and Advisory Activities' (AAA), these programmes rely on diagnostics carried through the country procurement assessment reports, which serve as an analytical tool to evaluate the suitability of existing systems, their compliance with best practices, and the major discrepancies with World Bank key principles. Specifically, CPARs are used to develop and establish action plans to improve procurement systems. After evaluating the existing system, the World Bank assists the borrower-country in developing or modifying its system.

in sub-Saharan Africa in the late 1990s and at the beginning of this century? Second, what measures have SSA countries taken to modify their existing procurement institutions and what are their accomplishments? Third, which organizational changes were implemented to improve the procurement system in some SSA countries and why? Underlying these questions are other issues of key concern—the major difficulties faced in the implementation of reforms, and the destructive impact failed reforms have on growth and the fight against poverty.

In Part I, we outline the conditions and forces leading to institutional change, in order to highlight the reasons for the efforts to modernize procurement and the risks related to each phase of the process. We explore these issues through an overview of the public procurement reforms, with special attention to reforms that took place in SSA in the late 1990s–early 2000s. In doing so, we also look at how countries endorsed substantial reforms at different levels: the legal and regulatory framework, the procedures and practices of procurement, the organizational settings, the devices implemented to check capacity to comply with the regulations, and the audits and anti-corruption mechanisms.[11] Keeping the declared objectives of transparency, competition, and accountability in mind, we examine and discuss these changes, and the instruments used to enhance them.

Part II focuses on institutional changes related to procurement systems. Drawing a framework based on contributions mainly from new institutional economists about the nature and significance of institutional endowments, we assess and discuss factors embedded in informal rules, which may explain why the progress towards modernizing procurement systems has been so limited in most countries in our sample. Our analysis shows a clear gap between the intentions of the reformer and the outcomes of reform, and provides explanations to why particular countries were able to reform faster than others.

Part III switches to the organizational arrangements that were created to support and implement institutional changes. North (1992a: 3) and North et al. (2009: 13 sq.) point out that institutional change is sustainable only if supported by organizations with an interest in their perpetuation. We take this view as our point of departure and focus mainly in this part of the book on the newly created administrative entities to which procurement functions were delegated. Public procurement is a way to organize transactions between public authorities and operators (be they private or public).

---

[11] The book recently edited by Quinot and Arrowsmith (2013) provides detailed analyses of the legal changes introduced in public procurement in major English-speaking countries in sub-Saharan Africa. It offers very useful insights on the legal dimension of institutional reforms for a subset of countries from our larger sample.

'Micro-institutions'—the entities in charge of translating general rules into specific ones and implementing them—play a major role in this transactional process. Although the design of administrative agencies has been a source of considerable interest among economists and legal scholars, the focus has essentially been on regulatory agencies in network industries. Little attention has been paid to the design of entities in charge of public procurement, and even less so with regard to sub-Saharan countries. Differentiating between suppliers that are responsible for the actual delivery of goods, works, and services under procurement from entities that oversee the procurement procedure, we focus on the latter. We pay special attention to the specific role of newly created procurement agencies, which we regroup under the generic term 'Procurement Regulatory Authorities' (PRAs).[12] Indeed, these 'mechanisms of governance', to use Williamson's terminology, provide a particularly useful example for studying the issues at stake in the design of entities in charge of reform.

We conclude with a summary of the main lessons derived from our analysis, which point to the difficulties in changing public procurement institutions and creating new modes of governance within a short timeframe. Changing formal rules is likely overemphasized in public procurement reforms while the role of informal rules and norms has been seriously underestimated. Similarly, the prominence given to formal procedures has been detrimental to the understanding of the importance of building human assets to implement them. On a more positive side, our research also brings to light institutional and organizational conditions that explain why some countries are capable of better performance than others, thus hopefully indicating the path for the future and successful reforms.

---

[12] We use PRA as a generic name. Actual names may vary among the countries.

Part I
Public Procurement Reforms in Sub-Saharan Africa: An Overview

> When humans understand their environment as reflected in their beliefs and construct an institutional framework that enables them to implement their desired objectives, then there is consistency between the objectives of those players in a position to shape their destiny and the desired outcomes.
>
> Douglass C. North (2005: 5)[1]

Reforming institutions is a long, slow, and demanding process that can hardly be planned in detail and is therefore subjected to a high risk of deviance. Nevertheless, there are situations in which powerful forces, often combining endogenous and exogenous elements, push towards reform, with results that often differ from what was expected.

It is a movement of this nature that we observe in the sub-Saharan countries that have made over the recent period substantial efforts, although of varying magnitude, to change their procurement systems and the institutions underlying them, particularly their legal framework. Why have these countries decided to engage in the process, often quite a radical one, of reforming these systems? What were the weaknesses of these systems that opened the door for reform? What did public procurement reform hope to achieve? And what are some major characteristics of a process that is still ongoing?

In the following chapters, we examine the conditions and forces that led to these reforms. We also identify some elements of these reforms which we will analyse in greater depth later in the book.

The core of our argument is that two sets of factors are central to these changes. On the one hand, endogenous forces had developed that pushed towards reform. The main components in that respect were (and still are): the debt burden of SSA countries, which substantially altered the costs of their financial resources; the uncertainties generated by inefficient public

---

[1] Douglass C. North, *Understanding the process of economic changes*, p. 116; © Princeton University Press.

procurement systems, which created increasing discontent among some key constituencies of existing political regimes; and the changes in civil society that introduced pressure on governments to reform. On the other hand, exogenous forces also played an important role, namely: the development of regional agreements that demanded greater transparency of public accounts and procurement procedures; and the conditions imposed by international donors when they were solicited to support ailing public finances. We shall argue that it is the combination of these two sets of factors that triggered the movement towards reforms, and that their varying intensity contributes to explain the differences in the amplitude of reforms implemented and the uneven record of their success.

1

Definition, Process, and Size of Public Procurement in Sub-Saharan Africa

Public procurement can be a somewhat vague concept encompassing a number of grey areas within the public finance sector. Among the many problems one has to face when trying to identify and measure the components of public procurement are issues related to why some public spending goes through the procurement process while other spending does not, as well as issues about the status and size of state-owned enterprises with respect to public procurement. We do not pretend to answer all these questions in this chapter, particularly since available data are limited and so sensitive to definition interpretation. However, we intend to introduce some clarification on the process of public procurement and to provide some indications about the magnitude of the budgets at stake in the countries of our sample.

In order to grasp the subject matter, we first define and discuss public procurement and its place in the broader public finance system. We follow with an explanation of how public procurement works and what processes are used. Finally, we propose an approximation of the size of public procurement in sub-Saharan Africa (SSA), which provides at least an initial understanding of the significance of these expenditures in the GDP of the countries under review at the time reforms were initiated.

1.1 What is Public Procurement?

Public procurement is the purchase of goods, works, and services, mainly from the private sector,[1] that uses public funds or guarantees from the government. It is part of the broader public financial system that includes two

[1] There are also situations in which procurement comes from (relatively) autonomous public enterprises, a fact which contributes to the difficulty of measuring the size of public procurement.

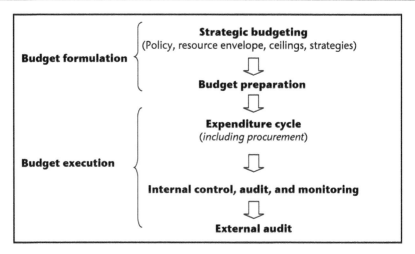

Figure 1.1 Budget formulation and execution
Source: Authors.

important phases: budget formulation and budget execution. In principle, these phases should go through the steps summarized in Figure 1.1. Of course, the sequence described in what follows is a *stylized representation* of what actually happens, and actual procedures may differ significantly depending on the country, its administrative and legal traditions, etc. Nevertheless, we believe that this representation captures the essential pieces of the puzzle that compose and delineate the configuration of public procurement.

1.1.1 A Stylized Representation

During *budget formulation*, the initial strategic budgeting stage involves several elements and establishes an overall macroeconomic framework to be used in the preparation stage. In this phase, national medium-term expenditure priorities are identified, and ideally they should be based on clear national targets. The resource envelopes as well as the ceilings and plans for budget users are determined for the years of the medium-term period. At the end of this phase, policy documents for the government and plans for budget users are produced, outlining the medium-term resource framework, a statement of expenditure policies, major strategic priorities of budget users and budget ceilings.

Based on the overall framework, the *budget preparation* then starts. During this phase, budget proposals are established by the different government departments and agencies—including procurement specialists or supply chain managers—taking into account economic policies and their associated assumptions. The different sectors review and price their programmes and sub-programmes, and undergo a process of prioritization to fit programme costs within available resources. This information is then provided to the ministry of finance or its equivalent and is used to develop the expenditure framework and ceilings, after which a series of hearings starts between the finance ministry and sector ministries. In conjunction with the macroeconomic framework and the sector review, a strategic expenditure framework is developed, enabling the analysis of trade-offs between and within sectors. On the basis of affordability and inter-sector priorities, medium-term sector resource allocations are made, and the revised budget is submitted to the government and the parliament for final approval.

Once the budget is adopted by legislature, *budget execution* can start. This phase encompasses the expenditure cycle as well as accountability processes and mechanisms such as internal control, audit and monitoring, and external audit. The expenditure cycle is composed of four main phases. The first phase is the release of funds to the spending units, and may be released through notification of cash limits, issue of warrants, etc. It might include authorization of advance procurement for large investment programmes which would require extensive studies, a complex procurement process, and are generally spread over several years. The second phase is the commitment phase, which is the stage wherein a future obligation to pay is incurred. A commitment consists of placing an order and awarding a contract for services to be rendered. It is a legal commitment and entails an obligation to pay only if the supplier has complied with the provision of the contract. The third phase is the acquisition and verification phase. At this stage, goods are delivered, works and services are performed, and their compliance with the contract or order is verified. The last phase is the payment phase, which can be made through various instruments.

1.1.2 A Complex Succession of Transactions

Public procurement is part of the whole budget cycle, from the planning to the execution phases. However, it is particularly significant at the execution phase and takes place when the government decides to purchase goods and services from the private sector. The UNCITRAL[2] Model Law on Procurement of Goods, Construction and Services (1994; updated 2011) defines public procurement as the governmental acquisition of any means of goods, construction, and services. Although this definition is accurate, it should be stressed that public

---

[2] The United Nations Commission on International Trade Law (UNCITRAL) adopted the Model Law on Procurement of Goods and Construction in 1994. An updated version was adopted on 1 July 2011. This model law, intended to help countries reform their systems of procurement, contains procedures and principles aimed at achieving value for money and avoiding abuses in the procurement process.

procurement is more than just the purchasing of goods, construction works, and services; it is a process and a complex succession of transactions within a political system that includes logistics and supply chain management.

Watermeyer (2004: 3) illustrates well how public procurement is more than the acquisition of goods and services. He defines public procurement as a process

> which creates, manages and fulfils contracts to the provision of supplies, services or engineering and construction works, the hiring of anything, disposals and the acquisition or granting of any rights and concessions. If procurement is indeed a process, it can be documented as a succession of logically related actions occurring or performed in a definite manner which culminates in the completion of a major deliverable or the attainment of a milestone.

This is to say that public procurement involves a complex succession of interdependent transactions, which makes its monitoring and control particularly difficult.

Wittig (1999: 3) emphasizes that this complexity comes largely from the central characteristic of public procurement as 'a business process within a political system'. He shows that the acquisition of goods, works, and services by public entities is different from acquisitions made by private entities. It is because

> Public procurement systems are the bridge between public requirements (e.g., roads, hospitals, defence needs, etc.) and private sector providers. Governments provide goods and services to meet a variety of citizens' needs. These items are obtained from either internal government organizations (hospitals, public works, departments, etc.) or from other sources external to the government in the private sector (domestic or international suppliers). In this sense, governments traditionally use their budget process to decide if they will 'make' something in-house or 'buy' it from other sources through their procurement system, just as private companies make similar decisions with regard to their enterprise resource plans.

However, unlike private sector procurement, public procurement occurs publicly under a political framework and thus has distinct considerations of integrity, transparency, accountability, national interest, and effectiveness.

In short, these three complementary definitions of public procurement converge to point out that public procurement is a complex acquisition process with important political components; thus public procurement is deeply embedded in its institutional environment.

1.2 Public Procurement as a Process

Public procurement begins at the planning phase and ends at the payment phase of the public expenditure process. Depending on the type of contract, it can also continue after payment is made and might include all logistics, storage, distribution, after-sale services, and maintenance to ensure proper use of the purchase. In the countries of our sample, there are two main approaches to public procurement. The prevailing one in anglophone countries is based on the UNCITRAL Model Law mentioned previously. Other SSA countries, particularly francophone and lusophone nations, adhere to a public procurement code (or system) based on a legal framework inherited from the Napoleonic system.

In what follows, we refer to the French system, as described in Bouley et al. (2002), to explain how the procurement system functions. We are aware that there may be non-negligible variations in the actual implementation of the procurement process among countries having inherited the Napoleonic tradition and even more substantial differences among those having inherited the Common Law system. Nevertheless, both approaches converge when it comes to the key 'nodes' of the public procurement process, and we believe that the process described here captures the essence of procurement systems and how they work.[3] Once more we emphasize that this is a stylized (and somewhat idealized) representation of the public procurement process.

1.2.1 Steps in the Public Procurement Process

Figure 1.2 helps to identify the main successive steps which constitute a public procurement process. Theoretically, the process starts with procurement planning. This stage coincides with the commitment stage (*financial control*) during which it is necessary to verify that the proposal to spend money has been approved by an authorized person and that money has been allocated for the purpose in the budget. The commitment stage also requires ensuring that sufficient funds remain available in the proper category of expenditure and finally that the expenditure is proposed under the correct category. Next, tenders are prepared and offers from bidders are evaluated based on certain predetermined selection criteria. The contract is then awarded to the selected bidder. After delivery or receipt of the goods, works, and/or services (*verification*), payment is made to the supplier (taking into account possible advance payments made at the beginning of the process). Before payment is disbursed (*accounting control*), it is necessary to confirm that a valid obligation exists, that a competent person has confirmed receipt of the goods, and that the works or services have been performed as expected. It is also necessary to verify that the invoice and other payment-related documents are correct and suitable for payment and that the creditor has been correctly identified. After

---

[3] For an in-depth discussion of the different features of the expenditure process system in francophone Africa, see Bouley et al. (2002: 15 sq.).

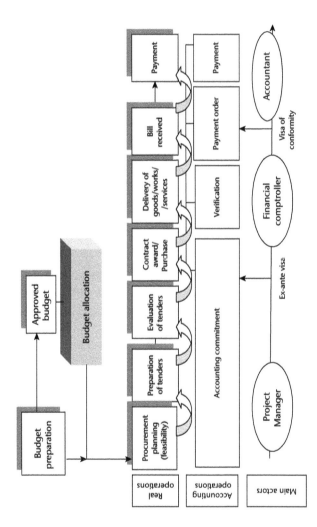

Figure 1.2 Procurement process from procurement planning to payment

Source: Bouley, Dominique, J. Fournel, and Luc Leruth, 2002. 'How do Treasury Systems operate in sub-Saharan Africa?' IMF Working Paper WP/02/58 (March). Washington, DC: IMF; and authors' own additions.

final payment is made, it is necessary to examine and scrutinize any expenditure and report any irregularities (audit).

The procurement process is thus a very long and complex sequence of transactions, involving many actors from the public sector: project managers, number of experts and/or engineers, financial comptrollers and accountants, and the private sector. Each transaction presents risks which we will examine more thoroughly in Chapter 3. These risks can result from deliberate action, particularly by policymakers but also by bureaucrats, and can generate immense opportunities for bribes, increasing the costs or reducing the quality of the goods, construction works, or services provided.

1.3 The Significance of Public Procurement in SSA

Generally speaking, the exact size of the public procurement market is very difficult to determine, and even more so when it comes to the countries in our sample. On a general level, public procurement is deeply embedded in the public budget. Thus it is not always easy to identify items that fall under public procurement precisely. Moreover, in some countries, goods, construction works, and services are produced and delivered within the public sector or through public enterprises while in others they are contracted out, which can have a significant impact on how items are listed and evaluated.[4] These problems are amplified in sub-Saharan Africa since accountability is often quite low, data collection limited, and reliability very hard to control.

1.3.1 A Significant Percentage of GDP

Nevertheless, all data available point in the same direction and suggest that public procurement accounts for a substantial percentage of public expenditure and gross domestic product (GDP). Based on a sample of twenty-three SSA countries for which disaggregated data were available,[5] we tried to estimate more precisely the level of procurement, i.e. the current and capital expenditure that could be subject to public procurement, in the year we took to represent our starting point in studying the reforms in public procurement. Data required for estimating public procurement were taken from IMF's publications (Statistical Appendix). Since the reporting differs among countries, for reasons summarized previously, the results are only estimates

---

[4] A good discussion of these methodological issues is provided in OECD (2013).
[5] These countries are Angola, Benin, Botswana, Burkina Faso, Burundi, Central African Republic, Chad, Republic of Congo, Côte d'Ivoire, Eritrea, Gabon, the Gambia, Guinea, Lesotho, Liberia, Mali, Mozambique, Mauritania, Mauritius, Nigeria, Rwanda, Tanzania, and Zimbabwe.

and in some cases would likely require significant adjustment if more and better harmonized data were available.[6] We also collected data on goods and services delivered by the public sector and on capital expenditure (since these two categories are the ones subject to public procurement). Our resulting data for 2002, summarized in the following figures, concur with previous estimations conducted for the period before 2002 (see Trionfetti 1997; 2000).[7] We double-checked the significance of these results by comparing them with much more recent information (see IMF Statistical Appendix 2012) as well as with data on the size of public procurement expenditures among OECD members and selected non-members (OECD 2013). With regard to their magnitudes, all data are consistent with what we found for the countries of our sample for the time when reforms were initiated. Public procurement consistently represents a non-negligible part of GDP, with variations around an approximate mean of 14 per cent.[8]

We provide two different figures that illustrate this result: the first one (Figure 1.3) indicates the weight of public procurement in GDP for the year for which we started collecting data on public procurement reforms, and the second (Figure 1.4) the weight of public procurement in total public expenditures for the same year.

Our estimate shows that at the beginning of the period under review, the mean for public expenditure subject to public procurement (capital expenditure and goods and services) accounted for about 15 per cent of GDP (with some significant variations, e.g. Mauritius, which had a low of 6 per cent, while Eritrea had a high of 34 per cent), which is pretty close to what was observed at about the same time in the European Union. Important variations across countries clearly suggest definitional as well as measurement problems. However, in all cases data support our main hypothesis, i.e. public procurement is significant with respect to GDP.

1.3.2 A Significant Part of Public Spending

Public procurement is also significant as part of public spending. It was on average responsible for 50 per cent of government expenditure in SSA (1.4).

[6] For instance, IMF's Statistical Appendix for the years under review includes net lending and transfers (which are not subject to public procurement) for Tanzania and Lesotho, but not for other countries.

[7] In order to make our evaluation more plausible, we also compared these data with the estimation of the weight of public procurement in the European Union (EU) at about the same time. The European Commission estimated that in 1997 public procurement in the EU accounted for €720 billion, that is, 11 per cent of the EU's GDP (Commission of the European Communities, 11 March 1998).

[8] According to the most recent study available (OECD 2013), procurement accounts for 12.8 per cent of GDP, representing, on average, 29 per cent of total general government expenditure across OECD members.

Public Procurement in
Per Cent of GDP

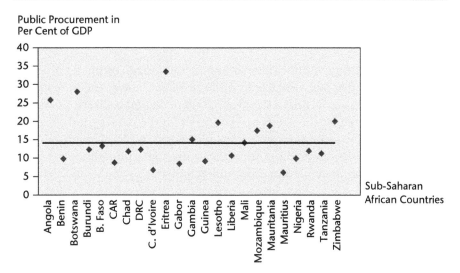

Figure 1.3 Public procurement in SSA as a percentage of GDP, 2002
Note: SSA includes the countries indicated on the graph: the horizontal line represents the mean.
Source: Authors' own calculation based on IMF (Statistical Appendix 2005).

Public Procurement in Per Cent of
Total Expenditure

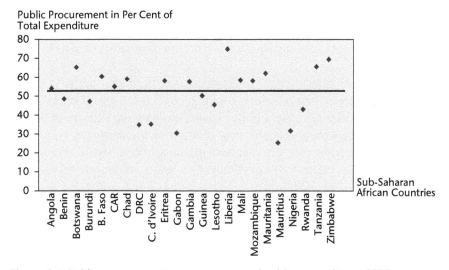

Figure 1.4 Public procurement as a percentage of public expenditure, 2002
Source: Authors' own calculation.

Note that the public procurement/total expenditure ratio varies quite a bit among countries, accounting for a high of 74.91 per cent in Liberia's total expenditure and a low of 25.52 per cent in Mauritius. Beside the definitional and measurement problems already mentioned, one possible explanation, in addition to the very weak quality of the data collected, for the abnormally high percentage of public expenditures in some countries likely relates to specific circumstances at the time (e.g. the civil war and its effects in Liberia).

Once more, although these calculations are only rough estimates, they are consistent with the data available in other research done at the time in several of our sample countries (Trionfetti 2000; Odhiambo 2003), as well as with data collected for the developed countries for the same period. They are also confirmed by the most recent data published by OECD. Notwithstanding the methodological reservations, these data converge to underline the significance of public procurement in economic activity.

1.4 Conclusion

Public procurement in sub-Saharan Africa accounts for a substantial percentage of public expenditure and GDP. Understanding the process of reform that could lead to improvement in this area is therefore critical for these countries. Due to different reporting methods, it is difficult to rigorously estimate the size of public procurement. The data available for twenty-three of the SSA in our sample at the beginning of the reform process shows that public procurement, on average, accounted for about 15 per cent of GDP and 50 per cent of government expenditure. This is confirmed by earlier as well as more recent data.

Part of the difficulty in data collection comes from the fact that public procurement is deeply linked to the budget cycle. It is a component of the execution phase of the broader public financial system that starts with budget formulation. Our review suggests that public procurement is a very long, complex process involving interdependent transactions, many actors, and various steps from planning to payment. As a result, numerous risks plague the system. It cannot be viewed only as the simple public purchase of goods, construction works, and services from the private sector as suggested in UNCITRAL (1994; 2011). Rather, it should be viewed as a process (Watermeyer 2004) and as a complex succession of transactions within a political system (Wittig 1999). It is a business process, but with very distinct considerations of integrity, accountability, national interest, and effectiveness, deeply embedded in institutions that frame this process, and it is often exposed to high risk of discretionary intervention from policymakers and bureaucrats who monitor those transactions.

Because the magnitude of public procurement is so significant and because it is so exposed to distortions, risk of corruption, and malpractice, there have been several attempts at reform. Over the past two decades, and particularly in the late 1990s and the early years of this century, reforms have been launched in sub-Saharan Africa (and other places) to make procurement systems more efficient. But before looking at the forces that have pushed towards this reform and shaped its characteristics, we turn to a closer examination of the major flaws and problems that plagued procurement systems at the time reforms were initiated.

2

Weaknesses and Flaws of Public Procurement Systems

Public procurement is a sensitive issue because of its weight in the economy, because it directly involves policymakers and high-ranking civil servants, and because it can have such an impact on users who are also constituencies of political regimes. In the 1990s, reform of public procurement systems was high on the agenda of several sub-Saharan countries as well as major international donors, as these systems were plagued by problems that could no longer be ignored because of their impact on the price of goods, construction works, and services, and on quality. Asymmetrical information emanating from dysfunctional procedures—ex-ante as well as ex-post—corruption in the allocation and monitoring of contracts, and problems of enforcement created uncertainty and hindered transparency, accountability, and equity, all indispensable aspects of an effective procurement system. These problems also increased the costs of the goods, construction works, and services provided during a period of severe public finance constraints. The magnitude of these problems challenged the support of constituencies that the political regimes in place badly needed.

This chapter develops a detailed diagnosis of these problems, with special attention to the issues of corruption, particularly at the implementation phase. We first identify the ex-ante conditions in which distortions are rooted, starting with the planning of procurement needs and ending with the contract award. Referring to several country cases, we specifically examine the lack of planning, the abuse of limited tendering as a primary method that distorts procurement processes, the poor preparation of bidding documents, the failure to advertise procurement opportunities, the insufficient time allowed for submitting appropriate bids, and the restrictions on the dissemination of the contract award. We then highlight the ex-post conditions which amplify these problems and which are essentially related to flaws in the implementation and enforcement mechanisms. We examine delays in the signature process; lack of or unusable appeals mechanisms for discarded bidders; payment delays; weak record keeping; the abuse of amendments to contracts; and the poor quality of delivery.

2.1 The Ex-Ante Characteristics

As shown in the previous chapter, public procurement is a succession of interdependent transactions. Each phase embodies risks and opportunities for inefficiencies or corruption that can jeopardize the credibility of the entire process. In what follows, we focus on the ex-ante characteristics linked to the planning and preparatory phases of the contract and show how the problems emerging during these stages can induce important transaction costs. Besides the risks attached to procurement when highly specific investments are at stake, as in the development of infrastructure, uncertainty arises from incomplete or asymmetric information which opens the door for misbehaviour among parties to the agreement. In principle, the procurement process provides the tools to impose rules and constraints, thus structuring the interaction between public authorities and providers of goods and services, and, ideally, making these interactions transparent. In the case of SSA, a key problem is that the actors' set of choices is not limited enough, nor adequately delineated, due to insufficient institutional constraints and/or poor implementation of existing rules. Black holes in the procurement process, combined with weak political commitment, feed opportunistic behaviour and multiply contractual hazards.

2.1.1 Lack of Planning and Advertising

Procurement planning is a critical stage in the procurement process, yet it is one of the weakest elements of the SSA process. This phase should be a major source of information during budget preparation. It should enable all technical specifications to be defined to allow the parties to prepare the appropriate bids. From the point of view of public authorities, it should support the identification of major investment expenditures, which in turn facilitates budgetary decisionmaking, and it should allow for better integration of procurement with other key elements in government policy (Evenett and Hoekman 2004; Lecat and Sanchez 2008: section II.C). More specifically, it should allow the different user departments: (i) to properly factor the cost of investment and disbursement forecast at an early stage of budget programming; (ii) to meet their needs in a timely fashion; (iii) to benefit from economies of scales; and (iv) to achieve value for money through packaging and timely use of funds. Ideally, procurement plans, among other things, should include:

(i) definition of requirements;

(ii) feasibility analysis, with technical specifications and/or design which often necessitates lengthy studies;

(iii) market research on what is available or what could be produced and delivered, with what possible delays and at what price according to the specifications;

(iv) specific contracts for goods, works, and/or services required to carry out the project;

(v) the proposed methods for procurement for such contracts;[1] and

(vi) scheduling.[2]

These plans should be monitored and updated on a regular basis throughout the duration of the project. A good procurement plan can prevent the need to use ad hoc procedures which usually lead to a non-transparent process and can have a negative impact on the price and quality of the goods or services delivered. A good plan also reveals all necessary information to potential bidders. The risk exists that procurement agents may retain information by not revealing early enough the different components of the projects. Evenett and Hoekman (2004) note that non-transparency at this stage can be due to: (i) administrative inefficiency or lack of administrative capacity (for example, due to lack of resources, the government does not make the investments necessary for a transparent regime, which makes the acquisition of information costly for firms); (ii) absence of hard budget constraints and oversight by the ministry of finance or its equivalent; and (iii) the self-interest of government officials who derive income from bribes.

Lack of advertising, or initial announcement and dissemination about a tender may amplify these problems. Indeed, this makes it difficult for parties to obtain information about available opportunities, thus generating asymmetries between public authorities and potential bidders, as well as among potential bidders themselves. Timely notification of bidding opportunities is a requirement of international procurement standards, such as those defined by UNCITRAL and the World Bank. According to international guidelines, a notice containing the scope and requirements of procurement should be

---

[1] Competitive bidding is not always the most efficient way of procuring goods and services, and transparent rules sometimes favour collusive practices (see discussion in section 2.1.4).

[2] For a detailed scrutiny of difficulties similar to those faced by public procurement in the attempt to meet these requirements, see Ménard and Oudot (2009) on the role of preliminary evaluation in public–private partnership.

published in newspapers and/or, nowadays, on the Internet. These forms of advertisement are often lacking, resulting in a less-than-transparent call for bidders.

This lack of procurement planning and advertising makes it difficult and costly for foreign firms as well as some local firms to overcome non-transparent contracting procedures. On the one hand, it favours opportunistic behaviour from public employees who can take advantage of this situation to capture personal benefits (e.g. seeking bribes, etc.). On the other hand, firms are unaware of potential opportunities offered by a government. As a result, only a few firms compete. In order to overcome non-transparency, foreign firms would need to have someone installed locally to obtain adequate information on bidding opportunities, an option which encourages bribery and increases transaction costs for these firms. Limited information about potential bids also favours the few firms (domestic and international) aware of the bidding opportunities, opening the way to higher prices.

Non-transparency due to the lack of advertising often results in oligopolistic situations, with a scarcity of sellers. As is well known from economic theory, such market structures usually produce three major effects. First, with limited transparency, prices offered by bidders will be higher, even without bidder misbehaviour, since prices will include the costs of obtaining inside information. Second, limited competition facilitates collusion among contractors so that prices are set by agreement rather than by supply and demand mechanisms. Lastly, this oligopolistic structure persists because the lack of planning and advertising contributes to the development of barriers to entry for new competitors.

Although not well documented, the lack of planning and advertising is a common weakness in the procurement process in SSA. Uganda provides a good illustration of the weaknesses that result from flaws in the planning phase. In that country, one of the first in our sample to adopt a reform of its public procurement system in the period under review, regulations specify that every procuring entity (user department) should prepare a 'multi-annual rolling work plan for procurements based on the approved budget' (Division II of the *Public Procurement Disposal of Public Assets* Regulation, Section 96).[3] Table 2.1 summarizes some key characteristics (as updated through several amendments to the initial reform) of how the procurement process should be implemented.

However, a World Bank study (Uganda 2004 CPAR), one of the key studies available on this issue for the SSA region at that time, shows that at least for the period reviewed by this report, procurement planning was rarely done

---

[3] <http://www.ppda.go.ug/>. First issued in 2004. Last consulted: March 2013.

Table 2.1 Properties of procurement methods in Uganda

Procurement methods	Characteristics	Threshold for application
Open domestic bidding	Public advertisement of tender or prequalification notice in national paper.	Below US$350,000 for goods, and US$3.5 million for works
Open international bidding	Public advertisement of tender or prequalification notice in international paper.	Above US$350,000 for goods, and US$3.5 million for works
Restricted domestic or international bidding	Without advertisement. Bids invited from shortlist developed from entities registration list or otherwise approved by contracts committee.	
Quotations and proposals	Without advertisement. A minimum of three quotations from a shortlist and approved by contracts committee.	Below US$15,000
Micro procurement (single source procurement) contract committee and PPDA	Direct procurement method without advertisement and without mandatory procurement records or any written documentation. Statistics reported to the contracts.	Below US$1,000
Sole-source procurement	In emergency situations and when only one supplier is available. Reported to the contracts committee.	At the discretion of the procuring entity if conditions are met.

Source: World Bank (2011a).

and, even when done, rarely followed the rules as stipulated in official documents.[4] The study, which updated a previous report from 2001, provides two reasons for these deficiencies: (i) lack of understanding of the value of proper planning due to low administrative and technical capacities; and (ii) lack of emphasis on planning as a facilitator in enforcing procurement rules and evaluating disbursement forecasts.

2.1.2 The Use of Limited Tendering

The choice of specific tendering methods, oriented bidding documents, or insufficient time for bid preparation are other ways to limit competition and increase collusion or corruption.

The discretionary power given to agents responsible for procurement in the absence of well-defined rules specifying ex-ante the procedures enables them to limit or bias competition by drawing on specific characteristics of the contract, for example limiting the use of tendering, drafting bidding documents oriented to favour one party, or allowing insufficient time for preparation of

---

[4] For a review of the available CPARs for SSA for the period 2000–8, see Lecat and Sanchez (2008). Their review focuses on a subset of twelve anglophone countries. A more general overview on public procurement reforms is provided in Abeillé (2011).

bids. Pope (2000: 208) describes some of these manoeuvres to restrict competition, thus precluding the government from getting best value from the process:

> Even if there is competition, it is still possible to tilt the outcome in the direction of a favoured supplier. If only a few know of the bidding opportunity, competition is reduced and the odds improve for the favoured party to win. One ploy is to publish the notification of bidding opportunities in the smallest, most obscure circulation source that satisfies the advertising requirements and hope that no one sees it. Cooperative bidders, of course, get first-hand information.

The type of methods used can also give the procurement entity certain discretionary powers. There are three main methods of formal procurement: open, limited (or negotiated), and selected.[5] Open tendering method means that any interested supplier may submit a tender. Limited tendering method occurs when an entity contacts a limited number of suppliers or contractors individually.[6] Under limited tendering, adopted in principle when only a few bidders are likely to qualify for the task to be performed, only pre-selected groups of suppliers are invited to bid. It should be noted that limited tendering does not include sole-source, single-source, or direct tendering, which are non-competitive methods reserved for exceptional cases.

The criteria for selecting one specific procurement method depend on the regulations of the individual country, so that there are significant variations also among the countries of our sample. In some countries, regulations state that the default procedure for conducting public procurement should be open tendering, unless specified prevailing conditions could warrant other types of tendering. This is the case for Ethiopia, where the procurement manual specifies that 'open tendering method is the norm' and the use of other methods needs to be justified (see Box 2.1 for an explanation of the different methods in Ethiopia). In other countries (e.g. Uganda, Angola), the type of procedure is defined according to the value of the procurement, with thresholds specified and updated on a regular basis. In Uganda, procurement methods are spelled out in the Act & Regulations, while the thresholds for applying the different procurement methods are defined in the guidelines.

Verdaux (2005) comments on the abuse that may result from the relative discretionary power in selecting procurement methods:

> ...although open competition is usually recognized as a principle of government contracting, practices and exceptions to the open competition principle have

---

[5] In addition to formal tendering procedures, countries also use 'informal' procurement methods, such as requests for proposals and quotations or newer tools such as purchase cards or electronic catalogues.

[6] These methods prevail in international and nationwide bidding. Nevertheless, other methods can be used and are sometimes better adapted to the situation. See Bajari et al. (2002) for interesting insights on outcomes under different methods.

Box 2.1 PROCUREMENT METHODS IN ETHIOPIA

Chapter 4 of the Procurement Manual adopted at the beginning of the reform of public procurement describes six approved methods of procurement, namely: *open tendering, two-stage tendering, request for proposals, limited tendering, request for quotations,* and *single-source procurement.* It is the responsibility of the public body in charge of procurement to select the most appropriate method in each case.

The *open tendering* method is the norm. The open tendering method may be with or without prequalification. The Tender Committee within the public procurement body will recommend the method of procurement to be used for the approval of the Head of the public body.

The use of methods differing from the *open tendering* is justified under the following circumstances:

Two-stage tendering is to be used only exceptionally, when (i) it is not feasible for the public body to formulate detailed specifications for the goods or construction or characteristics of services, (ii) it seeks various alternatives to meet its needs, and (iii) because of the complexity of the goods, works, or services, which will make it necessary for the public body to negotiate with suppliers and contractors.

Request for proposals is used most commonly for the procurement of *consulting services* apart from those services which 'include the production of goods in quantities sufficient to establish their commercial viability or to recover research and development costs'.

Limited (or Restricted) tendering is similar to the World Bank's limited international bidding (LIB) and is used for highly complex or specialized goods, works, or services, available only from a limited number of suppliers or contractors, or the 'time and cost to evaluate a large number of bidders would be disproportionate to the value of the goods, works or services'.

Request for quotations is similar to the World Bank's 'shopping' procurement method and is subject to limitations such as monetary thresholds and Tender Committee approval.

Single-source is similar to the World Bank's 'direct contracting' procurement method and is applied under similar circumstances such as 'proprietary' nature of goods; 'urgency' requirement; 'catastrophic event'; 'spare parts' available from original supplier, and 'extension of previous contracts'. In addition, section 4.11 of the Manual makes the method acceptable when the contract '*includes the production of goods in quantities to establish their commercial viability or to recover research and development costs*'.

Source: World Bank (2002: Vol. II p. 17) and Ethiopia: Procurement Manual, March 1999.

allowed other procurement methods, such as restricted bidding or sole sourcing to flourish. Actually, procurement practices have made sole-sourcing the most commonly used method of procurement in a majority of countries. [7]

This situation results from a lack of publicity because of the absence of proper means of publication, small number of national companies able to perform

[7] Sole-source, single-source or direct contracting consists of contracting without competition. The World Bank Guidelines: Procurement of Goods, Works, and Non-Consulting Services under IBRD Loans and IDA Credits & Grants (#3.6 in the initial version—2004; #3.7 in the last revised

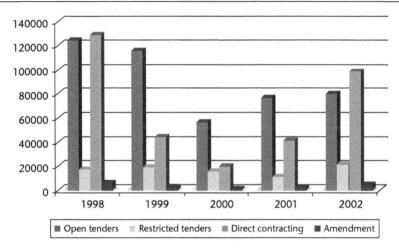

Figure 2.1 Methods of public procurement in Côte d'Ivoire at time of reforms (1998–2002)
Source: Côte d'Ivoire (2010).

government contracts in certain sectors, and at times collusion between the heads of public enterprises and businesses.

Although sole-source remains dominant in SSA,[8] it has declined in most of our sample countries, and tends to be better justified when used. However, this evolution is precarious, and difficult to assess because of important variations over time.[9] To illustrate, Figure 2.1 shows the different procurement methods used in Côte d'Ivoire, which was extremely active in reforming its government procurement system before the civil war that devastated the country. The figure provides a spectacular illustration of the significant variations in procurement methods in use over a relatively short period.

The single-source contracting method, which still tends to prevail in most sub-Saharan countries, has a strong impact on prices. As early as 1987, Domberger et al. developed an econometric model describing the relationship between the choice of the procurement method, the price, and the

version—2011) summarize the circumstances under which direct contracting is an appropriate method: (i) an existing contract for goods or works may be extended for additional goods or works of a similar nature; (ii) standardization of equipment or spare parts to be compatible with existing equipment may justify additional purchases from the original supplier; (iii) the required equipment is proprietary and obtainable only from one source; (iv) the contractor responsible for a process design requires the purchase of critical items from a particular supplier as a condition of a performance guarantee; and (v) in exceptional cases, such as in response to natural disasters.

[8] By comparison, at about the same time 'in most of the OECD countries, open procedures represent more than half of the tenders by public entities' (OECD 2003b).

[9] The problem is not limited to developing countries only. In a recent report the OECD notes important variations in procurement methods among the developed countries, particularly after the onset of the financial crisis in 2008 (OECD 2013: 13 sq.).

quality of services returned. From a sample of sixty-one contracts for cleaning services, they show that competition reduces prices significantly, sometimes by as much as 20 per cent, while maintaining or improving the quality of service. This result contradicts the generally accepted idea that a decline of prices is automatically associated with a decline in the quality of services.[10]

Avoiding competitive tendering can be achieved through well-known tactics. The 2004 World Bank CPAR report on Uganda (vol. II, p. 43) identifies several such tactics. One well-established tactic consists of splitting a contract in order to fall below the legal threshold in order to be able to apply another method. The splitting of tenders and the use of micro procurement to put bids under the threshold is an attempt at circumventing rules. Procurement packages intentionally split up also minimize record-keeping of the transaction to no other written records than the date and size of procurement.[11] Another tactic consists of claiming urgency as an excuse to forego competition and award the contract to a single supplier. Urgent procedures (e.g. repairing a collapsed bridge situated on a strategic axis) are often cited by contracting authorities to justify methods not based on competition. Generally such procedures are not justified, while real urgency is more a consequence of weak procurement planning and programming in the first place or of poor operations and maintenance. Moreover, the rather systematic absence of audits to determine if emergency procedures were truly justified, and what their impact was, tends to amplify the risk of favouritism, bribery, and corruption in using such procedures.

2.1.3 Oriented Bidding Documents

Bidding documents for goods, works, and services to be procured should provide all the relevant information and specifications necessary for a prospective bidder. Technical specifications should be based on characteristics and/or performance requirements. However, distortions are often introduced. For example, brand names are often mentioned in the bidding documents: goods with similar characteristics and equivalent performance will not be taken into consideration. As already noted by Pope (2000: 208), there are also subtler ways to restrict competition through oriented bids:

> Using the brand name and the model number of the equipment from the preferred supplier is a bit too obvious, but the same results can be achieved by including specific dimensions, capacities and trivial design features that only the favoured supplier can meet. The inability of competitors to meet these specifications,

---

[10] This idea has been theorized by Hart et al. (1997).

[11] Note that the use of micro procurement is sometimes justified, for example when it enables small local enterprises to bid.

which usually have no bearing on critical performance needs, are used as a ploy to reject their bids as being 'non-responsive'.

2.1.4 Insufficient Time for Preparation of Bids

Allowing sufficient time for the preparation and submission of bids by all interested parties is critical to attracting as many bids as possible. Specifically, the World Bank Guidelines provide that 'generally, not less than six weeks from the date of the invitation to bid or the date of availability of bidding documents shall be allowed for International Competitive Bidding (ICB)'. However, in practice, this time is often insufficient; in many cases, even when bidding opportunities are published in a newspaper and the theoretical period provided for bid preparation is reasonable, the issuance of the newspapers comes too late, preventing companies from submitting a bid. Electronic procurement can reduce this problem but does not solve all its aspects: besides its slow acceptance,[12] it may even provide incentive to shorten the time available for bid preparation, thus cutting the time for preparation even more.

In addition to specifications drawn up to favour specific firms, limited public circulation of bidding opportunities, or too short a time for responses, there are other ways to limit competition, for example, by discriminating against foreign suppliers. Discrimination usually takes place at the evaluation stage.[13] Evenett (2002: 20) explains the process:

> Governments may employ price preferences to inflate the bids of disfavoured suppliers. For example, a ten per cent price preference against foreign suppliers implies that their actual bids will be inflated by ten per cent before being compared to bids by domestic suppliers. This puts foreign firms at a disadvantage as raising a bid typically reduces the probability of winning a government contract.

Note that the lack of competition can result not only from the demand side (the contracting entities) as described so far, but also be induced by strategies on the supply side (the providers of goods, works, and services), with

---

[12] A recent OECD report notes the slow progress of e-procurement even in developed countries (OECD 2013: 9 sq.). In SSA, most countries are not fully equipped technically and do not have the human resources to generalize a fully fledged e-procurement system. However, several countries have successfully moved to: (i) posting advertisements online; (ii) transmitting bidding documents and proposal requests by email; (iii) providing information to bidders through emails; (iv) posting contract award decisions online; and (v) posting standard bidding documents and procurement newsletters online. Security issues regarding the confidentiality of bids, and flaws and abusive uses of the system, prevent the development of a fully fledged e-procurement system at this stage.

[13] Discrimination can be pursued by governments for: (i) macroeconomic management reasons: the increase in national income caused by a rise in government expenditures is smaller when the share of each dollar spent on goods produced abroad is large; and (ii) nationalism or outright protectionism (see Evenett 2000).

some well-informed providers taking advantage of the insufficient time to short-cut potential competitors and/or collude with friendly rivals. As is well known from the literature in industrial organization (IO), firms may have an incentive to conclude horizontal agreements to limit competition. The specific characteristics of the procurement market provide numerous opportunities for such behaviour. Among these opportunities, the following are particularly significant for the countries in our sample:

(i) the industry is concentrated, making it easy to identify and negotiate with competitors;

(ii) barriers to entry are significant, preventing the entry of new competitors;

(iii) market transactions are transparent so that the cartel can detect deviation from the cartel agreement. This is a paradox for arguments advocating extended transparency that could be attained through competitive bidding. There is a trade-off in public procurement between the need to provide transparency and the desire to avoid collusion. This trade-off makes the 'competitive bidding' methods sometimes inappropriate for certain types of transaction;

(iv) players compete with each other repeatedly either in a single market over time or simultaneously in several separate geographic markets; and

(v) the existence of a cartel agreement is easy to conceal.

It is also important to note that the resulting forms of collusion can vary considerably, which often makes it difficult to even recognize their existence. Among the most common forms of collusion, we find:

(i) simple price-fixing or 'bid-rigging', whereby a winning bidder and successful bid is pre-determined and other bidders are instructed to bid a certain amount higher;

(ii) market-sharing agreements under which customers are divided according to type or geographic location, and competitors agree to submit higher bids in markets assigned to other firms;

(iii) 'bidding fees', whereby the industry association charges a fee for the privilege of submitting a bid;

(iv) 'sharing the spoils', whereby the winning bidder agrees to compensate the losing bidders for the costs of submitting their bids.

Some of these forms are particularly hard to detect—for example, when foreign competitors are involved, when procurement bodies do not have adequate human resources, or when procedures are not well documented. These difficulties bring into the picture the problems associated with ex-post conditions of implementation and monitoring of public procurement.

2.2 The Ex-Post Conditions

The ex-post phase of procurement, when the contract is actually awarded, is as critical as the pre-contractual phase and is an aspect that the standard literature on optimal contracts has long underestimated or even ignored.[14] Indeed, fighting corruption and improving efficiency at the time of contract implementation is as important as measuring and correcting the negative impact and biases that come out of the ex-ante characteristics described previously.

2.2.1 Procurement and Corruption

Strombom (1998) and Pope (2000) emphasize that the contract performance phase is a critical stage in the procurement process. Indeed, notwithstanding the possibility of bribes in the ex-ante phase, the most extensive and costly corruption is likely to occur after contracts have been awarded.

A very simple example illustrates the point. Based on interviews with several public servants and operators from Senegal, Mali, and Burkina Faso, we have estimated the different cost elements in road construction and maintenance for five years after the projects were initiated. Figure 2.2 summarizes what happened with the (repeated) investments in those projects.[15]

The pre-emption due to corruption and malpractices may not accurately reflect what happens in all projects developed under procurement, but it does provide an important indication of a trend that can be observed, particularly with respect to the development of infrastructures. And this situation, of course, has a strong impact on costs.

First, costs induced by corruption tend to be included in the bidding price of a contract, and are thus passed to users, affecting the general well-being of the population. Indeed, the first consequence of corruption is to push prices upwards. As Strombom (1998) points out:

> ...winners have every intention of recovering their bribing costs, and they have a variety of ways to do so. The first stage, especially in collusive bidding, is by

---

[14] For example, Laffont and Tirole (1993) focus almost entirely on ex-ante conditions, with relatively few passages (e.g. in chaps. 10 and 11) on ex-post issues.

[15] This evaluation was presented by one of the authors (Abeillé, a former Regional Director for Procurement in Africa at the World Bank) at a workshop attended by civil servants and WB and AfDB staff members (March 2013). There was a consensus among the workshop participants that the evaluation reflected common practices.

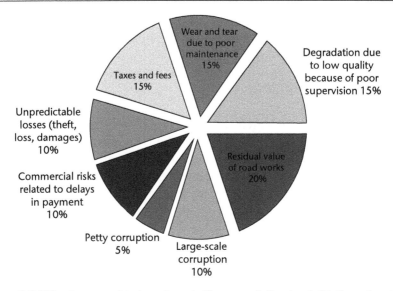

Figure 2.2 What happened to investments (five years following initiation of projects)
Source: Authors.

inflating their bid prices. Further, cost recovery can be achieved during contract performance by over-invoicing for quantities of goods delivered or work
performed, reducing the quality of materials used for construction or delivering
cheaper models of goods, and obtaining contract change orders to increase the
amount of goods sold or works performed at overpriced unit cost.

Another option for firms is to provide goods at a referenced price, e.g. world
price, but at lower quality without the knowledge of the contracting entities.
As a consequence, the impact of corruption can exceed bribes by far: as our
example suggests, rapid deterioration of a road system due to malpractices fed
by corruption during the construction process and in maintenance generates
significant extra costs ex-post.

Corruption also tends to maintain a monopoly situation, preventing, as
noted in the previous section, entry as well as innovation by outsiders. These
distortions can discourage useful investment and reduce growth (Shleifer
and Vishny 1993; Tanzi and Davoodi 2002). Moreover, corruption distorts
resource allocation, since it can provide incentives for the corrupted party to
increase demand for some goods and services. Looking at tentative reforms
in procurement, Tanzi (2000: 145) notes that: '[Corruption] increases public
spending: by promoting unnecessary or unproductive spending; by contributing to the overpayment for some services or goods that the government
buys; by making payments to individuals not entitled to these payments; and
in many other ways'.

Moreover, an unscrupulous contractor or supplier may take advantage of the possibilities opened by corruption to falsify standards certificates, to deliver over- or under-valued invoices, to pay bribes to contract supervisors, etc. As a result of this duplicity, the purchaser of the goods or services is likely to:

- fail to enforce quality, quantities, or other performance standards of the contract; and/or
- divert delivered goods for resale or for private use; and/or
- demand other private benefits (trips, tuition fees for children, gifts, etc.).

In sum, the initiative with respect to corruption can come from either side and always requires the active cooperation of the other party. The possibility of this union ultimately depends on the ex-post conditions of procurement implementation. We now turn to these conditions.

2.2.2 Insufficient Publication of Contract Award

Insufficient communication about the contract award is one of the ex-post flaws that can feed corruption. Without adequately publicizing the characteristics of a contract, without making the contract award known or motivating the decisions made, bidders lose the possibility to put pressure on decision-makers and lose the possibility to appeal.

This may explain why international organizations and donors have increasingly put pressure on the beneficiaries of financial support to make the usage of funds public knowledge. For example, contracts financed under the World Bank's funds must comply with Article 2.60 of the World Bank *Guidelines Procurement under IBRD Loans and IDA Credits*,[16] which stipulates that:

> Within two weeks of receiving the Bank's 'no objection' to the recommendation of a contract award, the Borrower shall publish in *UNDB online* and *dgMarket* the results identifying the bid and lot numbers and the following information: (a) the name of each bidder who submitted a bid; (b) the bid process as read out at the bid opening; (c) the name and evaluation process of each bid that was evaluated; (d) the name of bidders whose bids were rejected and the reason for rejection; and (e) the name of the winning bidder, and the price, if given, as well as the duration and summary scope of the contract award.

However, the impact of such conditions imposed on beneficiaries remains limited. There are many other situations—as well as donors—that allow local governments to escape obligations regarding publicity. Of course the capacity

---

[16] Initial version: May 2004. Last revised: January 2011.

to escape publication is amplified when contracts are not financed by foreign sources. Under these circumstances, bidders are often deprived of all relevant information on a specific bid as well as on strategies to adopt in future bids. It places potential bidders in an asymmetric position, which may push them to resort to corruption as a way to obtain information on a private basis.

2.2.3 Non-existent or Unused Appeal Mechanisms

In most African countries, there are no or very few contentious appeals introduced to a competent jurisdiction. The difficulty goes beyond the scarcity of competent jurisdictions. With the discretionary power that public authorities have over the procurement process, to challenge public decisions by going to court would put these bidders in a difficult, if not impossible, position in terms of all future bids.

In order to overcome such situations, Guasch and Spiller (1999) have proposed the creation of independent commissions that would work closely with developing-country agencies in charge of procurement, helping them to oversee the process. These commissions would provide a protest forum to which 'aggrieved bidders and governments could bring their grievances...and the commission would determine if there were grounds for proceeding with an investigation'. However, this proposal raises important political problems. It may offend national sovereignty if foreign experts are a part of such a commission (or, even worse, if they were to dominate them), etc. Moreover, the actual implementation of independent appeals mechanisms faces at least two major problems, as experienced in Burkina Faso, Cameroun, and Uganda, among others: they lack resources to become operational, thus losing their credibility, or those that do become operational are exposed to a burgeon of appeals without substantial content and the risk of bribery.[17]

In Part II, we come back to efforts being made in the context of the reforms under review to introduce a better-defined legal framework and more independent judiciary. However, we shall see that building well-designed institutions ex-ante does not resolve the ex-post problem of their operations, nor the capacity or incentive to use them.

2.2.4 Long Delays in the Contract Signature Process

Another weakness of procurement procedures comes from the often long period between the awarding of the contract and the last required signature, or in complying with all conditions for contract effectiveness. This can take

---

[17] During interviews with high-ranking civil servants and ministries, several described anti-corruption agencies as being the most corrupted ones!

several months, even a year in certain circumstances, before the interval between the time the winning bidder is announced and the time when the decision has been endorsed with all the necessary signatures and has run its course. As this is a well-known situation in SSA, companies prepare for it by inflating their prices ex-ante.

An alternative solution is for the bribing agents to speed up delays at each stage of the signature process, which feeds corruption and raises prices even higher. Agaba (2003) summarizes this pernicious process as follows: 'In other instances of government procurement, documents are "chased" by suppliers pushing them through the process in person'. The assumption is that 'chasing' will not be successful without bribes, commonly known in Uganda as '*kitu kidogo*' or 'speed money'.

Another practice used by contractors faced with long signature delays is to surreptitiously derail contract effectiveness, for example by retarding the mobilization of staff and materials, or by giving priority to another contract.

2.2.5 Abuse of Amendments to Contracts and Poor Quality of Delivery

Two other problems may arise during the execution of a contract. First, parties often abuse amendments to a contract in order to allow for the execution of works not initially planned. This can be the consequence of weak preparation and analysis in the preliminary phase (see section 2.1.1), or a strategy to boost prices, benefits, and even bribes once a contract has been approved.[18]

Second, the quality of the goods, construction works, and services delivered may not correspond with what was committed in the contract. This problem of low quality is best viewed from the perspective of local people who benefit from public investments only for a short period of time and who are the overall 'losers' of a weak procurement process. Investment in road construction is a famous example of poor execution of contract: in most SSA countries, roads have a very short lifespan, even when backed by high capital investment. Local people who should be the main beneficiaries of public investments become the main 'losers' of the procurement process that does not monitor implementation properly.

Only close supervision of the execution of contracts by competent and non-corrupt civil servants can guarantee that the quality of the delivered works meets contractual commitments. This raises the issue of the human assets needed for an efficient public procurement system.

---

[18] In an extensive review of concession contracts for public utilities in Latin America, Guasch (2004) discovers a rather systematic re-negotiation of long-term contracts after a relatively short period of time.

2.2.6 Delays in Payment

When bidders submit a bid, they need to take into account several factors, including the question of which goods and services to produce, the frequency of the type of transactions at stake, and uncertainty of the environment, a major issue in SSA. An important risk that bidders face in SSA is whether or not one will be paid in a timely fashion once the works or services are delivered. Arrears by the government, which underlie late or deficient payments, are detrimental to both the public and private sectors.

First, late payment constitutes a commercial risk for the bidders, endangering the cash flow situation of companies and posing a threat to the development of the private sector. It affects small and medium-size enterprises in particular, thus hampering potential development of entrepreneurship. Second, it also increases the price of bids, since bidders tend to introduce risk premiums—usually identified as commercial risk—as an umbrella against delays in payment. Through extensive discussions with numerous entrepreneurs in various SSA countries, we estimate that companies inflate their bids by as much as 45 per cent to hedge against such uncertainties. 'Speed money' is also used extensively, which pushes unit prices even higher. Bid inflation due to the anticipated delays in payment is especially widespread for locally financed projects. For foreign-financed projects, bidders know that the risk of not being paid is relatively small, since funds are usually kept in special accounts earmarked for the payment of specific projects.

Another distortion that payment delays introduce is the room it opens for 'bilateral' favours. If the contracting authority's payments to the bidder are late without compensating interest, the same authority will hardly be in a position to impose penalties for hold-ups incurred during contract execution. Thus, a regime of reciprocal tolerance develops, which once again is detrimental to both private and public sectors. Interestingly, the 2004 Malawi CPAR[19] indicates that contractors complained of late payments only in cases that continued for several months, which suggests that many contractors did not complain because they already had included the costs of such delays in their bid.

2.2.7 Weak Recordkeeping

The last aspect we want to mention with regard to ex-post conditions that generate flaws in the procurement process is weak recordkeeping. Recordkeeping is a key element of public procurement: it is an important tool for ascertaining at all times that a fair, equal, and transparent procedure has been used

---

[19] Malawi CPAR (2004: Volume II, p. 17).

throughout the process. Records provide evidence and therefore the means to make officials accountable, to prosecute offenders, and to improve processes. They are also critical to the appropriate management of public resources. Lack or limited availability of such records creates opportunities for fraud and makes it difficult to audit the procurement process and improve the system. In their survey of CPARs in several sub-Saharan countries, Lecat and Sanchez (2008, particularly par. #45) take special note of how poor record management is, despite laws mandating competent government authorities to do so.

2.3 Conclusion

The main weaknesses and flaws that we have identified at different stages of the procurement process are summarized in Table 2.2. Here we review the main impacts of these flaws on transparency, accountability, and competition. We also briefly indicate their consequences in terms of value for money.

Table 2.2 Main weaknesses in public procurement systems and their possible effects

Weaknesses in public procurement systems	Effect on			
	Transparency	Accountability	Competition	Value for money
Ex-ante characteristics				
– Lack of procurement planning	X	X	X	
– The use of limited tendering as a predominant method	X		X	X
– Oriented bidding documents	X		X	X
– Lack of advertising	X		X	X
– Insufficient time for preparation of bids			X	X
– Insufficient publication of contract award and therefore no possibility of appeal	X	X		X
Ex-post characteristics				
– Non-existent or unused appeals mechanisms	X	X		X
– Long delays in the signature process				X
– Abuse of amendments to contracts and poor quality of delivery		X		X
– Delays of payment				X
– Weak recordkeeping	X	X		X

Note: X indicates significant impact.
Source: Authors' summary.

In our examination of the different sources of weaknesses and flaws, we emphasized that ex-post characteristics matter at least as much as ex-ante ones. This implies that the central problems cannot be interpreted primarily as flaws in contractual design, a view that seems to dominate much of the economics literature.[20] To the contrary, we believe that the sub-Saharan African experience shows how the weaknesses and flaws, and the 'tactics' they feed on, develop during the different phases of the procurement process (more on this in the coming chapters).

Based on our analysis, the most common problems that emerge in the procurement process are: lack of procurement planning; use of limited tendering as the dominant method; preparation of oriented bidding documents; lack of advertising that leads to insufficient time for bid preparation; insufficient publication of contract awards; unused or non-existent appeal mechanisms; delays in the signature process; abuse of contract amendments and poor quality of delivered goods; lengthy payment delays; and weak recordkeeping. All of these problems create asymmetric information and facilitate or even favour fraud and corruption. They also hinder the transparency, efficiency, competition, and accountability that should characterize a healthy procurement system.

These problems—although present to some degree in all public procurement systems—are particularly significant and acute in sub-Saharan Africa. They have plagued public expenditures, particularly investment in infrastructures and essential services, to a level that is barely sustainable in a context of economic restrictions and public finance crises. Therefore, it is not surprising that there have been forces pushing towards reform of the procurement systems. We now turn to the examination of these forces.

---

[20] This position prevailed, for example, in Laffont and Tirole (1993). Laffont (2005, chap. 4) pays more attention to enforcement issues.

3

Drivers of Change in Public Procurement

The flaws and weaknesses that we have pinpointed in the previous chapter were spread widely in sub-Saharan Africa at the time reforms were implemented, and they continue to plague the development of the region. However, we have learned from several studies on the reform of public utilities that failures within a sector are necessary but not sufficient conditions to trigger reform (see, for example, Savedoff and Spiller 1999: chap. 1; Shirley and Ménard 2002: chap. 1; Laffont 2005: chaps. 2 and 4). A specific combination of endogenous and exogenous forces and factors must be at work, pushing actors towards the adoption of substantial changes. Identifying these forces and understanding how they converge is essential to understanding the forms of public procurement that developed in SSA in the late 1990s and early 2000s, and why these later developed unevenly and with varying degrees of success across the different countries involved. In this chapter, we address this central question—why did numerous countries in the same region start to reform their procurement systems in that period? A related question, to be explored further in Part III, is: why have some countries advanced further in that process?

This chapter can provide only partial answers to these questions, which will be examined again in later chapters from different perspectives. In what follows we make a distinction between the endogenous forces and factors inherent to public procurement reform, and the exogenous forces and factors that push towards reform even though they are not directly linked to public procurement. We emphasize in particular the push from domestic procurement stakeholders, the effect of the scarcity of public resources, and pressure from the international community. Some of these factors are already discussed in Wittig (1999), who examines both the domestic and international imperatives for procurement reform; in Savedoff and Spiller (1999: chap. 1) and Shirley and Ménard (2002: chap. 1), who examine the conjunction of micro- and macro-economic factors that push towards reform in public utilities; and in Lecat and Sanchez (2008), who emphasize the role of exogenous pressures in connection with changes in civil society in the case of sub-Saharan Africa.

In exploring the forces at work in the public procurement reform process, we draw lessons from countries that either played a pioneering role or have undergone particularly significant changes. We argue that while forces external to procurement might play an important role in giving the impulse to the movement towards reform, it is the endogenous factors pertaining to the public procurement sphere and its significance in public expenditures that ultimately had the crucial role. Our analysis goes beyond previous studies in its extension (our panel includes most SSA countries).[1] We use concepts emerging from the new institutional economics, and we take into account important institutional factors such as the role of the West African Economic and Monetary Union (WAEMU) or Common Market of Eastern and Southern Africa (COMESA), harmonization of procurement rules across several countries within our sample, weaknesses of legislative and institutional frameworks, the effect of asymmetrical information, the risk of corruption, as well as less perceptible effects such as the impact of international meetings and conferences on procurement reform in SSA.

We first examine the exogenous factors that contributed to the reform process in sub-Saharan Africa, factors not determined by parameters or variables related directly to procurement per se. In section 3.2, we focus on forces and factors that are directly related to public procurement.

3.1 Forces and Factors Exogenous (or Partially Exogenous) to Procurement

North (1990b: 86) argues that fundamental changes in relative prices, preferences, or ideas are the most important sources of institutional change. Change occurs when the contracting parties find it worthwhile to alter the game among them:

> Institutional equilibrium would be a situation when given the bargaining strength of the players and the set of contractual bargains that made up total economic exchange, none of the players would find it advantageous to devote resources into restructuring the agreements...The process of institutional change can be described as follows. A change in relative prices leads one or both parties to an exchange, whether it is political or economic, to perceive that either or both could do better with an altered agreement or contract. An attempt will be made to renegotiate the contract. However, because contracts are nested in a hierarchy

---

[1] Lecat and Sanchez (2008) and Quinot and Arrowsmith (2013) are significant contributions, although they focus almost exclusively on English-speaking countries.

of rules, renegotiation may not be possible without restructuring a higher set of rules.

The process through which institutional equilibrium is altered by changes in relative prices is then described as follows:

> But relative price changes alter the incentives of individuals in human interaction, and the only other source of such change is a change in tastes. All of the following sources of institutional changes are changes in relative prices: changes in the ratio of factor prices (i.e., changes in the ratio of land to labour, labour to capital, or capital to land), changes in the cost of information, and changes in technology (including significantly and importantly, military technology). Source of these relative price changes will be exogenous (such as the changes in land, labour ratios that resulted from the plague in late medieval Europe); but most will be endogenous reflecting the ongoing maximizing efforts of entrepreneurs (political, economic and military) that will alter relative prices and in consequence induce institutional change. The process by which the entrepreneurs acquire skills and knowledge is going to change relative prices by changing perceived costs of measurement and enforcement by altering perceived costs and benefits of new bargains and contracts (North 1990b: 84).

However, North (1989) also emphasizes that 'institutions do change, and changing relative prices have received most of the attention as the source of institutional change. But in addition to relative price changes, the ideas also matter in history...and are powerful instigators of change'.[2]

In what follows, we explore some of these fundamental sources of change that go beyond changes in relative prices and that are related to change in preferences. We do so by focusing on factors that are exogenous to public procurement per se.

3.1.1 Alleviating the Debt Burden: Pressure from International Organizations

One of the main factors that led to the reforms in public procurement is linked to the international monetary situation that African countries faced in the 1980s and early 1990s, which amplified scarcity in public resources and tensions on fiscal revenues. During the decolonization process and post-independence era in the 1960s and 1970s, African countries borrowed extensively from international lenders to stabilize their countries both politically and economically. In the 1980s, different economic shocks related to

---

[2] Summarizing the approach laid out by North, Furubotn and Richter (2005) explain that persistent changes in relative prices due to lasting exogenous changes (such as changes in total population, knowledge, or ideology) will cause actors to realize that they could be better off under alternative institutional arrangements; this awareness pushes towards institutional change.

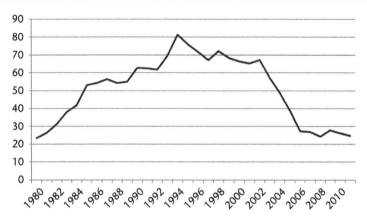

Figure 3.1 Debt to GNI ratio for SSA, 1980–2011
Source: World Bank (2013).

the oil crisis, rising interest rates, and falling prices for primary commodities increased the debt burden of African countries (see Figure 3.1). It became critical for international organizations to address the African debt crisis.

Structural Adjustment Programmes (SAPs), launched by the International Monetary Fund (IMF), which have dominated the reform landscape in Africa since the mid-1980s and which made financial support conditional to changes, particularly in public expenditures, illustrate this evolution well. About a decade later, in 1996, the World Bank and the IMF launched a debt initiative for Heavily Indebted Poor Countries (HIPCs), which created the framework for all creditors, including multilateral creditors, to provide debt relief to the world's poorest and most heavily indebted countries. As part of the debt relief effort, Poverty Reduction Strategy Papers (PRSPs) were drafted by the governments of these heavily indebted poor countries as a way to link debt relief with poverty reduction efforts. To qualify for HIPC status, countries had to meet certain criteria, including having a demonstrable history of economic reforms. These economic reforms had to reflect attempts to improve accountability and transparency in public expenditure, and public procurement, as part of public expenditure, was considered a key area where substantial efforts to reform should be made in order to qualify for debt relief.

An important step in this direction to reform was also the new language adopted by the World Bank, followed by other international organizations and donors, under the impulse of the then president of the Bank, James D. Wolfensohn. At a joint annual meeting with the IMF in 1996, Wolfensohn delivered a groundbreaking speech on the 'Cancer of Corruption', in which corruption was openly cited, for the first time at that level of decisionmakers in international organizations, as a major issue all around the world, affecting people's lives everywhere. This speech, by moving the issue of fighting corruption and improving procurement to the forefront of all national and international development dialogues, confronted head-on a topic that had long been ignored or kept under a bushel by the development community.

Consequently, countries had to demonstrate improvement in their public finance systems and in the fight against corruption in order to receive external financing from the international community. As emphasized by Lecat and Sanchez (2008), reform in the public procurement system became a key prerequisite after the mid-1990s for the delivery of financial support. It was also a necessary condition for certain countries in order to gain access to Poverty Reduction Support Credit, as illustrated by the cases of Uganda, Kenya, and Tanzania (Odhiambo and Kamau 2003).[3] With numerous public procurement improvement programmes being launched, indicators became increasingly necessary and were progressively developed to determine the level of aid to be delivered (the Country Policy and Institutional Assessment [CPIA] indicators were launched by the World Bank in 2005).

3.1.2 The World Trade Organization and the Trade Agreement in Procurement

Among the reforms required by international organizations and donors (and routinely as part of structural adjustment programmes) was the opening up of markets by countries that were benefiting from financial support. In that respect, the discussions with the World Trade Organization (WTO)[4] on procurement transparency and the Government Procurement Agreement (GPA) have, to some extent, contributed to procurement reform. The GPA, adopted in Marrakech in 1994 and which actually established the WTO, is a multilateral agreement which applies only to those WTO members who have signed it. Membership in the GPA remains limited; to date, no sub-Saharan country has endorsed it. However, SSA countries have participated in discussions concerning the GPA, adding to the hope that they may eventually sign the agreement. The trade liberalization trend also pushes in that direction, making it almost inevitable that countries review their procurement procedures and comply with the GPA.

---

[3] Poverty reduction programmes that developed after 2000 represent a revision of, and a complement to, the structural adjustment programmes of the 1980s–90s.

[4] The World Trade Organization was formally created in 1995. For discussions on the role of WTO initiatives at the time reforms were initiated, including the Government Procurement Agreement, the Working Group on Transparency in Government Procurement, and the General Agreement on Trade in Services, see Wittig (1999: section IIA), Lecat and Sanchez (2008: par. #10), and Arrowsmith et al. (2010: 186–203) who provide an extensive overview of the reforms introduced in the context of international trade with respect to public procurement.

3.1.3 The Push Towards Regional Integration

More important in the short run has been the movement towards building regional trade entities. As already noted by Wittig (1999: 3), 'a country may want to undertake public procurement reforms to support essential internal administrative improvements, to help qualify for internal financing from multilateral institutions or to help integrate a country into the multilateral trading system'. In that respect, regional integration is an active force pushing towards the reform of public procurement.

In sub-Saharan Africa, an important contribution to regional integration and the development of multilateral trading has been the creation of the West African Economic and Monetary Union (WAEMU)[5] and the Common Market of Eastern and Southern Africa (COMESA).[6] The aim of these regional unions or common markets is to fully integrate certain African countries into regional economic unions through trade and investment. In this context of integration and trade liberalization, procurement regulations and procedures needed to be harmonized and standardized across the free trade areas. The effort was also viewed as an opportunity to enhance competition and transparency in both private and public procurement arrangements. The reform of public procurement then became part of a comprehensive effort to develop a regional competition policy. Let us illustrate this with the measures adopted in the context of the two regional agreements mentioned previously.

In 2001 member countries of the COMESA embarked on a project funded by the African Development Bank (AfDB) to harmonize procurement rules and procedures. According to Karangizi (2003: 5), this initiative was intended to support COMESA member governments by:

(i) promoting regional harmonization of public procurement regulations and better access by enterprises in member states to public procurement markets as a means to increase intra-regional trade;

(ii) improving national public procurement systems through more transparent regulations and procedures, increased professionalism, and reduced opportunities for corruption; and

---

[5] WAEMU member states include Benin, Burkina Faso, Côte d'Ivoire, Guinea-Bissau, Mali, Niger, Senegal, and Togo. This union is also known by its French acronym, UEMOA (for *Union Economique et Monétaire Ouest-Africaine*). It was created in 1994, succeeding the old UMOA (*Union Monétaire Ouest-Africaine*) that had existed since 1962.

[6] COMESA was created in December 1994. As of 2012, COMESA member states include Burundi, Comoros, Democratic Republic of Congo, Djibouti, Egypt, Eritrea, Ethiopia, Kenya, Libya, Madagascar, Malawi, Mauritius, Rwanda, Seychelles, South Sudan, Sudan, Swaziland, Uganda, Zambia, and Zimbabwe. In the period under review, Angola and Namibia were also members, but Libya and South Sudan were not.

(iii) enhancing the capacities of recipient-country public procurement systems to take on responsibility and full accountability for aid-financed
procurement and to carry out more cost-effective procurement related
to infrastructure projects.

More recently, WAEMU and its member countries have committed to modernizing their public finance management (PFM) by harmonizing their
national systems and aligning them to international standards. Important
directives were adopted in 2005 and 2009[7] with the objectives of:

(i) installing budgetary discipline;

(ii) linking allocation of resources to public services performance; and

(iii) installing efficient external control.

Accordingly, reforming procurement has been an important part of this
programme, and it gives priority to the productivity of public expenditures,
transfer of resources to sector and decentralized authorities, harmonization
of procedures, and the opening of procurement to subregional competition.
The reforms were aimed at addressing 'governance and anti-corruption'
among WAEMU members so as to put in place efficient and transparent procurement policies and procedures, streamlining procurement in the budget
cycle and establishing transparent mechanisms of regulation and control.
Financial support provided by several international organizations[8] contributed to the implementation of the first phase (starting in 2010), oriented
towards strengthening competitiveness in the context of a free common market and harmonized legal environment.

However, promoting free trade was not the only purpose of these agreements. Underlying these general goals was the important issue of building
more transparent procedures and rules so that decisionmakers would become
more accountable for public procurement operations. In doing so, these trade
agreements, and accompanying reform, not only responded to pressure from
international organizations and donors or to the need to develop regional
exchange, but also responded to sociopolitical pressures from civil society.

3.1.4 The Growing Role of Civil Society and the Fight Against Corruption

Another factor accounting for the increasing concern in the public agenda
over procurement issues—and, correspondingly, procurement reform—is

---

[7] Two 'Community Public Procurement' Directives were adopted in 2005 and a 'Public Finance Management' Directive in 2009.

[8] Namely: the World Bank, the African Development Bank (AfDB), the Africa Capacity Building Foundation, and the *Organisation Internationale pour la Francophonie*.

the multiplicity of cases and allegations of corruption and fraud that surfaced, thanks to the diffusion of standardized diagnostic tools and the role of donors and independent NGOs (e.g. Transparency International) in pointing out corruption and fraud, and the resulting distortions. Consequently, public awareness has developed and fostered increased attention in the action of the government, as well as increasing reactivity of civil societies.

In their survey of the 'country procurement assessment reports' of twelve anglophone sub-Saharan countries, Lecat and Sanchez (2008: par. #16) note the high level of public mistrust towards procurement procedures that are opaque. As a consequence, there is growing belief within African societies, and particularly among constituencies of existing political regimes (or at least some of them), that corruption and fraud were—and still are—a plague challenging political stability and the potential for growth in these countries, and that efforts should be deployed to curb this phenomenon.

This awareness has been favoured by the rapid development and diffusion of the new information and communication technologies.[9] In some SSA countries, in the context of a growing public deficit, tight budget constraints, and squeezed income for large segments of the population, civil society (including religiously inspired movements, not all of them well intentioned) has increasingly influenced the political scene, demanding greater accountability and transparency from governments in how public funds are utilized. The ease that e-procurement provides in making information available on procedures, awards, stipulations of contracts, and relevant data for estimating their impact has pushed some governments towards reform of their procurement system. In the period under review, this was the case, for example, for Côte d'Ivoire, Ghana, Kenya, and Uganda.

With increased access to information, the end of civil wars that had long plagued several African countries, and the rise of democracy, concern for reforms has taken a prominent place, opening the door for citizens and various organizations to express their voice and to demand substantial change in the way public expenditures are decided and monitored, with direct repercussions for the public procurement area.

This is particularly so when it comes to the growing sensitivity with regard to corruption. Indeed, cases of corruption and their linkages to public spending and procurement have received increasing attention in SSA. Tanzi (1999: 10) establishes a direct link between corruption and procurement, and identifies several contributing factors.[10] More specifically, corruption can take several

---

[9] This role of information technologies found a spectacular illustration in the so-called 'Arab Spring'. For an assessment of the role of e-procurement among OECD members, see OECD (2013: section 2).

[10] Tanzi (1997) makes a useful distinction between 'political or high level' and 'administrative or bureaucratic' corruption. Corrupt behaviour that occurs during the budget preparation phase,

forms, occurring during any of the various procurement process stages described in Chapter 1. It can happen as a direct contractor–client pay-off for a contractual award, or it can occur when a firm develops strategies to become part of a restricted list of bidders or when firms collude and use bribes to circumvent competition regulation, etc. Soreide (2002) observes that factors such as the amount of money, complexity of the technology, the urgency to acquire the goods, the immediacy of the project, and discretion among public officials can be important elements in determining the risk of corruption in public procurement.

The widespread perception of these problems has supported the view that procurement reform, by setting appropriate rules and regulations and, even more importantly, by enforcing them, could become a key feature of anti-corruption efforts that could help promote good governance. Notwithstanding the scepticism that often accompanies these reforms, the widespread perception among donors, NGOs, and religious organizations that corruption undermines the whole fabric of economic and political life and leads to economic losses in public welfare has pushed towards reforms. The adoption of an agreement emphasizing the fight against corruption and impunity by the African Union in 2003, although it remains largely unimplemented, is an indicator of this growing awareness.

To sum up, factors exogenous or semi-exogenous to the restricted sphere of public procurement have converged to become the driver of change in the reform of public procurement. Figure 3.2 summarizes these factors.

Figure 3.2 Exogenous (or semi-exogenous) factors of change
Source: Authors.

a time when political decisions are made, reflects political corruption; corrupt behaviour and/or corrupt activities that take place during the budget execution phase will be mostly administrative corruption. According to Tanzi, in most cases corruption in public spending is connected with bureaucratic rather than political decisions.

3.2 Forces and Factors Directly Associated with Procurement

While the exogenous forces and factors are powerful ingredients in explaining the movement towards procurement reforms, they alone are not sufficient. As illustrated by several reforms of public utilities (see Shirley et al. 2002; Finger and Kunneke 2011), exogenous forces usually need to combine with endogenous factors. We identify as endogenous those forces and factors that are inherent to the public procurement sphere and which have a direct influence on public procurement reforms. Agaba (2003: 7), in referring to the public procurement reform initiated in Uganda in 1997, identifies two such factors:

> There were two sources of pressure on the government to review the performance of the public procurement system and to generate a restructuring plan. One was the realization by the government itself that the old system could not deal satisfactorily with the emerging demands on the system in terms of transaction numbers, expanding value of procurement budgets, scale and technical complexity of procurement activities. These demands were being made against a backdrop of a lack of bureaucratic accountability and transparency and the absence of a culture of value for money procurement.

In this section, we go further to examine more closely the role of these two domestic factors that combine with international forces to push towards procurement reform, and we also consider the role of another component: the better understanding of procurement among concerned constituencies as a way to achieve substantial savings, and as a social and economic policy instrument.

3.2.1 The Domestic Forces Pushing Towards Procurement Reforms

Facing severe budget constraints, the burden of public debt, and pressure from internal oppositions, several sub-Saharan governments became aware of the necessity to reform their national public procurement systems. There has been increasing recognition since the late 1990s that these systems were undeniably inadequate and outdated, as evidenced by several analyses (Lionjanga 2003; Nkinga 2003; Odhiambo and Kamau 2003). For instance, the thresholds determining which procurement method was to be used had not been updated for years; for countries such as Angola where inflation was high, these thresholds were totally meaningless. One important consequence was the inferior quality of delivered goods, works, or services. In other countries, public authorities had progressively acknowledged these flaws and the need to reform the institutional foundations of public procurement. At the same time governments faced the challenge of generally underdeveloped institutions.

Looking for explanations for this situation, Shirley (2008: 34) distinguishes four different arguments: (i) colonial heritage: countries inherited poor institutions from their colonial masters; (ii) factor endowments plus colonial heritage: colonizers saw human labour as one of the most valuable resources of the colonies, and thus created institutions designed for their exploitation; (iii) political conflict: countries had virtually no political competition with their neighbours or among their elites, resulting in institutions that served the self-interest of the rulers; and (iv) beliefs and norms: countries maintained beliefs and norms that were inhospitable to markets or engendered mistrust, preventing them from building institutions that would encourage trade and investment.

Although these arguments by themselves are insufficient, as Shirley points out, they provide a useful historical context to help explain why public procurement institutions are so underdeveloped. Discussing the case of Botswana, Lionjanga (2003: 4) describes a public procurement system in which rules and regulations had remained 'untouched' from 1967 until 2002:

> Upon the attainment of independence in 1965, Botswana was bestowed with a Supplies Regulations and Procedures (1963) by the departing British, promulgated on the basis of the Public Finance Act (1963). The Supplies Regulations and Procedures in question contained nine Parts, one of which, Part Four, dealt with procurement's organizational structures, principles, processes and rules. The Supplies, Regulations and Procedures was revised twice between 1967 and 1977 but interestingly, Part Four, dealing with procurement, remained untouched, except for Clause 11 which dealt with financial ceilings in relation to specific procurement methods and circumstances. The Supplies, Regulations and Procedures remained in force until 2002 when the present Act came into force.

The situation was pretty much the same in most SSA countries. However, this began to change in the late 1990s, albeit at a very slow pace. In Tanzania, among the first African countries to initiate the movement, the government analysed its procurement system and concluded that it needed to be reformed. Nkinga (2003: 8) summarizes the process as follows:

> The government's effort to undertake public procurement reform in Tanzania Mainland started in 1992 when the government commissioned a consultant to undertake a Public Procurement and Supply Management Study. At the conclusion of the study it was evident that the public procurement system in Tanzania had serious weaknesses and thus was in urgent need for reform.

In a similar vein, through a careful examination of procurement reforms in three countries (Kenya, Uganda, and Tanzania), Odhiambo and Kamau (2003: 15) conclude that these changes resulted from internal pressures from diverse stakeholders who were becoming aware of the major malfunctions in the system:

> The domestic push for reform came mainly from domestic procurement stake-holders. The procurement entities, the business community, professional associations, and the general public generally expressed dissatisfaction with the public procurement system. The stakeholders complained of misallocation of resources, inadequate infrastructure, inefficient services, high taxes, growing indebtedness and high risks.

These authors relate the stakeholders' complaints and dissatisfaction to moral hazard, adverse selection, and non-verifiability.[11] They point out that these informational problems limit competition, transparency, and integrity in the procurement system, with substantial consequences for transaction costs for firms as well as for governments.

Informational problems usually arise from asymmetries between the procurement parties. This asymmetry is routinely described as the core characteristic of the relationship between a principal and an agent. It may exist between the government (the principal) and the administration (its agent) in charge of implementing procurement as well as between public entities (the principal) and contractors (the agent). The economic literature has put much emphasis on the second aspect. However, the problem in public procurement is often located in the relationship between the government and the procuring entities.[12] For example, the procuring entity or, more precisely, procurement officers, possess information unknown or only partially known to the government (the principal):[13] in such a situation, procurement officers enjoy substantial discretion before and during the execution of their task, leaving room for a variety of private strategies (including corruption, fraud, etc.).

According to Marshall et al. (1993), these differences between the aims of the principal (the government) and the agent (the procurement officer) can be summarized as introducing: (i) *quality bias* (procurement official puts more

---

[11] Adverse selection means that the agent has some private knowledge about the cost or valuation that is ignored by the principal; it is often referred to as hidden knowledge and raises ex-ante problems in designing adequate contracts. Moral hazard means that the agent can take an action unobserved by the principal, or one that the principal cannot assess properly; it is also referred to as hidden action and raises ex-post coordination problems. Non-verifiability occurs when the principal and the agent share ex-post the same information, but no third party and, in particular, no court of law can adequately observe this information. For a detailed analysis see Laffont and Tirole (1993, particularly chaps. 4 and 8), and Laffont and Martimort (2002, chap. 2).

[12] For a discussion of the internal organization of government from the perspective of the agency theory, see Tirole (1994). It must, however, be noted that few contributions were developed later in this vein.

[13] As early as 1963, Arrow notes: 'By definition the agent has been selected for his specialized knowledge and the principal can never hope to completely check the agent's performance'.

weight on quality than price); (ii) *favouritism* (procurement officer favours a firm, for whatever reason); and (iii) *appropriation* problems (procurement official is not fully rewarded for any surplus gain resulting from his action, which makes him prone to corruption...or neglect). Similarly, Evenett (2000) and Evenett and Hoekman (2000) indicate that a procurement official is usually concerned with two factors: he tends to overvalue the quality of the goods his government agency is buying, because it has an impact on the size and prestige of his agency and because when he spends his agency's budget, he benefits from bribes from the supplying firms.

One important result of the tension between public authorities and their agents is that a government, even though well intentioned and sensitive to stakeholder pressure, may find itself deadlocked due to weaknesses, inefficiencies, or even blocking by the administration. Hence, as we shall see later on, procurement reforms require not only institutional changes, but also changes to the organization of the system.

3.2.2 The Potential Role of the International Community in Procurement Reform

In the previous section, we took notice of the role of international organizations and agreements in the push towards institutional reform, including procurement systems. The international community can also constitute an endogenous factor when, for instance, targeted initiatives and pressure from international donors to adopt specific standards or implement specific rules pertain to the sphere of public procurement itself. We are concerned here with the initiatives aimed at improving aid effectiveness by relying on reformed public procurement systems to channel overseas development aid. Although the actual impact of this factor has been seriously challenged (see Rodrik 2004; Shirley 2008: chap. 4), it remains a non-negligible component, at least as far as formal reforms such as the adoption of new laws and rules are concerned.

Let us illustrate with an influential initiative from a key international organization. In January 2003, the Development Assistance Committee (DAC) of the OECD and the World Bank initiated a joint procurement round-table whose goal was to promote partnership approaches for conducting aid-related procurement.[14] This initiative was based on the principle that by using national fiduciary systems (rather than donor rules and regulations), the impact of aid on the ground would be improved. This concept implies a greater reliance on a country's procurement system, that is, the country's legal and institutional framework as well as the micro-institutions in charge

---

[14] One of the authors of this volume, Bernard Abeillé, was a part of this initiative.

of implementing laws, regulations, rules, and procedures. The underlying idea was that national fiduciary systems should be used to channel overseas development aid, with participating countries required to improve their procurement system substantially in order to receive funds directly into their national accounts.

The initiative was based on the diagnosis that flawed public procurement systems are a major factor in slowing down project execution and contributing to the low disbursement ratio.[15] Due to the weaknesses of flawed procurement systems, foreign-financed projects are often isolated or 'ring-fenced' from the government system, as is well illustrated by the creation of project implementing units (PIUs).[16] These PIUs deal with all aspects of a project, including the procurement process. As a result, they often weaken line departments, create parallel super-ministries, reduce morale in the civil service, and contribute to donor ownership rather than national ownership (UNDP 2003). More generally, donors' fiduciary responsibility for their projects creates a costly parallel system, justified by donor reluctance to submit to fiduciary risks by relying on national systems for project implementation. Lionjanga (2003: 4) summarizes the challenges that result from the different requirements, particularly when multiple donors are involved, as follows:

> One such challenge involved the multiplicity of bidding documentation which remained in use…A particular example in Botswana is that tied assistance (80.0 per cent of all aid in 1981) meant the procurement practices of funding agencies had to be followed virtually to the letter by the procuring entities. As a result, as late as 2001–02, one department in the ministry of education at the time of the review was simultaneously using four different types of bid packages, e.g., the ADB, the EU, SIDA and the RSA.

The initiative under review was undertaken by the international community to strengthen country systems in an effort to avoid high transaction costs associated with outsiders' control and enhance the impact on development. It relied on the assumption that development can be successful only if the country itself owns the process and the government leads the development efforts. Using country procurement systems could speed up disbursements for both domestic and foreign-financed projects, could lead to substantial savings for the country, and would avoid parallel structures such as PIUs in adhering to donors' fiduciary requirements.

---

[15] The World Bank, like other development institutions and agencies, is required to 'ensure that the proceeds of any loan are used for the purposes for which the loan was granted, with due attention to considerations of economy and efficiency and without regard to political or other non-economic influences or considerations' (World Bank, IBRD, Articles of Agreement, Article III, Part 5(b); and World Bank, IDA, Articles of Agreement, Article V, Part 1(g)).

[16] The effectiveness of aid and PIUs is discussed in several papers (e.g. World Bank papers 2000, 2001, 2004; Banerjee et al. 2002; Danielson et al. 2002).

These well-intentioned goals, however, necessitated a successful reform of public procurement, and particularly of the organization of the system—a task that was much more arduous than expected, as we see in the subsequent chapters. A legalistic approach has tended, and continues, to prevail, to the detriment of the development of performance indicators. As a result, double checks (by local authorities and by foreign donors) have often been implemented, which translates into transaction costs being higher rather than lower.

3.2.3 Reform as a Social and Economic Policy Instrument

Public procurement has been recognized as an area where substantial savings can be made, thus contributing to the improvement of public finance while benefiting the population through better services at lower prices. In that respect an efficient procurement system can contribute to fiscal discipline. Studies have shown that improvements in public procurement management systems and procedures can reduce prices by up to 20 per cent—or even up to 40 per cent or more, according to Abeillé (2011)—while improving the quality and performance of products and services. This can have a substantial impact on national budgets (value for money), allowing for better public services and contributing to the poverty reduction agenda. In addition, more transparent procedures would facilitate more realistic economic investment decisions, thereby making investments by foreign as well as local investors more attractive because risks and uncertainty are reduced.

As a consequence, there is a growing appreciation among stakeholders of the linkages between specific national objectives and public procurement practices. Improved procurement policies could be part of an industrial policy or the instrument for attaining social objectives (for example, support for small and medium-sized enterprises, minority-owned businesses, disadvantaged ethnic groups, or geographic regions) through set-asides and preferences policies (Evenett and Hoekman 2004; Quinot 2013). In combination with the other factors already listed, this may provide the incentive for decision-makers to reform. It may even become a strong political argument in democratic countries or those leaning towards such a regime.

We sum up these endogenous drivers of change in Figure 3.3.

3.3 Conclusion

In this chapter, we examined some of the main factors and forces that push towards reform that could help meet the declared goals of transparency, accountancy, and integrity. We made a distinction between the exogenous

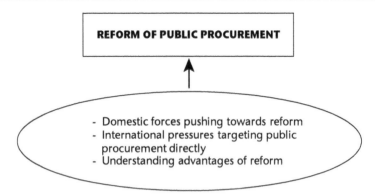

Figure 3.3 Endogenous factors of change
Source: Authors.

factors, i.e. those not determined by parameters or variables related to procurement per se; and the endogenous factors, i.e. those directly related to procurement.

On the exogenous side, we emphasized elements that can change relative preferences, with corruption at the top of the agenda; the debt burden from the 1980s and the pressure it induced on public budgets; the push towards regional integration; the growing role of civil society; and pressure from international organizations striving for trade liberalization, with a particularly influential role from the World Bank, the IMF, the WTO, and the GPA.

On the endogenous side, we highlighted the domestic factors pushing for procurement reform: greater interest in public procurement among the international donors in relation to the development of more attentive strategies for mobilizing local or regional resources and a better understanding of procurement as a way to achieve substantial savings, thus reducing pressure on taxpayers and simultaneously providing improved procurement as a social and economic policy instrument.

Our central hypothesis is that the combination of these forces (see Figure 3.4) makes reform more probable and that the nature and intensity of these forces are key elements for the plausibility of the implementation of reform. In isolation, none of these factors is unlikely to have a significant impact on public procurement.

All these forces and factors have an unambiguous political dimension. However, their political embeddedness varies according to the country, its political regime, and its traditions and beliefs, depending, for example, on whether they operate through competing political parties in a democratic regime or through constituencies supporting authoritarian regimes or whether they operate through a movement oriented towards more transparency and

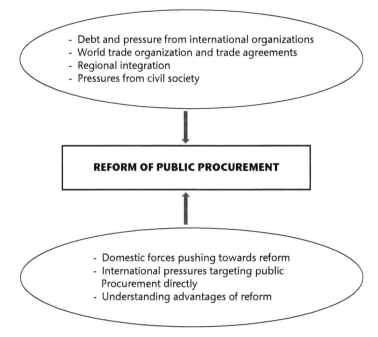

Figure 3.4 Drivers to change summarized
Source: Authors.

greater freedom, or through religious communities fighting to impose their own agenda.

Despite these differences, procurement reform pressures in SSA are heading in the same direction: the need for substantial changes in the ways the development and operation of public procurement are organized and in the institutions framing these modes of organization. We now turn to these aspects.

4

Modalities of Institutional and Organizational Changes

The combination of internal forces pushing towards reform in conjunction with pressure from international donors to do so, as described earlier, initiated a wave of transformations in public procurement systems in Africa in the late 1990s and the first decade of this century. These changes in public policies developed along two axes: (i) changes in the public procurement institutions; and (ii) the creation of a new type of organization to oversee public procurement.

Ultimately, the objective of these reforms was to modify institutions that frame human interactions in the context of public procurement. In order to reach that goal, reforms focused on changing the institutions 'that foster exchange by lowering transaction costs and encouraging trust' (Shirley 2005/2008: 611). More specifically, they targeted the conditions under which contracts are prepared and negotiated (ex-ante) and, to a lesser degree, how they are implemented and monitored (ex-post). This effort involved changing the legal framework, the procedures and practices supporting public procurement, the organizational framework within which they would be developed, the controls and audits, and the implementation of anti-corruption measures. Reforming these different components should work to restructure the interaction among the parties involved by imposing limits and conditions on the actors' set of choices while opening new opportunities for more transparent and less costly transactions.

We review these reforms, first by examining the modalities of the institutional changes implemented (section 4.1), and then by considering the associated organizational changes (section 4.2). In this chapter, we focus on the changes needed along these two axes and their underlying objectives. It should be noted upfront that in the reform of public procurement in SSA, the emphasis has been on ex-ante conditions, i.e. changes in the prevailing legal framework. The actual implementation and performance of these changes tell another story, to be explored in subsequent parts of the book.

4.1 Institutional Changes and Expected Results

4.1.1 Changing the Institutional Framework

The explicit objective of institutional reform in public procurement is to modify the structure of transactions between public authorities and private operators to reduce uncertainty and to increase transparency, competition, and accountability. However, through procurement reform, governments might also promote other interrelated objectives. Schooner (2002) identifies six other goals that could be partially embedded in the broad objective defined previously:

(i) Efficiency: a procurement system is efficient when it minimizes the amount of resources spent on the purchase of needed goods and/ or services while simultaneously using these resources in a timely manner;

(ii) Uniformity: compelling all government agencies to purchase in the same manner, following the same laws, rules, and practices. This can be a source of efficiency because sellers do not need to learn new rules in order to do business with different agencies or departments;

(iii) Risk avoidance: avoiding undue risks by filtering out undesirable contracts;

(iv) Best value: getting the best deal or value for money;

(v) Satisfaction for end users; and

(vi) Wealth distribution: utilizing procurement as a policy instrument, e.g. supporting domestic firms, redistributing goods or services in favour of some constituencies, or supporting social policies.[1]

CHANGES IN THE LEGISLATION
Changing the formal rules to reach these goals (or at least some of them) implied that new legislation had to be developed which would constitute an ex-ante framework to facilitate cooperation with suppliers as well as with international donors. This objective was considered a priority in the reform of public procurement in SSA, as is well illustrated by the triggers which define the conditions of financial support and which primarily always refer

---

[1] See Quinot 2013 for a discussion of this later aspect.

to rules and procedures. It meant adopting internationally accepted standards, such as those defined by organizations like the World Bank, the African Development Bank, or the European Union, as the basis for the design of the new laws. For example, the World Bank procurement guidelines indicate that:

> ...a clear, comprehensive and transparent legal framework is characterized by: the presence of legal rules that are easily identifiable ... At a minimum, such rules should provide for: wide advertising of bidding opportunities, maintenance of records related to the procurement process, pre-disclosure of all criteria for contract awards, contract awards based on objective criteria to the lowest evaluated bidder; public bid openings, access to a bidder complaints-review mechanism, and disclosure of the results of the procurement process. (World Bank guidelines, CPAR Instructions, Attachment 1).[2]

Hence, the reformed public procurement legislation would encompass rules concerning the *process* of acquiring goods, works, and services as well as an appeals mechanism to address complaints from aggrieved bidders. Wittig (1999), Everett and Hoekman (2004), OECD (2003a), and many other sources consider that internationally acceptable public procurement legislation should normally contain the following conditions:

- open tendering as the preferred procedure;
- detailed description of the steps involved in open tendering (preparation of invitations to tender and tender documents, advertisements, submission and opening of tenders, examination and evaluation of tenders, award and conclusion of contracts);
- definition of the circumstances under which methods other than open tendering could be used (for example, limited tendering, request for quotations);
- description of other procedures;
- explanation of the rules concerning essential elements in the process (for example, qualification of tenders, technical specifications, records of proceedings, evaluation of tenders); and
- an independent appeals system that would address complaints from aggrieved bidders and provide solutions against violations of the legislation.

Depending on the legal origin of the country, these ex-ante conditions may be embedded either in its rules or in regulations. Countries with civil law systems are likely to include these conditions in a code, whereas common law countries are likely to use regulations as the means to change ex-ante

---

[2] World Bank (2002, last revised 2011).

conditions. In most common law countries, government procurement regulations are a part of financial regulations and are therefore part of a broader set of financial instructions, with a particular role for the judiciary as the ultimate recourse. In civil code countries, procurement is usually a part of a legislative structure, ultimately determined by the parliament: it is embedded in a code accompanied by regulations and standards specifying the general conditions for different kinds of contracts.

CHANGES IN PROCEDURES

An important aspect of the reform process focuses on modifying procedures and practices, with the underlying objective to limit the actors' selection of choices, thereby restructuring the interaction of these actors. A significant step in this direction is the simplification of the procurement process. This can be achieved by attempting to attain uniformity in contract documentation and delivery systems in order to produce a homogenous system. Although seemingly a minor step, this can have a major impact, as it eliminates the previous document proliferation that has resulted from the parallel sets of rules developed by contracting entities, which made the control (ex-ante) and the monitoring (ex-post) of agreements particularly difficult.

It was assumed that by bringing uniformity to the procedure through the use of standard bidding documents, uncertainty in procurement would decrease. This would foster higher participation, with lower costs for bidders as well as for the public entities in charge of monitoring the bids. In the case of sub-Saharan countries, these reform efforts resulted in the development of standard bidding documents and manuals on procedure. These manuals, developed at the national level with the assistance of development partners (mostly the World Bank), prescribe the mandatory steps, including how information should be given with regard to:

- defining and disseminating the criteria used to evaluate the quality and competitiveness of a given bid; and

- the availability of avenues for challenging given awards.

Lastly, an important part of institutional reform has to do with capacity-building. Indeed, it is essential not only to have guidelines that support transparency and accountability, but also to implement conditions that will guarantee the actual application of ex-ante agreements through adequate enforcement mechanisms. In that process, well-trained and motivated procurement staff is central to ensuring proper application of the procurement system, i.e. a cadre of staff possessing the technical proficiency to implement the function (World Bank guidelines, CPAR Instructions). As we will see, underestimating this dimension has been a major factor in the reform difficulties experienced by the countries under review.

CHANGES IN CAPABILITIES

In addition to human capabilities, enforcement mechanisms require several interdependent components: organizational support, monitoring procedures, control over the actual implementation of an agreement, and capacities to sanction deviations. It also means that ex-post institutional laws and regulations must be complemented by an action plan.

Developing robust mechanisms for enforcement is indeed a key aspect to the successful reform of a procurement system:

> ...clarity of rules and institutional arrangements may be of little value if there is no means to enforce the rules and if the rules are not, in fact, enforced. The means of enforcement include the right to audits by the government of the procurement process and a bidder complaints-review mechanism in which bidders have confidence (World Bank, CPAR Instructions, 2002/2011: Attachment 1).

Enforcement is usually linked to the design of anti-corruption measures specifically targeted to public procurement, with a special emphasis on increased accountability.

4.1.2 Expected Results: Transparency, Competition, and Accountability

Indeed, the procurement reforms aimed to improve transparency, competition, and accountability. Although this terminology is now familiar to all those concerned with reform—scholars, policymakers, consultants—the content and associated expectations are not always clear. The underlying assumption of these three goals is that by increasing ethical behaviour in the procurement process, countries would be able to lower public spending, increase the quality of delivery, and improve confidence in the procurement process to attract the most reliable bidders.

TRANSPARENCY

Transparency means that the procurement system employs procedures through which bidders and contractors (and even the public at large) can ascertain that government business is conducted in an impartial and open manner (Arrowsmith 1998; Schooner 2002; Quinot and Arrowsmith 2013: 17–19). Clear information about the various steps of the procurement process enables potential suppliers to make informed decisions on whether or not to bid. The following effects are to be expected from increased transparency:

- Lower prices: (i) More firms (domestic and international) can participate in the bidding process, and an increased number of bids should result in stronger competition and lower bidding prices; and (ii) firms do not have to pay/bribe to obtain information on bidding opportunities and can reduce their bidding price accordingly. The government and the taxpayers should benefit from these lower prices, provided that the gains are not ripped by corrupted agents.

- Increased quality: Greater transparency should also facilitate requirement specifications (ex-ante) and control of the goods and services delivered (ex-post), thus improving quality as well as after-sales services and maintenance.[3]

- Increased confidence and investment of firms in procurement practices. A transparent procurement system allows competing enterprises to better evaluate the risks of doing business with the government.[4]

- More efficient allocation of resources: With increased visibility, it becomes more difficult for contracting entities to justify the purchase of certain favoured goods or services.[5]

In sum, the introduction of transparent procurement procedures leads to smaller costs for firms and increased competition, and a reduction in bribery, factors which in turn lower the bidding price and enhance national welfare. In addition to contributing to budgetary savings for governments and taxpayers under certain conditions, and enhancing the efficiency of domestic suppliers or contractors and the quality of the goods, works, and services supplied, transparent procedures can also attract more investment by lowering risk. As summarized by an OECD (2003b: 9–10) report on good governance:

> ...transparent and predictable procedures are a vital element of good economic governance. They help build public confidence in the management of government affairs...Transparent procurement systems can provide an important tool to combat corruption in government procurement. While transparent procedures are not sufficient in themselves to eliminate corruption, an effective system of monitoring, procedural checks, and proportional penalties can render penetration of fraud and corruption more difficult.

---

[3] However, robust supervision is essential to avoid situations where bidders, relying on poor supervision or corruption, artificially reduce prices to secure contract awards and later try to recoup losses through lower quality or quantity delivered.

[4] Transparency, however, does not necessarily imply stronger competition if, for instance, (i) there are barriers at entry (discrimination) or (ii) transparency enhances collusion.

[5] These effects on firm costs and government expenditure develop under certain conditions: (i) there should be a broader local and international market for the goods, works, or services at stake; increased transparency then enables competing firms to supply the government; (ii) publication of bidding opportunities should be circulated widely enough to ensure that existing firms are aware of these possibilities; and (iii) international firms should be allowed to bid so as to allow for more competition.

Box 4.1 ANTICIPATED BENEFITS FOR NIGERIA FROM PROCUREMENT REFORM

- The procurement system will become transparent and create equal access for bidders of public sector contracts;
- Through efficient and effective management of Nigeria's economic resources, all avenues of wastage and leakage in the economy as a result of inefficiency in the award of government contracts and procurements will be minimized, thereby increasing the government revenue base;
- It will enable contractors to have a fair hearing, as there will be a statutory contract appeal board where aggrieved contractors and suppliers would file their protests; and
- It will assist in the codification of all the relevant laws in the aegis of procurement as already done under the Corrupt Practices and other Related Offences Act (2002).

Source: Ekphenkhio (2003).
Note: At that time, Ekphenkhio was the Permanent Secretary in the Office of the Secretary of the Government of Nigeria.

The case of Nigeria provides an illustration of the possible benefits that countries can expect from securing greater transparency through procurement reform (see Box 4.1). It is one of the few available documents explicitly outlining the benefits expected for SSA countries from procurement reform.[6]

However, increased transparency does not necessarily lead to lower transaction costs, an issue that can moderate the anticipated benefits. Indeed, better transparency can also mean more procedural rules, increased delays in decision-making, and may introduce contractual rigidities that make adaptations difficult and costly.

INCREASING COMPETITION

Despite the importance of transparency, which makes it a necessary aspect of the procurement reform, its existence in a procedure is not sufficient on its own to ensure the success of reform. In order for transparency's full effects to emerge, it needs competitive pressure. A government may undertake the following action to increase competition:

i) Increase the knowledge and capabilities of procuring agencies in order to design an efficient procurement process;

ii) Ensure that the obligation to publish bidding opportunities is mandated through legislation, as the success of a high degree of transparency in market transactions is conditional to the evaluation of bids through procedures and evaluations that are well defined ex-ante and credible, particularly with respect to corruption;[7]

---

[6] Of course Nigeria also illustrates the gap that can exist between well-intentioned reforms and the actual outcome.

[7] There is some debate over the virtues of publishing the details of procedures ex-ante, since it may in some cases facilitate collusion.

iii) Reduce barriers to entry by removing constraints on regional and foreign participation in procurement, as well as eliminating discriminatory practices from the legislature; and

iv) Create rules which ensure competitive tendering as the primary or default method. Other methods are still to be allowed, but need to be duly approved and rationalized, making the unjustified use of other methods (such as direct contracting) difficult.

However, it is not always obvious that by maximizing the effective use of competition, the government receives its best value in terms of price, quality, and contract terms and conditions (Schooner 2002). As Hart et al. point out (1997), there are situations in which there is a trade-off between costs and quality, which may challenge the expected benefits from competition or some of it. Moreover, while corruption tends to disturb a competitive result, competition does not necessarily impede corruption (Soreide 2002; Soreide and Rose-Ackerman 2012). Competition might provide additional opportunities for rent-seeking behaviour. Rose-Ackerman (1999, 2007) observes that whenever regulatory officials have discretion, the incentive for bribery exists. Indeed, even though competition might be the default method of procuring goods, the discretionary authority of public officials can open up opportunities for bribery (Della Porta and Vanucci 1999). Also, competition (removing the discrimination provision) without transparency (publication of bidding opportunities) can hinder price effects, since firms will not be able to compete or may have to offer bribes in order to become aware of available opportunities.

REDUCING NON-ETHICAL BEHAVIOUR AND IMPROVING ACCOUNTABILITY

Efforts to reduce non-ethical behaviour underline the importance of laws or regulations explicitly targeting corruption, such as codes of ethics, laws or rules facilitating controls and audits, and mechanisms to implement higher sanctions. Accountability matters in that respect, and the term has become central to the good governance dialogue. It refers essentially to the capacity to monitor and assess the responsibilities of decision makers. It can be more or less formal, ranging from answerability to liability. In a sense it is the opposite of unethical behaviour. A key role for accountability with respect to public procurement is, of course, the fight against corruption.

The basic guideline in that respect is to implement laws, rules, and incentives that increase the transaction costs of corruption and favour integrity (understood as the exclusion of bribery, favouritism, or unethical behaviour).

The following benefits can be expected from an efficient reform that eliminates corruption:

i) Decreased prices, for two reasons: firms no longer have to resort to bribery in order to secure a contract or speed up the procurement process, and existing firms that had refrained from bidding because the odds of winning were too small are now bidding, thereby increasing competition;

ii) Increased quality: with more stringent controls, firms have to fulfil their contracts;

iii) Less complexity: in all cases of corruption, projects tend to develop into bigger and more complex undertakings than necessary, so that the end result is either higher costs or a project of inferior quality that will not perform according to expectations and will require costly upkeep and repairs.

iv) Increased efficiency in resources allocation: corruption affects the allocation of public spending. Investment decisions and projects are influenced by opportunities to secure bribes and not by the project's rate of return, as calculated in a cost-benefit analysis. Corruption is costly because it creates distortions entailed by the necessary secrecy (Shleifer and Vishny 1993). The need for secrecy can shift investments away from the highest value projects, such as health and education, into potentially useless projects, such as defence and oversized infrastructure, if the latter offer better opportunities for hidden corruption.

v) Greater firm presence: the level of corruption limits the attractiveness of investments in a country. Pervasive corruption may weaken international interest in both trade and foreign direct investment, resulting in lower GDP growth and a reduction of qualified competitors in procurement projects. Better control of corruption can lead to an increase of foreign enterprises promoting trade or greater investment expenditures (Soreide 2002; Wei 1997, 2000).

vi) Lower inflation: local or international bribe-paying firms will inflate their prices to compensate for their losses, even when they do not get the contract (transferring the costs to other activities), which leads to an increase in domestic inflation.

To sum up, the necessary institutional changes are complex because they need to extend beyond the formal aspects (indispensable measures such as reforming contract laws, the judiciary, etc.). Change is also needed in the less formal components, such as the conditions of implementation and support of norms and rules that can modify the behaviour of agents. It is the combination of institutions supporting transparency, accountability, and competition while keeping corruption in check that can create an environment favourable to the success of procurement reforms. But even more is needed: adequate organizational arrangements must also be in place.

4.2 Modalities of Organizational Change

The central message of this section is that institutional changes need to be embedded in adequate organizations to make public procurement reforms successful. In the previous section, we examined the lines along which the legal and regulatory framework should be transformed to increase transparency, competition, and accountability in public procurement. This approach provided the guidelines along which new laws and regulations were formulated in SSA countries and have subsequently led to the reorganization of procurement systems. We now turn to the enactment of new procurement legislations through the organizational changes that resulted from these reforms.

A determinant aspect of these changes was the creation of the 'new players' in charge of implementing and monitoring the new rules of the game. These new players, which we identify as 'micro-institutions', operate within the reformed framework and are in charge of implementing and monitoring the rules of the game in the relationship between public authorities and the operators actually delivering goods or services under public procurement. These organizations share substantial characteristics with private organizations (role of the hierarchy in the coordinating process, importance of adequate incentives, problems of control due to bureaucratization, etc.). But they also have specific characteristics, particularly in their decision making process, since their domain of action is determined and controlled by the political system and, in many cases, by the judiciary as well. This is why they can be considered as 'micro-institutions', with a special status on the fringe between the institutions fixing the rules of the game and organizations playing within these rules.

4.2.1 Overview of Procurement Regulatory Authorities

We focus in what follows on one aspect that illustrates well the logic of these changes: the creation of new independent procurement organizations or administrative agencies that we group under the generic expression *Procurement Regulatory Authorities* (PRA).[8] Indeed, PRAs were created to provide

---

[8] Some precaution is needed when using this generic expression because the entities under this label do not necessarily have all the usual properties of regulatory agencies as described in the economic literature (e.g. Laffont 2005).

support in the implementation of the new legislations, to promote greater transparency and accountability in public procurement, and to improve efficiency in the management of the procurement system. At the country level, PRAs have a pivotal role in managing and overseeing the implementation of procurement regulations and practices, and in driving initiatives to improve procurement systems. Table 4.1 presents an overview of these organizations in SSA.

In the initial phase of reforms (2001–4), sixteen out of forty-seven sub-Saharan countries created a similar organization through legislation, regulations, or decrees, and ten of these PRAs rapidly became operational. Similar organizations have been developed after this initial wave, with limited success: as of 2012, there were thirty-five SSA countries with such 'micro-institutions' in charge of implanting reforms in procurement.[9]

The organizational setting in which these arrangements are embedded varies among countries, with PRAs taking the form of agencies, directorates, offices, regulatory entities or independent bodies.[10] Depending on the individual country, these bodies also have different roles and levels of competence. Notwithstanding these differences, these entities all share one fundamental characteristic: they were designed and implemented to embody institutional changes in order to make them operational. In that respect they provide the arms and legs, so to speak, to the new legislations or regulations: they operate as micro-institutions in the sense that they give substance to the general rules defined at the broad institutional level and they provide the means to implement these rules (more or less successfully) in the interaction between public authorities and operators in charge of delivering goods, works, and services under procurement.

Procurement regulatory authorities is therefore a generic term that can refer to a variety of administrative agencies taking several different forms. For example, this type of organization in Gambia is called the Gambia Public Procurement Authority, in Ethiopia the Public Procurement Board, and in Sierra Leone

---

[9] Many of these entities have experienced problems in establishing themselves as effective organizations in monitoring and regulating procurement activities. More specifically, they have had limited success in establishing the coalitions required to overcome resistance to implementing or developing the organizational practices and capabilities needed to consolidate and institutionalize reforms. Many of these also suffered from a severe lack of effective management, thus losing their credibility in the effort to change practices and/or mobilize citizens to support their efforts. More on these issues in Chapters 8 to 10.

[10] To illustrate the significance of these micro-institutions beyond their variation in names and forms, there are approximately sixty independent agencies in the United States: an agency in the United States government is created by an act of Congress and is independent of its executive departments. In France, these bodies are Independent Administrative Authorities (AAI); in a report from 2001, the *Conseil d'Etat* counted thirty-four Independent Administrative Authorities. Contrary to the French administrative tradition, these entities are not subject to the authority of a minister.

Table 4.1 Procurement regulatory authorities (PRA) in SSA in the initial phase of reforms

Country	Creation of a PRA is under discussion	PRA was created by law, regulations, or decrees	Date of creation	Name of the PRA	PRA is operational
Angola	***				
Benin		***	2004	Agence de Régulation	
Botswana		***	2002	Public Proc. and Asset Disposal Board	***
Burkina Faso *					
Burundi					
Cameroon		***	2001	Agence de Régulation des Marchés Publics	***
Cape Verde					
Central African Republic*					
Chad		***	2004	Organe Chargé des Marchés Publics (Secr. Gal du Gvt)	
Comoros					
Congo (Brazzaville)*					
Congo (Democratic Republic)					
Côte d'Ivoire	***				
Equatorial Guinea*					
Eritrea					
Ethiopia		***	2004	Public Procurement Board	***
Gabon					
Gambia		***	2003	Gambia Public Procurement Authority	***
Ghana		***	2003	Public Procurement Board	***
Guinea*					
Guinea-Bissau*					
Kenya		***	2001	Public Procurement Department at Ministry of Finance	***
Lesotho*					
Liberia	***				

(Continued)

Table 4.1 Continued

Country	Creation of a PRA is under discussion	PRA was created by law, regulations, or decrees	Date of creation	Name of the PRA	PRA is operational
Madagascar		***	2004	Direction de la Réglementation des Marchés Publics (DRMP)	
Malawi		***	2004	Department of Public Procurement (DOPP)	
Mali*					
Mauritania*					
Mauritius	***				
Mozambique	***				
Namibia					
Niger		***	Sept.04	Agence de Régulation	
Nigeria		***	2003/2007	Bureau of Public Procurement	
Rwanda*					
Sao Tome and Principe*					
Senegal	***				
Seychelles*					
Sierra Leone		***	Law Dec. 04	National Public Procurement Authority	
Somalia*					
South Africa		***	2003	Supply Chain Management Office	***
Sudan*					
Swaziland*					
Tanzania		***	Law Jan.04	Public Procurement Regulatory Authority	***
Togo*					
Uganda		***	Law Feb.03	Public Procurement and Disposal of Public Assets Authorities	***
Zambia					
Zimbabwe*					
Total out of 47 countries	7	16			10

* Countries that do not have a PRA and are not planning to set up a PRA in the near future.

*** This indicates 'yes'.

Source: World Bank staff and government authorities.

the National Public Procurement Authority. In most francophone countries, they are called '*Agence*' or '*Autorité*' *de Régulation des Marchés Publics* (ARMP). These different forms of 'micro-institutions' can be characterized as follows. An *agency* is an administrative unit of government, such as the Central Intelligence Agency, the Census Bureau, or the Office of Management and Budget in the United States. Procurement agencies belong to the executive branch, but are outside of executive departments. For example, in 2001 Cameroon created (Decree No. 2001/48) a procurement agency called the *Agence de Régulation des Marchés Publics*. A *directorate* is a group of persons chosen to govern procurement affairs. The Public Procurement Directorate in Kenya was thus created in 2001 also as a governmental organization to serve as the central organ for policy formulation, implementation, human resource development, and oversight of the public procurement process. An *office* is an executive agency that advises the head of the State on procurement-related issues. An *authority* is an entity that has the power or right to give orders or make recommendations and decisions, issue regulations, and impose sanctions. Botswana's Public Procurement and Asset Disposal Board (PPADB), established through an Act of Parliament, is such an independent authority.

4.2.2 Independent Procurement Regulatory Authorities Around the World

Independent procurement regulatory authorities are not unique to the African region. Indeed, many countries in other regions of the world have set up such administrative agencies. Figure 4.1 shows the great disparity that exists among the geographical region. Europe and the Central Asia region have been very active in creating such entities since the 1990s. As of 2010, Africa[11] has sixteen PRAs, East Asia three PRAs, the Middle East/North Africa two, Europe and Central Asia eleven, Latin America and the Caribbean two, and South Asia two. Clearly, Africa, Europe, and East Asia are the regions with the highest numbers of PRAs. In proportion to the number of countries in the region Europe and East

---

[11] We use the world classification compiled by the World Bank. The Africa region has forty-seven countries. The East Asia and Pacific region includes Cambodia, China, Fiji, Indonesia, Kiribati, Korea, the People's Democratic Republic of Lao (Lao PDR), Malaysia, Marshall Islands, FS Micronesia, Mongolia, Palau, Papua New Guinea, the Philippines, Samoa, Solomon Islands, Thailand, Timor-Leste, Tonga, Vanuatu, and Vietnam. The Middle East and North Africa region (MENA) includes Algeria, Bahrain, Djibouti, Egypt, Iran, Iraq, Israel, Jordan, Kuwait, Lebanon, Libya, Malta, Morocco, Oman, Saudi Arabia, Syrian Arab Republic, Tunisia, United Arab Emirates, and West Bank and Gaza. The Latin America and the Caribbean region (LAC) includes thirty countries. The South Asia region includes Afghanistan, Bangladesh, Bhutan, India, Maldives, Nepal, Pakistan, and Sri Lanka. The Central and Eastern Europe region includes Albania, Armenia, Azerbaijan, Belarus, Bosnia-Herzegovina, Bulgaria, Croatia, Czech Republic, Estonia, FYR Macedonia, Georgia, Hungary, Kazakhstan, Kosovo, Kyrgyz-Republic, Latvia, Moldova, Poland, Romania, Russian Federation, Serbia and Montenegro, Slovak Republic, Slovenia, Tajikistan, Turkey, Turkmenistan, Ukraine, and Uzbekistan.

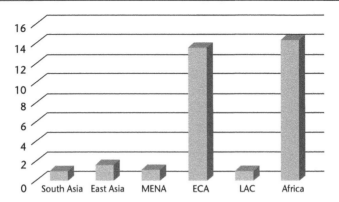

Figure 4.1 Overview of independent procurement regulatory authorities around the world (2010)

Note: Countries of Eastern Europe and North America are not represented. Data is not available for Afghanistan, Bhutan, Cambodia, China, Malaysia, Papua New Guinea, Iran, Hungary, Trinidad, and Tobago.

Source: World Bank, Procurement Policy Services Group, Operations Policy and Country Services.

Asia have the highest concentration of PRAs, while the Latin American region has the smallest number of PRAs.

One important question is, of course, how countries operate or oversee their procurement activities when they do not have an independent procurement regulatory authority. There are two main possibilities: these countries either (i) have a department, or a unit in an agency, which is responsible for overseeing procurement; or (ii) they have no PRA or department at all. In this case, the tasks normally carried out by the PRA are split among several agencies, or are not undertaken at all. For instance, the ministry of public works would carry out training activities, complaints would be handled by the courts, and procedures (bidding documents) would be designated to each procuring agency.

Figure 4.2 summarizes the different procurement bodies in different regions around the world. Europe and East Asia have the highest percentage of PRAs for the countries of these regions.[12] In Latin America, oversight procurement functions are handled mostly through units or departments in ministries. South Asia, India, Nepal, and Sri Lanka have no PRA, department, or unit operating as a procurement agency.

To sum up, and in spite of the differences across countries, there has been a trend worldwide towards creating relatively independent entities to implement new public procurement rules, to supervise and monitor the operations

---

[12] Due to a lack of full information regarding PRAs for the entire Africa region, we have not included Africa in this graph.

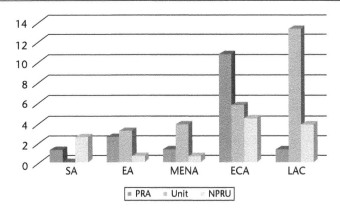

Figure 4.2 Public procurement oversight authorities around the world (2010)[1]
Note: PRA = independent procurement regulatory authorities; Unit = unit or department in an agency; NPRU = no procurement regulatory unit.
Source: The World Bank, Operations Policy and Country Services.

of public authorities in their procurement activities, and to often create an interface between public authorities and the operators actually in charge of delivering goods and services under government systems. However, there has also been significant resistance, so that the number of these independent entities remains limited and those existing are often weakly operational or not operational at all.

The issue is challenging. It is closely related to the emerging concerns about 'good governance', with transparency, competition, and accountability as the declared goals of reform, and to the capacity of public authorities to reach these goals. Public procurement reforms in SSA must be understood with this background in mind. In this context, measuring the impact of the newly created entities on the performance of public procurement systems should be high on the agenda of decisionmakers. Unfortunately, it remains largely a neglected dimension, for reasons to be explored in the following chapters.

4.3 Conclusion

In this chapter we have argued that institutional changes involve modification of the formal rules by developing new legislation that constitutes ex-ante agreements with respect to cooperation and procurement. They also involve changing the procedures and practices of procurement. Finally, capacity-building is needed not only to improve the application of ex-ante agreements, but also to strengthen enforcement mechanisms. Procurement reforms also deal with ex-post mechanisms of enforcement. These mechanisms focus on several aspects of procurement, such as the organizations needed to implement the rules; the human capacity that needs to be built to make the changes efficient; and monitoring, control, and sanctions that determine the actual course followed by public procurement reform. The anticipated results of these changes are increased transparency, competition, and accountability.

In the aftermath of institutional changes, the restructuring of the procurement organizational system induced the creation of new organizations or administrative agencies which we describe as 'micro-institutions'. Typically, these organizational changes resulted in the development of procurement regulatory authorities (PRA) or similar arrangements. In this chapter and more generally throughout Part I, we have examined the objectives and components of public procurement reform and the support they need from laws and regulations on the one hand, and from adequate organizational arrangements on the other. We have also suggested that the actual development of these reforms varies across sub-Saharan countries, as among other regions of the world. Nevertheless, we observe a powerful trend everywhere towards such reforms.

These variations across countries bring the following questions to the agenda: What explains the differences among countries? Why are some countries reforming faster than others? What have countries achieved from the implementation of public procurement reform? We turn to these questions next.

Part II
Institutional Changes at Work: Assessing Successes and Failures

> The foreign aid community generally assumes that institutions are malleable and can be changed through aid within the three to five-year life span of a development project, or at most the 15 to 20-year span of several projects. Another premise is that well-intentioned outsiders can discover needed institutional changes and persuade governments to implement reforms and sustain them...These assumptions are wrong: (i) most institutional change is well beyond the timeframe of even a series of aid projects; (ii) institutional change requires alterations in beliefs that, short of invasion, cannot usually be pushed or purchased by outsiders; (iii) successful institutional adaptations have been engineered by insiders and sometimes work quite contrary to the conventional wisdom or best practice touted by the aid community; and (iv) aid in the absence of a supportive institutional framework can create perverse incentives and prop up rulers who are opponents, not catalysts, of reform.
>
> Shirley (2005/2008: 632–3)

North (1990b: 3) defines institutions as 'any form of constraints that human beings devise to shape human interaction'. Institutions are meant to 'reduce uncertainty by providing a body to everyday life' and by providing the 'rules of the game'. They are 'the underlying determinant of the long-term performance of the economies'. Many studies emphasize the importance of institutions for long-term growth and the significant impact they have on income (Rodrik 2004; Acemoglu et al. 2001; Easterly and Levine 2003; North et al. 2009; Acemoglu and Robinson 2012). The quality of institutions is of paramount importance: institutions can rule or trump, meaning that their role needs to be recognized (Rodrik 2002). Creating or improving institutions may lead to substantial economic gain and is therefore important for a country's development.

However, the difficulty in theoretically modelling and empirically assessing this relationship between institutions and economic development, and even more so in identifying the type of institutions that matter the most, must be acknowledged upfront. One dimension of the problem is, of course, the timeframe: institutions change slowly and interact with the economy through mechanisms that are not well understood. The ongoing debate about institutions and growth exceeds the purpose of this book.[1] Our goal is more modest: through the public procurement example, we explore in the following some venues through which institutional changes have an impact on the running of the economy.

More precisely, we examine the substantial changes that affected public procurement institutions in twenty-eight SSA countries,[2] with a special emphasis on the initial phase of reform, the period 2001 to 2004. A few studies have looked at the specific-country experience of that period, e.g. Ekphenkhio (2003) on Nigeria, Lionjanga (2003) on Botswana, or Nkinga (2003) on Tanzania. However, there has been no analysis focusing on reform processes and covering a period of several years since the time these reforms were initiated. More generally, we are unaware of any systematic comparative analysis of public procurement reforms for a relatively large sample of countries similar to the one we use.[3] Our analysis also differs from existing studies because of its emphasis on how procurement reforms are deeply embedded in institutional changes or constrained by the lack of such change across SSA.

Our empirical evaluation pays particular attention to the period 2001–4 because in that period substantial procurement reforms were adopted and/or began to be actually implemented in SSA, thus facilitating a comparative approach. We are well aware that a four-year period is very short for assessing institutional changes. We are nevertheless convinced that there are valuable lessons to be learned from these experiences because this time span corresponds to expectations embedded in the action plans designed to support reforms of public procurement, and because it allows us to take advantage of the homogenous dataset available for this period, which provides a means to capture part of the dynamics of these reforms.

---

[1] Elements of the controversy can be found in Sachs (2003); Jutting (2003); Rodrik et al. (2004); Pande and Udry (2005), and Shirley (2008).

[2] The twenty-eight countries are: Angola, Benin, Burkina Faso, Burundi, Cameroon, Chad, Côte d'Ivoire, Ethiopia, Gambia, Ghana, Guinea, Guinea-Bissau, Kenya, Lesotho, Madagascar, Malawi, Mali, Mauritania, Mozambique, Niger, Nigeria, Rwanda, Senegal, Tanzania, Togo, Uganda, Zambia, and Zimbabwe.

[3] Lecat and Sanchez (2008) use a comparative approach to assess procurement reforms from 2000 to 2008, focusing essentially on legal changes in nine anglophone SSA countries. Abeillé (2011) proceeds to an extended review of public procurement reforms, but does not develop a cross-country analysis.

5

Interpreting Institutional Change in Public Procurement: Our Theoretical Framework

The idea that 'institutions matter' and that reforming them is key in overcoming poverty and slow growth was and remains an important element in the revision of public policies and strategies of international organizations and donors. The late 1990s–early 2000s can be considered the period when this issue became high on the agenda of researchers, policymakers... and consultants! The World Bank report (2002) on *Building Institutions for Markets* summarizes this reorientation well. Until that period, little attention had been given to understanding the 'institutional framework' that provides the backbone to the process of change.

Douglass North was a pioneer in that respect, emphasizing early on that: 'The major role of institutions in a society is to reduce uncertainty by establishing a stable (but not necessarily efficient) structure to human interaction. The objective of a reform is therefore to institutionalize the structure of exchange in such a way as to reduce uncertainty' (North 1990b: 16). North's contributions to the analysis of institutions and his active participation in public debates on issues of institutional reform and growth had a significant impact not only on the scholarly research agenda, but also among policymakers.[1]

Major reform initiatives that occurred in public procurement in sub-Saharan Africa were influenced by this emerging concern and have generated new institutions that are reflected in new sets of laws and regulations. Since the 1990s, various SSA countries, under pressure from political constituencies and the civil society as well as from international donors, have acknowledged

---

[1] Another influential factor that should be mentioned here is the key role of the development of regional integration (e.g. the European Union) in the awakening among policymakers to the importance of institutions. Although this factor has already been referred to as an important force pushing towards public procurement reform in SSA (see subsection 3.1.3 in Chapter 3), its analysis is beyond the scope of this book.

the need for reform which would improve the institutions, providing support to their public procurement systems. How deeply have these institutions changed? How have these changes affected the process of procurement reform? And what achievements have been accomplished?

In dealing with these issues, social scientists, lawyers, and economists have focused mostly on public procurement from a contractual and/or trade perspective and on the compatibility of the new regulations with international best practices (Arrowsmith 1998; Hoekman 1998; Laffont 2005; Quinot and Arrowsmith 2013: 269 sq.). They have paid little attention, aside from the possible exception of the legal framework, to the complex netting of institutions within which these reforms take place and how much their characteristics and changes determine the outcome of reform. Understanding the role of this institutional background and the process of institutional change within which public procurement reform is embedded is essential, but problematic. As one might suspect, institutional change is vastly more complicated than a naïve vision suggests.[2] It is a long-haul process that requires time as well as considerable resources and commitment. Institutional change is 'hard' and resists dramatic change under most circumstances (Shirley 2005/2008; 2008, chap. 2 and conclusion). Changing formal rules is only one aspect of the process: informal rules and enforcement mechanisms are just as important, if not more so.

In what follows we propose a framework to capture these dimensions that remains close to North (1990b, 2005) and Levy and Spiller (1994), followed by numerous contributions partially synthesized in Ménard and Shirley (2005/2008). These contributors have introduced to the agenda of researchers and policymakers the urgent need to take into account the different dimensions of the institutional endowment of a nation when one is trying to understand or implement reforms. Building on this framework enables us to see that public procurement reforms have largely remained at the level of formal rules, overlooking the necessity to change the informal rules and to implement enforcement mechanisms, or have been postponed vaguely to the future.[3]

Figure 5.1 illustrates the dimensions that ideally should be taken into account for an extensive understanding and/or the appropriate design of institutional changes.

---

[2] Unfortunately, this naïve approach tends to dominate among well-intentioned reformers wanting to take institutions into account.

[3] Initiatives to tackle informal rules were not perceived as essential at the time public procurement reforms were initiated. They were left on the side as something that does not belong to the procurement sector. Despite constant efforts from one of us (Abeillé, Regional Director for the World Bank at that time) to develop synergies between civil services and public financial management reforms, establishing a real partnership between these dimensions remained at the level of lip service.

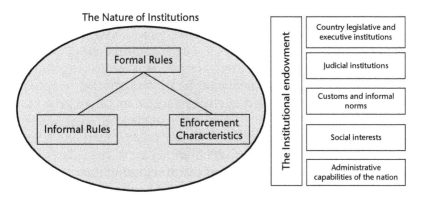

Figure 5.1 The nature of institutions and institutional endowments
Source: Authors.

Section 5.1 of this chapter focuses on the nature of the institutions and their implications (left-hand side of the figure) by summarizing some major aspects of the analytical framework initially outlined by North. Section 5.2 focuses on the endowments defining an institutional environment (right-hand side of the figure). Section 5.3 draws some lessons that will support our analysis of public procurement reforms.

5.1 Institutions: Which Ones Matter?

In our view, two streams of literature played a particularly significant role in highlighting the status of institutions in the design and implementation of reforms on the agenda of researchers and policymakers.[4]

First, beyond the pioneering work of Coase (1960), who points out the role of legal systems in the organization and development of transactions, the new institutional economists and especially the contributions by North (1981, 1990b, 2005, among others) provide a conceptualization of institutions which encompasses several dimensions and insightful views on how informal rules complement formal ones, and of the key role of enforcement mechanisms. An important step towards making the concept operational comes from Knack and Keefer (1995), who explicitly test the correlation between institutions and development and show the significance of a specific set of institutions in explaining growth, namely: the institutions surrounding and supporting property rights.

---

[4] For a review of the literature, see Pande and Udry (2005), Shirley (2008: chap. 3), and Acemoglu and Robinson (2012: chap. 2).

Second, Acemoglu et al. (2001) and Acemoglu and Robinson (2012) have proposed an analysis of factors, related mostly to political processes, which could explain the differences in institutions that developed in various colonies and the resulting divergent performance across colonial and post-colonial economies. Their argument, particularly their emphasis on the so-called 'extractive institutions' implemented by colonizers to exploit resources in countries where they did not implement large settlements because of environmental constraints (as signalled by mortality rates), has been seriously challenged (Easterly 2006; Shirley 2008: chap. 3). Besides the controversy, the point we want to make with respect to their perspective is that it adds little to the actual identification and analysis of specific institutions that could help us in analysing the context of public procurement reforms.[5]

Thus, although we make some reference to the second stream, in this chapter (and book) we refer mainly to the 'northian' tradition as the background to our analysis of the institutional context of reforms. Initially, North (1981) focuses on the structure and performance of economies through time and observes that human cooperation requires rules of behaviour which provide support to the organization of transactions and which function as institutional constraints. These constraints, including the role of violence, define the opportunity set of individuals acting in a world of positive transaction costs and imperfect foresight (North 1990b: Part I; North et al. 2009: chap. 1).

However, there is another side to the coin: institutional constraints also play a positive role in reducing the uncertainty of human interaction and the costs of cooperation. North captures these complex effects through the now classical distinction between formal institutions, which include rules specifically devised by people, and informal institutions, which are mostly built through social interaction over time. North (1990b: chaps. 5 to 7) adds another dimension, which has already been noted at the micro level by Williamson (1985: chap. 3) and one which is essential for understanding why the impact of institutional change is often so small or so counterproductive, i.e. the nature and role of enforcement mechanisms (and their accompanying organizational arrangements) with respect to both formal and informal constraints.

5.1.1 Formal Rules and Informal Constraints

As already mentioned, North (1990b: 3–4) provides the influential definition of institutions as: '... the rules of the game in a society or, more formally, the

---

[5] It should be noted that more recent developments proposed by Acemoglu and Robinson are getting close to the analysis provided by North (1990b) and North et al. (2009).

humanly devised constraints that shape human interaction [...]'. In the same passage he goes further, emphasizing that 'institutions reduce uncertainty by providing a structure to everyday life. They are a guide to human interaction [...]. Institutional constraints include both what individuals are prohibited from doing and, sometimes, under what conditions some individuals are permitted to undertake certain activities'.

Formal rules are one component that shapes institutions and determines their capacity to adapt. They include political rules (such as electoral ones), judicial rules (for example, contract law), economic rules (such as competition policies), and administrative rules (for example, procedures for opening a bid in public procurement). These rules can be part of constitutions, statute laws, common laws, or even regulations framing contracts. They do not change at the same pace. Constitutions are more costly to alter than statute laws and the latter are more costly to alter than regulation, but constitutions also tend to be more stable. Therefore, there is a constant trade-off for policymakers between rules that restrict discretionary power of agents but introduce more rigidity, and those that are more flexible but are also more prone to opportunistic behaviour.

Equally important, although too often neglected by reformers, are the *informal* and often tacit *rules* that structure social conduct and determine preferences and their changes.[6] Informal institutions are conventions and codes of behaviour: 'they range from conventions of neighbourhood conduct to ethical norms defining degrees of honesty in information exchange between the parties involved'. North (1989: 239) defines 'convention' more precisely as a way of coordinating human interaction in which all parties have a stake in seeing that they obey certain types or protocols. Conventions include *norms of behaviour* that 'are socially sanctioned types of activity which are agreed upon and which are enforced by community sanctions'. They can be partially understood as *self-imposed codes of conduct*, i.e. 'standards of behaviour that are ingrained in individuals, usually through learning, schooling and family life, and define how people should behave and which therefore define the degree to which individuals will live up to the standards of conduct. These informal constraints constitute much of what is called culture in a society' (North 1989).

Both formal and informal constraints are of utmost importance in shaping human interactions, determining the conditions under which transactions develop. In that respect, 'the institutional constraints define the opportunity set of individuals [...]. They make up an interconnected web that, in various combinations, shapes choice sets in various contexts'

---

[6] For an extensive discussion of informal rules, see Jutting (n.d.).

(North 1990b: 39). These rules and constraints also determine the stability of institutions and their (variable) capacity to reduce uncertainty. In the same passage (North 1990b: 41), North emphasizes that 'stability derives from the fact that there are a large number of specific constraints that affect a particular choice [...]. Significant changes in this institutional framework involve a host of changes in a variety of constraints, not only legal constraints but norms of behaviour as well'. This complex netting of rules and constraints also creates room for continual change at the margin, changes that may be cumulative, thus altering or even revolutionizing institutional endowments. Hence, the stability that generally characterizes institutions combines with marginal incremental changes in relative prices and/or in preferences that may induce substantial realignment within the institutional framework. Indeed, from the observation deck of the economist, constraints and the support they provide to transactions change over time, mainly because of changes in relative prices and changes in preferences. Analysing the forces behind these changes is, therefore, central to understanding how reforms are born and the reasons for their success or failure. Unfortunately, our knowledge of these processes is still rudimentary, to say the least.

5.1.2 Enforcement Characteristics

In his paper 'Institutional Change and Economic History', North (1989: 239) also discusses a third dimension of institutions: 'institutions consist of informal constraints, formal rules, and the enforcement characteristics of both'. Enforcement is a key issue and one that has long been neglected in the economic literature. New institutional economics makes an exception here. The theme was already introduced by Williamson (1971) in his seminal paper on contracts. And it was also present early on in North as well (Davis and North 1971: 27). North (1989) summarizes the issue with an analogy to a competitive sports team: if there is no umpire and no cost to the teams violating the rules, one could expect a very different sort of game than the one in which the umpire enforces the rules and imposes stiff penalties on players who violate them.

However, enforcement is difficult to achieve. In a world of perfect enforcement there would be a neutral third party (the 'umpire') impartially evaluating disputes and awarding compensation to the party injured by contract violation. In such a world, opportunism, shirking, and cheating would never pay. But such a world does not exist because flaws in design and the costliness of measurement make it difficult to determine whether a contract has been awarded and executed in full compliance with the rules and contractual obligations. Nevertheless, North argues in his paper 'Government and the Cost of Exchange in History' (1984) that an impersonal body of law, the courts, and the coercive power to enforce judgments are fundamental factors in permitting the complex contracting that is essential in a world of specialization and impersonal exchange.

Enforcement can be achieved in several ways and depends on the degree to which potential hazards such as shirking or opportunism can be controlled by institutions. In early societies, agency problems were typically solved through kinship or other close ties. Greif (1993) notes how eleventh-century Jewish traders in the Mediterranean trade network enforced codes of conduct by maintaining close social relationships, using the threat of ostracism as a disciplinary device. Later, standardized weights and measures, units of account, methods of exchange, and procedures to resolve disputes such as merchant law courts supported the expansion of trade by lowering information costs and easing enforcement.

In 'Ideology and the Free Rider', North (1981: chap. 5) argues that we all live in a Hobbesian world and the only way economies can operate near the frontier is to keep bad behaviour in check. Laws governing behaviour are established and governments are given the authority to police, including through the usage of violence (an idea developed further in North et al. 2009). However, individuals can still engage in behaviour that undermines the very foundations of the system: the potential for chaos and economic collapse exists. The development of particular ideologies and norms such as those related to family values or binding individuals to groups (i.e. tribes, clans, churches) complements formal institutions as the means to reduce behaviour that imposes negative externalities on society. Individuals are not perfectly rational: their behaviour is rooted in belief systems, and the persistence of flawed political and economic structures cannot be understood without extended assumptions about the role of subjective perceptions. Although institutional structure remains important in checking opportunistic behaviour, individuals and groups can act on deeply held beliefs in ways which affect the socioeconomic fabric of a society. Ultimately, only the exercise of 'controlled violence' can secure rights and reduce uncertainty, making enforcement credible (North et al. 1989: 13 sq.).

In sum, integrating enforcement in the analysis is both essential and challenging. On the one hand, enforcement mechanisms are essential to make rules and their implementation credible, as so well illustrated by the difficult fight against corruption. Putting into practice the constraints needed to make enforcement operational, on the other hand, means imposing restrictions on the choice set of agents in order to control opportunistic behaviour, with the risk of slipping into extortion.

5.2 Institutional Endowments

The resulting combination of formal rules, informal constraints, and enforcement mechanisms defines an institutional environment. As stressed by Shirley (2005/2008: 610):

> ...to meet the challenge of development, countries need an institutional framework that supports a market economy, which includes two distinct and not necessarily complementary sets of institutions: (i) those that foster exchange by lowering transaction costs and encouraging trust, and (ii) those that influence the state and other powerful actors to protect private property and persons rather than expropriate and subjugate them.

These two institutional sets require different components, as summarized in Box 5.1. The first set includes rules framing transactions, contracts and contract enforcement mechanisms, habits, beliefs, and values regarding economic activities. The second includes constitutions, electoral rules, the judicial system, laws governing speech, and education, norms which motivate people to abide by the laws and cooperate in monitoring the government.

Following North (1990b) and others, Levy and Spiller (1994) focus their attention on formal rules and their support which they identify as 'the institutional endowment'. They show how political institutions interact with regulatory processes and argue that the credibility and effectiveness of choices are constrained by a nation's specific institutional endowment. In their view, there are five decisive components in that respect:

i)   The country's legislative and executive institutions that are the formal mechanisms (a) for appointing legislators and decisionmakers and for making laws and regulations; (b) for implementing these laws;

Box 5.1 COMPONENTS OF THE INSTITUTIONAL FRAMEWORK

Institutional framework includes two sets of institutions:

Those that foster exchange:	Those that influence the state and other powerful actors:
• Commercial norms and rules framing transactions	• Constitutions
• Protection of property rights	• Electoral rules, laws governing speech and education
• Contracts and contract enforcement mechanisms	• Courts and the judiciary
• Habits and beliefs favouring shared values and the accumulation of human capital	• Norms that motivate people to abide by laws and cooperate in monitoring government

Source: Authors.

and (c) that determine the relations between the legislature and the executive.

ii) The country's judicial institutions, which comprise formal mechanisms (a) for appointing judges and determining the internal structure of the judiciary and (b) for impartially resolving disputes among private parties, or between private parties and the state.[7]

iii) Customs and other informal but broadly accepted norms that are generally understood to constrain the action of individuals or institutions.

iv) The character of the contending social interests within a society and the balance between them, including the role of ideology.

v) The administrative capabilities of the nation.

However, less formal rules matter just as much. Satisfactory performance can be reached through a wide range of regulatory procedures and norms and beliefs embedded in the institutional endowment, as long as three complementary mechanisms restraining arbitrary administrative action are in place: '(i) substantive restraints on the discretion of the regulator, (ii) formal or informal constraints on changing the regulatory system, and (iii) institutions that enforce the above formal constraints' (Levy and Spiller 1994: 205). In the subsequent chapters, we refer to these components in order to assess the progress achieved in public procurement, the new mode of governance introduced to circumvent some institutional flaws, and the obstacles reforms faced.

5.3 Implications for Our Analysis of Procurement Reforms

Within the framework defined previously, the way politics and politicians operate is of particular importance because it determines how so many economic rules of the game are defined and enforced...or ignored!

Understanding the political economy and the characteristics of the politics of SSA countries is essential to fully grasp the balance of forces at work in the efforts to reform public procurement. In the following chapters, we will come back to our framework and the particular role of political institutions. For the time being, let us refer to the characteristics and expected role of formal and informal rules embedded in institutional endowments and their implications for development and growth as emphasized by North (1992b: 8):[8]

---

[7] On the nature and role of the judiciary, see also Hadfield (2005/2008: chap. 8).
[8] See also Bates (1987, 1989) for an emphasis on the role of informal structures.

i) Political institutions will be stable if and only if they are supported by organizations with an interest in their perpetuation. Therefore, an essential part of political/economic reforms is the creation of such organizations.

ii) It is essential to change both institutions and belief systems for successful reform, since it is the mental models of the actors that will shape choices.

iii) Developing norms of behaviour that will support and legitimize new rules is a lengthy process and in the absence of such reinforcing norms, polities will tend to be unstable.

iv) While economic growth can occur in the short run with autocratic regimes, long-term economic growth entails the development of the rule of law, guarantees of property rights, and the protection of civil and political freedoms.

v) Informal constraints—norms of behaviour, conventions, and codes of conduct—are necessary (but not sufficient) conditions for good economic performance. Societies with norms favourable to economic growth can sometimes prosper even with unstable or adverse political rules. The key is the degree to which there is enforcement of the adverse political rules.

Drawing on these five elements, we show in the following chapters that reforms in the area of public procurement were only partial and that by not tackling all the aspects embedded in institutions, sustainability of the reforms remains fragile.[9]

5.4 Conclusion

Reform of public procurement is part of the process of institutional change. This process encompasses two dimensions. The first dimension relates to the nature of the institutions themselves. Institutions rely on formal, informal, and enforcement characteristics that shape the behaviour of actors. The second dimension relates to the institutional endowment of a specific country. Although institutional endowments frame the domain within which choices are made, it is not static: actors influence the way components combine and change over time, particularly through their action in the political system.

---

[9] Controls, enforcement, and sanctions, not to speak of efforts to modify beliefs and norms, were and remain at best postponed and most of the time neglected or rejected.

This theoretical framework sets the stage for the analysis of the public procurement reform developed in the subsequent chapters. Our analysis emphasizes in particular the need for reformers to understand that institutional change is a broad process that includes several dimensions, not just rules and regulations. Changing formal rules is only one aspect of the process: informal rules and enforcement mechanisms are just as important if not more so. As North points out (2008: 27–8),

> ...even when we have a 'correct' understanding of the economy and the 'correct' theory about its operation, the policies at our disposal are very blunt instruments. They consist of alterations in the formal rules only, when, in fact, the performance of an economy is an admixture of the formal rules, the informal norms, and their enforcement characteristics. Changing only the formal rules will produce the desired results only when the informal norms are complementary to that rule change and enforcement is either perfect or at least consistent with the expectations of those altering the rule.

Institutional change is an alchemy that still remains a mystery and one that includes path dependence, favourable initial conditions, political will, ideas, and ideologies. Specific components of the social, political, and institutional environment need to be carefully analysed in order to identify which changes can be introduced with chances to succeed. Based on our framework, the next two chapters look at ways to capture these changes and deliver some lessons about the limits to institutional changes when too much emphasis is put on formal rules.

6

Assessing Progress in Public Procurement Reforms

The previous chapter posited the general framework underlying our analysis of the process and flaws of public procurement reforms in sub-Saharan countries. In what follows, we deal with a problem that our model as well as alternative models face—that of measuring the progress (successes and failures) of these reforms. Progress is related to the design of reform as well as to their enforcement; it has a formal dimension, but also depends on informal factors, which means that it is necessarily multidimensional. It can also be a very fuzzy concept.

In order to better delineate the problem, we examine the monitoring tools and the methodology put into place by the World Bank at the beginning of this century, later modified jointly by the World Bank Africa Region Procurement Group and the OECD, and adopted by several international organizations and governments, to follow and assess public procurement reforms.[1] Notwithstanding the limits of this methodology, of which we are aware, it allows us to better identify the institutional issues at stake and explain the difficulties reform faces. It also provides the foundation for the empirical analysis proposed later. The first section of the chapter focuses on a relatively detailed description of the tools elaborated for assessing public procurement reform in SSA, while the second section develops five leading indicators used to do so.

6.1 Tools to Assess the Results of Reforms

Since the late 1990s, the World Bank, in partnership with governments and other development partners such as the European Union and the African

---

[1] Two of the book's authors, Christine Léon de Mariz and Bernard Abeillé, have been actively involved in the development and implementation of this methodology.

Development Bank (AfDB), has been deeply involved in assessing procurement systems and advising public authorities on conducting reforms of these systems in SSA countries. It has supported these reform efforts by providing technical assistance and by helping the countries assess their procurement systems through the *country procurement assessment reviews* (CPARs).

Various approaches are used to assess country procurement systems. Some are based on performance and results approaches while others focus on rules, regulations, and compliance (Jensen 2004). To monitor progress, and subsequently to adjust its assistance, the World Bank developed a database, starting in 2001, referred to as the *public procurement reform progress index* (PPRPI), abbreviated to *progress index* hereafter. This index, which corresponds to the second type of approach, is the first and the only one to date to provide information on the period that followed the implementation of procurement reforms. We provide a relatively detailed analysis of the progress index, including the rationale and the methodology behind this index, since the resulting database provides key information on the national procurement systems of SSA countries as well as key indicators on the reliability of institutions and the credibility of the reformers in the countries under review.

6.1.1 The Progress Index as a Way of Obtaining Information about Procurement Systems

To follow up on procurement reform, the World Bank developed in the early 2000s an *observatory* based on the CPARs (see Box 6.1 for a detailed explanation). Given its fiduciary responsibility—for projects financed by the World Bank, borrowers have to adhere to WB procurement guidelines and allow the World Bank to supervise project implementation—the World Bank has a particular interest in assessing procurement systems through the CPARs.

First, these reports help to ensure that national procurement procedures are suitable for use in Bank-financed investment projects and also to identify unacceptable discrepancies among these procedures. Second, the reports allow the World Bank to do a comprehensive analysis of a country's procurement system and to evaluate its performance. Third, CPARs are also important for non-earmarked lending such as adjustment lending, debt relief, and poverty reduction support credits, delivering some assurance that the fiduciary framework for fund management provided is sound. To sum up, CPARs ensure that the national competitive bidding mechanism to be used in cases below the internationally competitive bidding threshold is acceptable for use in Bank-financed investment projects; they provide a basis for decisions on the supervision of Bank operations; and their diagnosis serves as a decision making tool for governments eager to improve their procurement system. Although initially meant to improve World Bank project execution,

---

Box 6.1 COUNTRY PROCUREMENT ASSESSMENT REPORTS

Since 2002, *country procurement assessment reports* (CPARs) have served as an analytical tool developed by the World Bank to diagnose the health of the existing system in a country and, in the process, generate with the government a dialogue that focuses on needed reforms. The main purpose of the CPAR is to establish the need for and guide the development of an action plan to improve a country's system for procuring goods, works, and consulting services.

The objectives of a CPAR are to: (i) provide a comprehensive analysis of the country's public sector procurement system, including the existing legal framework, organizational responsibilities, and control and oversight capabilities, the current procedures and practices, and how well these work in practice; (ii) undertake a general assessment of the institutional and organizational risks associated with the procurement process, including identification of procurement practices unacceptable for use in Bank-financed projects; (iii) develop a prioritized action plan to bring about institutional improvements; and (iv) assess the competitiveness and performance of local private industry with regard to participation in public procurement, and the adequacy of commercial practices that relate to public procurement.

The *public procurement reform progress index* (PPRPI) is based on these CPARs and more specifically on action plans. An action plan includes recommendations both for the country and for any Bank operational matters. The main measures included in the action plan are sometimes a part of annual conditionality triggers of poverty reduction support credits (PRSCs), or other budgetary support instruments.

Source: Authors' compilation based on World Bank, CPAR Instructions

---

CPARs progressively moved to the more global objective of improving national procurement systems.

Araujo, Director of the World Bank Procurement Policy and Services Group at the time, explains the objectives and rationale for CPARs as follows:

A key objective of the new procedures [...] was to promote dialogue with governments on how to strengthen their public procurement systems. A further objective was to assess, in practice, the efficiency, transparency, and integrity of a country's entire procurement system and the risk it may pose to the use of Bank funds. The CPAR was also intended to provide a key input to the Country Assistance Strategy (CAS) for the Bank to support public procurement reform as part of an agreed implementation strategy [...] [T]here have been a number of important developments that make such a revision timely. First, with transparency and broader governance concerns having become an integral part of country assistance strategies, the efficiency and transparency of public procurement systems has been seen increasingly as an important component of public sector management. Second, changes in the Bank's business over the years, including the increased use of adjustment lending and the introduction of poverty reduction support credits (PRSC) and debt relief initiatives, has resulted in the need to undertake a comprehensive diagnostic of the country's fiduciary accountability environment, including an assessment of the country procurement system, as part of the process for agreeing to such lending. Finally, in July 2000 the CPAR was officially designated as economic and sector work (ESW) requiring revisions to the instruction to comply with Bank business processes for ESW.

(Araujo, CPAR Memorandum, May 2002)

6.1.2 The Progress Index as a Way to Measure the Credibility of the Reformers

In continuity with the CPARs, an *observatory of procurement reforms in the Africa region* was created by the World Bank Procurement Group in the Africa Region in 2001. The rationale for creating this observatory emerged from an internal study from the Africa Procurement Group that focused on the status of procurement reforms in twenty-eight of the forty-seven countries of the region (for the remaining nineteen countries, there was either no information available or no noteworthy procurement reform occurring). Through a careful examination of the CPARs prepared for twenty-one of these twenty-eight countries over the previous five years, the study concluded that an *observatory* was needed because of the difficulty of gathering information on ongoing procurement reforms: related documents were dispersed among a variety of locations and layers of bureaucracy, making a comprehensive and up-to-date overview of the procurement reforms taking place almost impossible. The creation of the observatory would: (i) act as a central oversight tool to continuously maintain a complete database on procurement reforms; and (ii) be the means to monitor progress of the reforms and to identify areas for further improvement and the steps needed to achieve that purpose.

It is in this context and striving for these aims that the *public procurement reform progress index* (PPRPI) has been developed. It was intended to assess the credibility of reformers and their commitment to implement reform. It became a comprehensive tool used in discussions with key policymakers at the country level as well as with international organizations and major donors, in particular in the formulation of policy triggers attached to budgetary support programmes. The observatory was used as a monitoring device until 2006, when it was discontinued, following the emergence of OECD indicators covering similar issues for a more extensive set of countries.[2] In its short life, the observatory permitted the Africa Procurement Group to keep up to date on the status of all procurement reforms underway in the region, and to examine reasons for delays and ways to accelerate or introduce programmes where needed. It is a unique source of information about progress

---

[2] Indicators partially derived from the index have been provided by OECD since 2006, while countries are conducting self-evaluations in the context of annual reviews carried out jointly with development partners. See next footnote.

in a major set of institutional reforms and it is the main source of information for our empirical analysis on the emergence and development of those reforms.

6.2 Indicators to Monitor Progress in Procurement Reforms

The progress index is the unweighted average of specific indicators corresponding to areas identified as the five 'pillars' of national procurement reform. These pillars intend to capture different dimensions of national procurement systems, allowing to measure the ongoing reforms, and of changes in institutions in which they are embedded. The indicators associated to these 'pillars' are aimed at measuring different components of institutional progress in public procurement reforms. Initially, countries were expected to establish action plans to modernize their procurement systems based on measures relating to these five pillars. After the harmonization of the index jointly established by the World Bank and the OECD (see Annex), indicators became more the source of guidelines to assess the level of conformity and/ or progress in procurement.

The first pillar refers to the *legal and regulatory framework*. It is a set of indicators on procurement laws, institutions, and the existence or creation of a distinct procurement authority and its responsibilities, that is, oversight, policy, audit, and recourse functions separate from the procurement implementation function. The second pillar refers to the *procurement procedures*. The related indicators are linked to the need (and the institutional capacity) of a country to develop guidelines, standard bidding documents, transparent bids-evaluation and award procedures, and transparent contract management. The third pillar is about *procurement capacities*: it refers to the need to have proficient procurement staff in place in order to apply regulations and procedures efficiently and transparently. The fourth pillar is concerned with *independent fiduciary control*, which refers to the existence of regular audits with possible application of sanctions, an independent judiciary for recourse, and a procurement oversight separate from procurement implementation. The last and fifth pillar relates to *anti-corruption measures and application of efficient sanction systems*, which focuses on anti-corruption measures that should be incorporated in procurement laws accompanied by an effective sanctions system.

The initial five pillars were reduced to four after an agreement between the OECD and the World Bank to install the 'procurement round table' initiative, with the objective of addressing key capacity development needs and 'building procurement systems in developing countries around which donors can harmonize their procedures' (Manning 2003; see also OECD/

World Bank 2005: vol. 3). In the new typology, pillar I remains focused on the *legal and regulatory framework*, pillar II has been redefined as *institutional framework and management capacity*, and pillar III as *operational practices*, while pillars IV and V were merged into *control and transparency*. Notwithstanding the changes introduced after 2006 (see Annex for a more detailed comparison), the specific indicators associated to the different pillars remain pretty much the same. Each indicator is in turn broken down into subindicators and sub-subindicators to which are associated several 'scoring criteria'. Therefore, the index aggregates these scores[3] at the indicator level, then at the pillar level. Assessors can also go a step further and aggregate the scores of the different pillars in order to obtain an integrated evaluation of the global progress accomplished in the procurement reform in relation to the action plan adopted by the reforming country.

This is what the *progress index* does. It was not and is not a measure of level of efficiency or performance of a public procurement system. It rather assesses progress made in reform with respect to initial targets agreed upon. In sum, the indicators, subindicators, and sub-subindicators associated to the different pillars intend to capture through qualitative assessment the different dimensions of the institutional reform programme that countries in our sample committed to do. Table 6.1 provides a list of the main indicators in use in the initial phase of reforms under review.[4]

6.2.1 Objective of the Progress Index

The initial progress index existed only in the African region; moreover, it was the only database at that time that was aimed at tracking public procurement reforms. The objective of its implementation in SSA countries was to rate each country's effort to modernize its public procurement system. The methodological strategy underlying the index basically intended to capture the gap (and its evolution over time) between the action plan adopted by a country in agreement with the World Bank (and possibly other donors and international organizations) and the actual implementation of reform. Five degrees or 'stages' were identified as central in measuring reform progress, and ranged from no progress or decline, to maturity.

i) *No progress, decline, or not rated (country progress=1)*: At this stage, the country has not started to implement any measures articulated in the

---

[3] The World Bank/OECD scoring for each sub-subindicator is on a scale from 0 (failure to meet the proposed standard) to 3 (full achievement of the stated standard). Until 2005, the scoring scale of the World Bank Africa Region Procurement Group was slightly different (a scale of 1 to 5).

[4] Details on the indicators, sub-indicators, and sub-subindicators after the World Bank/OECD harmonization adopted in 2005, with explanations for users, can be found in OECD (2010c).

Table 6.1 Pillars and their main indicators (until 2005)[a]

Pillar I: Legal framework and regulations
Indicator 1. Procurement Law complies with applicable obligation.
Indicator 2. Availability of supporting regulation and documentation.

Pillar II: Procurement procedures
Indicator 3. Mainstreaming procedures into public financial management.
Indicator 4. Functional regulatory body at the Centre.
Indicator 5. Existence of institutional development capacity.

Pillar III: Procurement capacity
Indicator 6. Efficient procurement operations and practice.
Indicator 7. Functionality of public procurement market.

Pillar IV: Independency of fiduciary control
Indicator 8. Effective control and audit systems.
Indicator 9. Efficiency of appeals mechanism.

Pillar V: Effectiveness of anti-corruption measures
Indicator 10. Ethics and anti-corruption measures.

[a]See Annex for a comparison of Pillars before and after 2005.

Source: B. Abeillé, presentation to fiduciary week, World Bank (Washington, DC) 8–11 March 2004.

procurement reform action plan, or after some preliminary efforts, the country has stopped implementing reforms for various reasons. Not rated (or unrated) means that a country has decided not to reform its procurement system and, as a result, the status of the country cannot be reviewed for possible action (CPAR or comparable review action to be launched).

ii) *Initial progress of the reform (1<country progress<2)*: Initial procurement reform measures are being taken, essentially at the formal level (e.g. introducing a law or a regulation, or initiating that process), but the law has not been published in the national gazette or progress remains weak in disseminating and/or applying the law. Proactive involvement by both the Bank and the target country is needed to get the reform process under way.

iii) *Average progress of the reform (2<country progress<3)*: The reform process is under way, but sustained action by both the government and the Bank is needed to maintain momentum. Sustainability remains an issue.

iv) *Advanced stage of the reform (3<country progress<4)*: Criteria for the maturity stage are actively being pursued, but have not yet been fully achieved. Some criteria (such as independent fiduciary control and effective anti-corruption measures) need further improvement.

v) *Maturity stage of the reform (4<country progress≤5)*: At this stage, the country has performed all the actions called for by the procurement action plan. The overall procurement system has therefore been improved. This does not mean that the procurement system is perfect

(or fully acceptable based on internationally best practices), but rather that the country has made substantial efforts to modernize its system based on a predetermined action plan.

6.2.2 Limitations of the Progress Index

With reference to the framework introduced in the previous chapter, it should have already become obvious that the index focuses strongly on reforms in formal institutions and procedures, which corresponds to only one dimension of those identified in our framework, an issue to be discussed further in the next chapter.

For the time being, let us examine some technical aspects more closely that will help to assess the limits of this index. In order to do so, let us start with a fictitious example. A country, 'Wonderland', adopts a plan for reforming its procurement system at time T_0. The ranking for the next four years, according to the pillars described previously, is summarized in Table 6.2.

The logic behind this 'score' is based on ordinal variables. If we focus on the bottom line ('PPRPI Total'), which aggregates the grading of the different pillars, in T_1 Wonderland showed some initial progress in the implementation of its T_0 action plan on public procurement. By T_4, Wonderland has reached the maturity stage of reform. It had performed most actions stipulated in the procurement action plan. It is also possible to decompose the global result into the different pillars, so that the specific characteristics of a country's institutional environment can be taken into account (we explore this further in the following chapter). For example, in this fictitious case, Wonderland had difficulties in making significant progress on pillar V.

Using such an index to measure reform progress has flaws and limitations. First, it rates the progress in the implementation of an action plan, adopted in T_0, between T_1 and T_4; it does not rate the system per se. Therefore, one should be cautious not to make a comparison among countries to determine

Table 6.2 Example of a PPRPI for 'Wonderland' during four consecutive years

Country: 'Wonderland'	T_1	T_2	T_3	T_4
Pillar I (Legal and regulatory framework)	2	3	4	4.5
Pillar II (Procurement procedure)	2	3	3.5	4
Pillar III (Procurement capacity)	2	3	4	4.5
Pillar IV (Independent fiduciary control)	0.5	1	2	3
Pillar V (Anti-corruption measures)	0.5	1	1.5	2
PPRPI Total	**1.4**	**2.2**	**3**	**3.6**

Source: Authors.

which system is the most advanced. Comparisons can only be made in terms of the progress or achievement of a specific action plan. In that respect, the progress index has been a useful tool since its inception for commenting on the procurement reforms in the SSA countries; however, it only rated the achievements made and the pace of reform over a limited period of time. The index did not provide an annual evaluation of public procurement systems; rather it assessed *progress* (or *lack of progress*) of the procurement reform (versus the system itself) based on an action plan prepared jointly by the World Bank and the respective government. It remained an internal tool for monitoring the progress of institutional changes articulated in the action plans, and it relied almost entirely on the World Bank's CPARs. In sum, it provided limited information on a procurement system.[5] Nevertheless, it remains a unique dataset for assessing progress achieved in major institutional reforms.

Second, this progress index was compiled by different procurement experts who might have been more or less severe in their ratings of the progress made by the countries they supervised, thereby creating a bias in the ranking. This flaw, however, was mitigated somewhat by the fact that all the ratings were reviewed by a panel of specialists, chaired by the same person for the period under review.

Third, one might also argue that some countries reached an advanced stage of reform because their action plan was less complex (fewer components to implement) or because reform had started much earlier than the initial date chosen to measure progress, so that in the period under review, it was much easier for that particular country to make the final push towards reform. This argument is related to the concept of path dependency, with institutional changes exhibiting characteristics derived from past history (for a discussion, see North 1990b: chap. 11).

Fourth, many of these limitations and flaws originate with the methodology of the index. Indeed, the index is based on ordinal variables and the synthetic result is the simple arithmetic mean of the five pillars, which of course is a very simplified way, with non-negligible distortions, to capture the different dimensions of reform and their interaction. In particular, the possibility to sum the values of the different pillars is based on an equivalence assumption (that is to say: an increase from 1 to 2 is technically equivalent to an increase from 2 to 3). However, different scales applied to the different pillars could introduce other biases and controversial issues without necessarily

---

[5] Rating a system is much more demanding: it requires well-defined benchmarks that allow for a comparison at the system level. Tentative benchmarks were established by a World Bank/OECD/ DAC working group and adopted at the so-called Paris Declaration in March 2005.

producing a clear gain in what the index is trying to measure, i.e. the trend in relation to the initial adopted plan.

The analysis of our database in the following chapter needs to take these arguments into consideration. However, despite its limitations, the progress index provides an important and useful indication of the achievements made in reforming institutions, particularly the legal framework and the procedures associated to public procurement. And more generally, it can provide the means to approximate trends and to make comparisons, although cross-country comparisons should be used with caution.[6]

6.3 Conclusion

In this chapter we have examined the monitoring tools and methodology used at the initiative of the World Bank to assess the public procurement reforms in SSA. The resulting database relies on five 'pillars' subsuming a complex set of indicators which are themselves based on sub-indicators: legal framework, procedure and practice, institutional capacity, independence of the fiduciary control, anti-corruption measures, effectiveness of the sanctions system, and handling of complaints. This database represents a unique experiment to monitor progress in the public procurement area. This experiment, initially developed by the World Bank Africa Region Group, laid the groundwork for the development of country indicators ('benchmarks') to assess the quality of a national procurement system subsequent to the signing of the Paris Declaration, updated by the Cusco Declaration of May 2011.[7]

Indeed, notwithstanding the limitations discussed previously, the progress index delivered important lessons. It showed that institutional change needs an environment that is conducive to reform, with a key role for strong institutions, political stability, and freedom. This is to say that reforming public procurement is particularly difficult for those countries that need it the most.

---

[6] For a discussion of the challenges of cross-country comparisons, see Shirley (2008: chap. 5). More recently, assessments based on the same methodology have been developed to evaluate procurement risks ('Country Procurement Risk Assessment') and institutions and policies ('Country Policy and Institutional Assessment'). See Abeillé 2012 for a summary of recent results for the Africa region.

[7] See <http://www.oecd.org/dac/effectiveness/parisdeclaration/members>. The Paris Declaration from 2 March 2005 is an international agreement which over one hundred ministers, heads of agencies, and high senior officials endorsed, committing their countries and organizations to increase efforts for the harmonization, alignment, and management of aid, using a set of monitorable indicators. The pillars and the related indicators before and after the Paris Declaration are listed in Annex. In May 2011, the OECD/DAC Task Force on Procurement met in Cusco and took stock of the accumulated knowledge in its Declaration, opening the door to the second-generation procurement reforms.

The methodology and indicators associated with the initial 'five pillars' later synthesized under 'four pillars' provide unique tools to identify these difficulties and the obstacles reforming countries face, and to assess changes through a comparative approach. In the next chapter, we develop and discuss some evidence based on the data thus collected.

7

Institutional Changes and Their Limitations in Sub-Saharan African Countries: Some Facts

Based on the theoretical framework laid out in Chapter 5 and the database presented in the previous chapter, which we complement with data from other sources, we now present empirical evidence, essentially of a statistical nature, on the public procurement reforms implemented in twenty-eight countries in sub-Saharan Africa and their limited success.

Our analysis focuses essentially on the years 2001 to 2004 in order to capture the changes and progress that happened shortly after action plans were adopted. We also take advantage of the homogeneity of the data collected during that period. We do so by making use of the five synthetic pillars to present the progress made along each marker. Our empirical evidence highlights the feasibility and some of the achievements gained through public procurement reform when this is accompanied by institutional changes, especially as far as the legislation is concerned. However, the analysis of our database also gives indications of heterogeneity in reforms among the different countries in our survey and of limited achievements, which we attribute to inadequate institutional changes with regard to informal institutions (particularly norms) and enforcement. In that respect, the expectations of the earlier reform years in terms of the more efficient use of public resources were far from being met at the end of the period. There is an especially wide gap between the initial intentions of the reformers and the ultimate outcome.

Of course it can be argued that our data are relatively short term. Nevertheless, we observe flaws that question the sustainability of reform when the emphasis was almost exclusively on formal changes, with too little concern for establishing different norms through adequate enforcement of the new rules. More specifically, our analysis suggests that most progress was in the area of laws and regulation, overlooking the informal constraints (norms of behaviours, conventions, and self-imposed code of conduct) and their enforcement, which did not substantially improve during the period under review. As such, this made the sustainability of the achievements problematic because only one dimension of these institutional reforms was in place. We present an overview of the reforming countries in section 7.1, and we examine the limitations of the achieved gains in section 7.2.

7.1 Institutional Change: Progress of Reforms in the Countries of Our Sample

In what follows, we first summarize the progress[1] in the implementation of public procurement reforms in the twenty-eight countries of our sample after they had adopted the action plans to reform. We then turn to a closer examination of the progress occurring in the different areas that make up the procurement system, with reference to the 'pillars' and their associated indicators as identified in the previous chapter.

7.1.1 Progress in the Implementation of the Reforms

Procurement reform is a complicated process and is often associated with words such as 'obstacles', 'barriers', and 'resistance to change' (Hunja 2003); however, opportunities for successful change can arise, as evidenced by the progress index (PPRPI).[2] Table 7.1 summarizes changes in the institutional structures that support procurement reform in the initial reform period under review, according to the ranking discussed in Chapter 6. We focus on the period 2001–4 because of the multiplicity of changes adopted at that time and because of data availability through the progress index for the twenty-eight sub-Saharan countries (out of forty-seven) that continued with the reforms already initiated at the beginning of the period.

The average of the five synthetic pillars in the progress index confirms a trend towards change as articulated in the action plans of our sample countries. The unweighted average for the twenty-eight SSA countries modifying their country procurement systems went from 1.9 in 2001 to 2.3 in 2004. This means that, on average, countries exhibited improvement from the level of 'initial progress' (adoption of initial reform measures, mainly at

---

[1] 'Progress' is measured as the capacity to reach the goals outlined in the action plans of the reforming countries. See our discussion in the previous chapter.

[2] Components and indicators of the index are described in the Annex.

Table 7.1 Progress status in 2004 (compared to 2001) for countries in sub-Saharan Africa

Score	Stage of reform implementation	No. of countries (out of 47)	Countries
1	No progress	1	(Eritrea)
1<country progress<2	Initial progress	12 (+3)	Angola, Benin, Burundi, Cameroon, (Cape Verde), (Congo DRC), Côte d'Ivoire, Gambia, Guinea, Lesotho, (Liberia), Rwanda, Sierra Leone, Togo, Zimbabwe[a]
2<country progress<3	Average progress	14	Burkina, Chad, Ethiopia, Guinea-Bissau, Kenya, Malawi, Mali, Mauritania, Mauritius, Mozambique, Niger, Nigeria, Senegal, Zambia
3<country progress<4	Advanced stage	5	Ghana, Madagascar, South Africa, Tanzania, Uganda
4<country progress≤5	Maturity stage	0	
	Not rated in 2001	12	Botswana, Central African Republic, Comoros, Congo (Brazza), Eq. Guinea, Gabon, Namibia, Sao Tome & Principe, Seychelles, Somalia, Sudan, Swaziland

Note: Countries with partial data for the period under review in parentheses.

[a] Zimbabwe went through a notable decline in its index over the period. See Table 7.2.

Source: Authors.

the formal level) to the level of 'average progress' (implementation of some measures, but with support from the World Bank and/or other international organizations).

According to the index, at the end of the review period, no country had fully implemented its reform programme as initially projected in its action plan; that is to say, no country had reached the maturity stage of reform (meaning a score equal to or exceeding 4 on a scale of 1 to 5).[3] Twenty-eight countries out of forty-seven were rated during the period in question, and out of these twenty-eight countries, only four—Ghana, Madagascar, Tanzania, and Uganda—had reached the advanced stage, meaning that they had actively reformed their procurement system and were not far from completing the set of measures outlined a few years earlier.

One question that necessarily comes to mind is the significance of this status in 2004 compared to what the situation was at the beginning of the period, since the rate of progress is as important as the level attained. Table 7.2 gives

---

[3] Reaching the maturity stage does not mean that the procurement system of the country is perfect, but rather that its procurement system has improved significantly. Do remember that the index does not rate the country system but its reform in terms of progress made. The category 'maturity' means that the country is committed to reform and that most measures decided in partnership with the World Bank have been fully applied.

Table 7.2 Political/administrative structure and evolution of public procurement reforms

	Government type	Administrative divisions	Legal system based on:	Evolution of public procurement reforms		
				2001* (A)	2004* (B)	2004–01(B-A)
Angola	Republic; multiparty presidential regime	18 provinces	– Portuguese civil law system and customary law	1.1	1.7	0.6
Benin	Republic	12 departments	– French civil law and customary law	1.9	1.9	0.0
Botswana	Parliamentary republic	9 districts + 5 town councils	– Roman–Dutch law and local customary law	NR	NR	
Burkina Faso	Parliamentary republic	45 provinces	– French civil law system and customary law	1.3	2.5	1.2
Burundi	Republic	17 provinces	– German and Belgian civil codes and customary law	1.0	1.7	0.7
Cameroon	Republic; multiparty presidential regime (formerly federal State)	10 provinces	– French civil law system, with common law influence	1.4	1.8	0.4
Cape Verde	Republic	17 municipalities	– the legal system of Portugal	NR	.1.3	NR
Central Africa Republic	Republic	14 prefectures	– French law	NR	NR	NR
Chad	Republic	18 regions	– French civil law system and Chadian customary law	1.8	2.3	0.5
Comoros	Republic	3 islands + 4 municipalities	– French and Islamic law in a new consolidated code	NR	NR	NR
Congo (Brazza)	Republic	10 regions + 1 commune	– French civil law system and customary law	NR	NR	NR
Congo (DRC)	Republic	10 provinces + 1 city; (subdivided into 26 new provinces in 2009)	– a new constitution was adopted by referendum 18 Dec. 2005	NR	2.0	NR
Côte d'Ivoire	Republic; multiparty presidential regime	19 regions	– French civil law system and customary law	1.2	2.0	0.8
Eq. Guinea	Republic	7 provinces	– Spanish civil law (partially) and tribal custom	NR	NR	NR

Eritrea	Transitional government	6 regions	– primary basis is the Ethiopian legal code of 1957	NR	1	NA
Ethiopia	Federal republic	9 ethnically based states + 2 self-governing administrations	– civil law	1.8	2.1	0.3
Gabon	Republic; multiparty presidential regime	9 provinces	– French civil law system and customary law	NR	NR	NR
Gambia	Republic	5 divisions + 1 city	– combination of English common law, Islamic law, and customary law	1.3	1.7	0.4
Ghana	Constitutional democracy	10 regions	– English common law and customary law	2.2	3.4	1.2
Guinea	Republic	33 prefectures + 1 special zone	– French civil law system and customary law	1.8	1.9	0.1
Guinea-Bissau	Republic	9 regions	– French civil law	1.2	2.4	1.2
Kenya	Republic	7 provinces + 1 area	– Kenyan statutory law, Kenyan and English common law, tribal law, and Islamic law	2.6	2.5	-0.1
Lesotho	Parliamentary constitutional monarchy	10 districts	– English common law and Roman–Dutch law	1.6	2.0	0.4
Liberia	Republic	15 counties	– dual system of statutory law: Anglo-American common law for the modern sector and customary law, unwritten tribal practices for indigenous sector	NR	1.2	NA
Madagascar	Republic	6 provinces	– French civil law system and traditional Malagasy law	2.4	3.1	0.7
Malawi	Multiparty democracy	27 districts	– English common law and customary law	2.0	3.0	1.0
Mali	Republic	8 regions	– French civil law system and customary law	2.6	2.7	0.1
Mauritania	Democratic Republic	12 regions + 1 capital district	– combination of Islamic law and French civil law	2.5	2.6	0.1
Mauritius	Parliamentary democracy	9 districts + 3 dependencies	– French civil law system with elements of English common law in certain areas	NR	2.2	NA

(Continued)

Table 7.2 Continued

	Government type	Administrative divisions	Legal system based on:	Evolution of public procurement reforms 2001* (A)	2004* (B)	2004–01(B-A)
Mozambique	Republic	10 provinces + 1 city	– Portuguese civil law system and customary law	2.0	2.2	0.2
Namibia	Republic	13 regions	– Roman–Dutch law	NR	NR	NR
Niger	Republic	8 regions + 1 capital district	– French civil law system and customary law	2.3	2.3	0.0
Nigeria	Federal republic	36 states + 1 territory	– English common law, Islamic law (in 12 northern states), and traditional law	2.0	2.3	0.3
Rwanda	Republic	5 provinces	– German and Belgian civil law systems and customary law	2.6	2.0	-0.6
Sao Tome & Principe	Republic	2 provinces; Principe, Sao Tome *note*: Principe has had self- government since 29 April 1995	– Portuguese legal system and customary law	NR	NR	NR
Senegal	Republic	11 regions	– French civil law system	2.2	2.5	0.3
Seychelles	Republic	23 administrative districts	– English common law, French civil law, and customary law	NR	NR	NR
Sierra Leone	Constitutional democracy	3 provinces + 1 area	– English law and customary laws	NR	1.3	NA
Somalia	Transitional parliamentary federal government	18 regions	– a mixture of English common law, Italian law, Islamic Shari'a, and Somali customary law	NR	NR	NR

South Africa	Republic	9 provinces	– Roman–Dutch law and English common law	NR	2.1	NA
Sudan	Power-sharing government under the 2005 Comprehensive Peace Agreement	25 states	– English common law and Islamic law	NR	NR	NR
Swaziland	Monarchy	4 districts	– South African Roman–Dutch law in statutory courts and Swazi traditional law and custom in traditional courts	NR	NR	NR
Tanzania	Republic	26 regions	– English common law	2.6	3.2	0.6
Togo	Republic	5 regions	– French-based court system	1.0	1.1	0.1
Uganda	Republic	69 districts	– common law and customary law	2.7	3.6	0.9
Zambia	Republic	9 provinces	– English common law and customary law	2.3	2.3	0.0
Zimbabwe	Parliamentary democracy	8 provinces + 2 cities	– mixture of Roman–Dutch and English common law	2.0	1.4	–0.6

* *Scores:* Scale from 1 to 5; a high value on the scale means that a country has made substantial progress in reforming its procurement system.

NR: not rated in the period under review; *NA:* not available.

Source: Authors' own compilation based on: The World Bank, Africa Procurement Group; and CIA—The World Factbook (https://www.cia.gov/library).

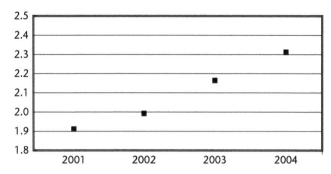

Figure 7.1 Public procurement reform progress in Africa, 2001–4
Note: Only with countries included in the PPRPI dataset in 2001.
Source: The World Bank, Africa Procurement Group, PPRPI.

the details on this evolution, as well as on the political systems and administrative structures prevalent in forty-seven African countries.[4]

For a very broad picture of the progress made, the data can also be utilized to aggregate the five pillars for all countries under review over the period considered. Figure 7.1 provides this summary: progress starts in 2001 at an average of 1.9 and reaches 2.3 in 2004. The index does not start at 1 (lowest score) because in 2001 some countries had already taken steps to initiate their reform programme. This explains why only a few countries were at the 'no progress' stage on that date. For instance, CPARs had been carried out for Burkina Faso, Cameroon, and Chad in 2000, with the result that certain measures had been taken prior to the period under review. In fact, some country system assessments were already being conducted in the 1990s, although technical assistance from the World Bank became more consistent and systematic later in the decade, making the data, essentially after 2000, more appropriate for a sufficient number of countries in our sample.

Seven additional countries began to reform their procurement systems after 2001, but are not included in Figure 7.1. It is also worth noting that some countries (such as Botswana) started to update their procurement system without the assistance of the World Bank, or with the support of the World Bank and other multilateral organizations (such as the African Development Bank) and bilateral donors (such as France, Germany, and the Netherlands). For lack of available data, we focus only on the countries monitored by the World Bank Index.

---

[4] South Africa is included in this table for informative purposes only; it is NOT included in our analysis.

7.1.2 Progress According to Indicator Pillars

As indicated in the previous chapter, the measure of progress in procurement reforms was established through five main pillars: (pillar I) the *legal and regulatory framework*, (pillar II) *procurement procedures*, (pillar III) *procurement capacity*, (pillar IV) *independent fiduciary control*, and (pillar V) *anti-corruption measures and the application of efficient system of sanctions*. The implementation of each component was monitored by the progress index (PPRPI). The aggregated index on which Figure 7.1 is built is a simple average of the five pillars for the countries under review so that it reflects only a very broad trend for the entire region. However, as pointed out in the theoretical framework, understanding reforms, their flaws, and their successes requires a more careful look at the components of reform and their evolution. Table 7.3 is a step in that direction, in which progress is broken down by pillar, while Figure 7.2 visualizes the average progress made within each pillar. We are, of course, aware of the arbitrariness that can be caused by summarizing the events and progress of such a diversified set of countries where each undertook its public procurement reform at a different pace. On the other hand, this measure of the averages provides insight into what happened in the global development in procurement reform in SSA for the period under review.

At the end of that period, the twenty-eight sample countries had reached the 'average progress' level in the implementation of the first reform component, which means these countries had made moderate progress in reforming their procurement legal systems.[5] Regarding the other pillars, they remained at quite a low level.

Indeed, in addition to the country differences already mentioned, there was also diverging development across the different reform components. Not all indicators evolved similarly during the period under review: some

Table 7.3 Procurement reform: average progress and breakdown according to indicator pillars

Pillar	2001	2002	2003	2004	(2004–2001)
Pillar I	2.3	2.5	2.7	2.9	0.6
Pillar II	2.0	2.1	2.1	2.3	0.3
Pillar III	1.7	2.0	2.1	2.2	0.5
Pillar IV	1.9	1.8	2.1	2.0	0.1
Pillar V	1.6	1.7	1.9	2.0	0.4

Source: Authors' own calculations.

[5] It needs to be remembered that 'average progress' is measured as a value between 2 and 3 on our 1-to-5 scale. Average progress implies that the reform process is under way, but sustained action by the government and donors is needed to maintain momentum.

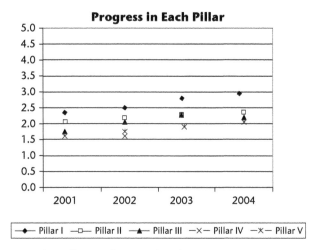

Figure 7.2 Progress by pillars in the period under review
Source: Authors' own calculations.

components of the reform programme were implemented, broadly speaking, while others were only very partially undertaken. For instance, the component for creating new laws and regulations was implemented faster than the components that focused on setting up new procedures and practices, improving the control system, institutional capacity, and anti-corruption measures. Pillar I (the formal legal framework) progressed much faster than pillars II–V. In other words, even though pillar I improved over this period, the lack of attention to capacity-building, independent fiduciary control, effective anti-corruption measures, and enforcement explains why overall progress has not been as substantial as was expected, as already shown in Table 7.1. This is of course to be related to the issues emphasized in our theoretical framework, i.e. the difficulty in changing informal institutions and in enforcing new rules of the game.

Let us substantiate this point through a brief review of the evolution of the different pillars in order to get a better picture of the reforms in their different dimensions.

PILLAR I: LEGAL AND REGULATORY PROCUREMENT FRAMEWORK
During the period of implementation of reform,[6] the emphasis was on pillar I, the procurement legal and regulatory framework, which is the *formal* side of institutional reforms, and significant progress was made in that respect. During this period, many countries drafted new procurement laws and

---

[6] This was also the case later on, as illustrated by the different scenarios reviewed in Lecat and Sanchez (2008) and Quinot and Arrowsmith (2013).

Table 7.4 Enactment of public procurement legislation

	Countries in sub-Saharan Africa	Date of public procurement law or decree
1	Burkina Faso	May, 2003
2	Chad	November, 2003
3	Ethiopia	July, 2004
4	Gambia	February, 2002
5	Ghana	December, 2003
6	Guinea Bissau	November, 2002
7	Madagascar	July, 2004
8	Malawi	August, 2003
9	Senegal	July, 2002
10	Sierra Leone	December 2004
11	Tanzania	July, 2004
12	Uganda	February, 2003

Source: The World Bank, Africa Procurement Group, PPRPI.

regulations to modernize their procurement systems. The legal and regula-tory framework was changed often using the United Nations Commission on International Trade (UNCITRAL) model and/or guidelines from the World Bank and other international organizations. Table 7.4 indicates that within four years, twelve of the twenty-eight sample countries had enacted new pro-curement legislation or regulations (laws or decrees).[7] Other countries had also worked actively on their procurement legislation, preparing drafts etc., but did not enact any new legislation (this was the case for Angola, Côte d'Ivoire, Kenya, and Mozambique).

In relation to our theoretical framework, it is clear that various countries have sought to change their formal institutions. Overall, progress was made in the legal and regulatory procurement framework and new sets of formal rules were developed with respect to the process of acquiring goods, works, and services by public sector entities.

The resulting procurement regimes differed according to the prevailing legal and administrative traditions of each country, but they also followed a number of general principles, reflecting the influence of international models such as the UNCITRAL Model Law and the World Bank guidelines. It should also be noted that in many cases, an important aspect of this formal aspect of reforms was the creation through legislation of *procurement regulatory authori-ties* (PRAs) or similar arrangements, in charge of implementing and monitor-ing the reforms, providing links between public authorities and operators (see

---

[7] This is the number of countries that did enact new legislation or regulations, not to be mis-taken for the larger number of countries that initiated reforms and, for some of them, developed new organizational arrangements to implement reforms (see Table 4.1 in Chapter 4 for more details).

Part III). However, much less has been accomplished with regard to changing the less formal constraints and enforcement characteristics, as partially captured through the other pillars.

THE OTHER PILLARS

Pillar II, which concerns *procurement procedures*, also exhibited progress, although significantly less rapidly than pillar I. In many of the countries in our sample, little progress, if any, was made with respect to pillar II. Although numerous manuals on procedure, guidelines, and bidding documents exist in the countries of our sample, most documents do not conform to international standards. Usually, the preparation of these documents is done in conjunction with the drafting of the regulations, but their use can be effective only after the enactment of new procurement laws. After adopting the new laws Ghana, Guinea-Bissau, Kenya, and Mali prepared standard bidding documents and, in some instances, users' guides during the period under review. Tanzania issued an extensive set of standard bidding documents in November 2002, and Uganda, to a lesser extent, issued guidelines for regulations and some standard bidding documents in 2004. The other countries of our sample registered little progress, if any at all, with respect to this pillar.

Some progress can also be noted in pillar III (*procurement capacity*), although not very substantial. This is an important observation because it happens in the context during which many of the sample countries had invested resources (although less than in pillar I) in capacity-building. In some cases, a capacity-building plan had been prepared and training given at various levels (central, decentralized, and for private sector representatives); visits to countries with better-developed capacities were organized to gain insight from their experiences, and investments were made in computers to facilitate monitoring of the procurement process. Nevertheless, this pillar overall remains one of scant attention; this represents a serious challenge to the sustainability of procurement reforms in the long run.

Progress in pillar IV (*independent fiduciary control*) is even weaker, with countries devoting very little resources and energy to improving fiduciary controls. Similarly, the last pillar on *anti-corruption measures and application by efficient sanctions system*, which relates also to the handling of complaints, has seen very little progress, and this only in a handful of countries. In Burkina Faso, the High Authority against Corruption (*Haute Autorité de Coordination de Lutte contre la Corruption*) published its first report in 2004 on contract management for certain projects. The report was sent to the prime minister and sanctions for mismanagement were rapidly applied against civil servants.

More generally, it should be emphasized that pillars III, IV, and V are closely linked, as effective audits and anti-corruption measures need to be carried out by trained personnel. Generally civil servants within the entities responsible for control (the *Tribunal de Contas* for lusophone countries, the *Cour des Comptes* for francophone countries, or the *Auditor General* for some anglophone countries) have no specific training in public procurement, so their capacity to identify and implement effective measures is very limited. This situation makes the enforcement of new rules fragile.

To sum up, despite some progress, particularly in the formal legal framework (pillar I), there is wide discrepancy between the intentions of the reformers at the beginning of the process and the outcome after four years of reform. Reformers backed by international organizations sought to change five dimensions of the procurement system within a relatively short period; yet, at the end of the period, only one dimension has improved substantially. It confirms a lesson emphasized long ago by new institutional economists: institutions change very slowly, and the actual implementation of formal changes even more so.

Moreover, it is important to note that important heterogeneities exist among the countries. During the period under review, some countries undertook substantial reform of their procurement systems while others did not deliver what they promised: they stagnated or even regressed. Digging deeper into our database and looking at the evolution of the score of the different countries of our sample for the different pillars shows these differences among the countries.[8] Burkina Faso, Ghana, Malawi, and Uganda, i.e. the fastest reforming countries, made significant progress and those that reached reform's advanced stage included Madagascar, Mauritius, Tanzania, and Uganda. It is worth noting that the fastest reformers were not necessarily the ones that reached the 'advanced stage' of reform. One possible explanation is that some countries had already started the update of their system before the inception of the index, and had thus reached a more advanced phase by that time. However, in all cases, variations in progress along the different pillars and across countries remain significant, with the most important progress mainly concentrated on formal reforms (Pillar I).

7.2 Limited Achievements and the Problem of Sustainability

Indeed, our examination of the achievements from the reform of public procurement systems among the twenty-eight sample countries indicates important gaps between the progress made in reshaping formal institutions and the slow pace at which changes were introduced or observed in informal institutions and their enforcement procedures. The uneven development along the dimensions corresponding to our 'pillars' helps to understand the limitations

---

[8] Database available from the authors.

of these reforms. Changing one dimension only imposes limitations and/or has negative implications for the entire reform process, as was already mentioned in Chapter 5 (section 5.3).

We come back in Part III to the issue of supportive organizations, or 'micro-institutions', and the impact they can have on the success or failure of reforms. In what follows, we focus on the implications that changes in formal rules have on the procurement reform, as compared to changes in informal rules, as well as the implications of issues relating to enforcement and to the problem of human capital.

7.2.1 The Gap between Formal and Informal Rules

At the beginning of the movement towards procurement system reforms, there was the hope that this could be done within a four- to five-year reform programme (which is why we focus on the initial period of reforms). However, the evidence provided in section 7.1 shows that out of the twenty-eight SSA countries, not a single country had succeeded fully in implementing its action plan in that short timeframe, and only twelve countries had been able to change their formal rules, a process that alone took several years (see Table 7.4). Notwithstanding North's affirmation (1992a) that 'formal rules can be changed overnight by the polity', it is clear that changing even formal rules is not easy. It is often a long and tedious process, and a highly politicized process. In our sample, despite intentions to amend formal rules, most countries were unable to accomplish the change during the initially planned period. Furthermore, the impact of most measures in the countries that did reform was limited. This observation suggests the existence of major obstacles, even with respect to changing formal rules, due to limited human capabilities and poor political commitment.

The initial emphasis on creating new laws and regulations reflected four ambitions: (i) to give an impulse to reform; (ii) to initiate more transparency in procurement systems; (iii) to move towards regional harmonization (Verdeaux 2005); and (iv) to meet the triggers agreed upon with international organizations or through bilateral agreements as conditions for gaining access to various budgetary support programmes. Changes in the formal rules, however, did not necessarily produce the desired outcome. As was seen in section 7.1, the impulse to reform took longer than expected; harmonization faced numerous obstacles even at the formal level; and transparency, largely identified as the existence of mandatory advertisement and measures against corruption, remained limited because it was defined by the thresholds for selecting procurement methods, which favoured contract 'slicing'.

Beyond these difficulties is the more general issue of the 'sustainability' of reforms when reform is basically limited to changes in formal institutions. As already argued in the theoretical framework, changing formal rules is a necessary but not a sufficient condition to successful and sustainable reform. Even if formal rules could be changed overnight, which they cannot (although rare exceptions might exist), informal constraints embodied in customs, traditions, and codes of conduct are much more impervious to sustainable reform. The difficulties of the sample countries that did reform formal institutions in reaching the second level (which implies that the reform process is underway but depends on sustained action by the government and outside forces, in our case the World Bank) illustrate the importance of time in assuring the sustainability of reform. In that respect, a time span of five years, as targeted in the action plans endorsed by the reforming countries, was unrealistic. Institutional change is incremental and consists of marginal adjustments to complex rules, norms, and enforcement which are integral parts of reform: it takes time for these adjustments to become cumulative (nor does it happen automatically) (Shirley 2008: chap. 2 and 3). As noted by North (1990b: 43):

> ... perhaps most important of all, the formal rules change, but the informal constraints do not. In consequence, there develops ongoing tension between informal constraints and the new formal rules, as many are inconsistent with each other. The informal constraints had gradually evolved as extensions of previous formal rules. An immediate tendency is to have new formal rules supplant the persisting informal constraints. Such change is sometimes possible, in particular in a partial equilibrium context, but it ignores the deep-seated cultural inheritance that underlies many informal constraints.

Changes in beliefs and norms require a period of gradual learning, which makes the understanding of traditional social organizations, culture, and politics a key issue of the process of institutional change.

7.2.2 The Politics of Reforms: Enforcement Issues

One important requirement in that respect is to understand the political forces at work, and this needs identifying the 'winners' and 'losers' of the reform and creating incentive mechanisms to ensure institutional change. These mechanisms are not well understood and too often neglected, which might explain why so many reform attempts have stalled (Cox et al. 2000; Shirley and Ménard 2002). Understanding the political economy of a country is as important as changing the formal rules in public procurement. Changes are resisted and ultimately not enacted because of political conflicts arising from redistribution of the post-reform rents involved. Such resistance, if not anticipated and/or wrongly estimated, could paralyse the implementation of reform and could explain the slow progress in pillars II to V in the countries of our sample that adopted new formal rules.

These lock-in situations bring the issue of enforcement and the effectiveness of its accompanying rules into the picture. Without adequate formal and informal constraints and incentives, self-serving behaviour might preclude implementation of the desired changes, thus generating uncertainty about the future of reform. The transaction costs will reflect this uncertainty and will include a risk premium, the magnitude of which might prevent further advancement with the reform process.

Corruption illustrates this problem well. Some SSA countries have made efforts to adopt laws and/or regulations to improve public procurement transparency and combat corruption. But enforcement mechanisms have been neglected or they lack the basic capacities and/or power needed to be effective. North (1990b: 48) explains that 'rules are generally devised with compliance costs in mind, which means that methods must be devised to ascertain that if a rule has been violated, to measure the extent of the violation, and to apprehend the violator'. As Figure 7.2 suggests, the reform process in our sample countries has not been very successful in transforming these 'pillars' aimed at improving enforcement mechanisms. Two reasons might explain this situation. First, the sequencing of the reform made these pillars a secondary phase of the process, a miscalculation amplified by the unrealistic expectation that the first phase (formal reforms) would be short. Second, the procurement system is much broader than assumed and encompasses a variety of institutions over which procurement reform does not have full control. In many cases, institutions besides those directly involved in the procurement reform (e.g. *Cour des Comptes, Tribunal de Contas,* or Attorney General) were too weak or not within the scope of reform's jurisdiction. Lack of effective third-party enforcement made it extremely difficult to achieve sustainable reform. This also underlines the complementarities of a public procurement system with the institutional framework of a country, and points to the fact that procurement reforms can hardly be achieved without other institutional reforms.

7.2.3 The Problem of Human Capital

One major aspect that is critical for the success of reform relates to human capital. Human capital is indeed a vital factor in ascertaining compliance to rules and agent performance. Although some progress was made during the period under review, and notwithstanding the difficulties in assessing this progress, training programmes to improve public procurement skills clearly remained insufficient. Some public officers were trained, and there was even some attempt to develop capacity-building programmes, but these efforts faced three obstacles: (i) the lack of dissemination: only a few agents were aware of the institutional change and were willing to invest in building adequate capacities, while most agents were not in compliance. This clearly raises the issue of incentives such as: (ii) job mobility of the agents: some of the trained staff moved onto other positions; and (iii) lack of academic curriculum: training programmes were not integrated into a broader academic curriculum, so that from a long-term perspective there was little incentive for agents to invest in this capacity-building.

This lack of capacity introduces serious issues of compliance and enforcement. Cost of the human resources needed to make public procurement reform effective was not adequately taken into account despite the importance of the matter. One way to overcome the capacity problem would be to concentrate available resources in one main organizational structure, for example, a procurement regulatory authority (more on this in Part III). Klitgaard proposes a framework based on the observation that laws and controls are insufficient if there is no adequate organization with well-endowed human capital to implement them. The fight against corruption is typical of the issues at stake (Klitgaard 1998: 6):

> When corruption becomes systematic, fighting it must go beyond implementing liberal economic policies, enacting better laws, reducing the number and complexity of regulations and providing more training, helpful though these steps may be. Fighting systematic corruption requires administering a shock to disturb a corrupt equilibrium. It might include such steps as the following: (i) formation of a national coordinating body that is responsible for devising and following up on a strategy against corruption, along with a citizens' oversight board; (ii) identification of a few key agencies or areas on which the anti-corruption effort might focus its attention in the first year, in the hope of achieving some momentum-building successes; (iii) a capacity-building strategy within key ministries that takes the problems of incentives (including incentive reforms) and information seriously; and (iv) identification of a few major offenders whose cases will be prosecuted.

In sum, human capital with respect to public procurement is a major issue that deserves more attention; enforcement of a new institutional framework can be possible only if public procurement officers and people working in public procurement (including staff at supreme audit institutions) are given proper training and adequate incentives to make changes effective.[9]

7.3 Conclusion

In this chapter, we have shown that some (but not all) countries improved their formal procurement systems after the reform movement was initiated in the late 1990s. We have also shown that most progress was made in the area

---

[9] See Shirley (2008: chap. 7) for a converging view.

of formal rules, while other dimensions were sidestepped. The enforcement mechanisms and informal constraints (norms of behaviours, conventions, and self-imposed codes of conduct) did not substantially improve during that period. As such, sustainability of the gains is problematic, as only one dimension of the institutional reform is in place. Therefore, the reforming countries are now at a critical juncture: these new rules need to be complemented by a change in beliefs and enforcement mechanisms through extensive training and monitoring.

Indeed, despite some progress, there is wide deviation between the initial reform intentions to change several dimensions of the procurement system (i.e. legal procurement framework, procedures and practices, institutional capacity, fiduciary controls, and anti-corruption measures and sanctions) and the outcomes achieved after four years. Reform took longer than originally planned and concentrated on the formal ex-ante rules: among the countries that changed their legislation, the target has been more or less attained in only one out of the five identified pillars. Reform has not tackled the informal constraints or the effectiveness of the enforcement mechanisms. This is due to the sequencing of the reform and a general lack of human resources, but also because of pressure from organizations and donors who focused largely on making changes to the formal rules within a relatively short period. One should also add that little attention has been paid to the relationship between formal and informal constraints and enforcement mechanisms because the expertise in this area is weak or not properly appreciated.

Table 7.5 summarizes the approach that was taken to reform procurement systems.

The focus during the first phase has been on changing the formal rules and creating new oversight organizations. It was expected that at a later stage the 'reformers' would address issues related to performance, efficiency, and enforcement mechanisms. But graduation to the second phase is problematic, due to a combination of political interference, cultural pegging rooted in norms and behaviours, corruption, and control of violence.

Table 7.5 The two stages of the public procurement reform

Environment: Political interest + delivery of public services	
Pressure conducive to reform; civil society + international community	

1st Stage of the Reform	2nd Stage of the Reform
Adequate Institutional Environment	Compliance
Changes in the formal rules	Enforcement
	Performance
Creation of new micro-institution/organization	Player using the new rule of the game

Source: Authors.

North et al. (2009) provide us with interesting political economy elements for understanding how these obstacles crystallize. They distinguish between two types of societies, identified as *limited access orders* and *open access orders*. Open access orders control violence through open access and competition, while limited access orders resolve the problem of violence by granting privileged control to political and/or military elites. These authors argue that transplanting institutions from open access orders into limited access orders, such as markets, elections, and rule of law, often fails because it challenges the rent-creation system that holds the limited access order together, and thus creates risk of violence: the groups losing from the reform will resist change, while those who might benefit hesitate to support changes that could end in violence.

Another dimension needs to be taken into account: feasibility of the reform. As rightly emphasized by Levy and Spiller (1994) in their discussion of reforms in telecommunications, the key to making markets work effectively lies not just in introducing market competition, but in introducing it sensibly. In that respect, not fully understanding the political dimension in which these reforms would take place, reformers were too optimistic in setting up a timeframe that was too short. Given the cost of enforcement, the problem of resources, and more broadly political economy considerations, 'second- or third-best solutions', although less efficient from an abstract point of view, might have survived better than the one viewed as optimal. This approach would suggest that, for example, strengthening inefficient bodies to improve their internal mechanisms or concentrating on the enforcement of existing rules and training may be more efficient than moving away from existing systems.

Last, in the complex netting of factors involved in institutional changes, one cannot neglect the role of actors, and particularly those organizations that are the key 'players' of the game within the institutional environment. Indeed, institutional changes require 'engines' to overcome the obstacles to the adoption of new rules, to implement these new rules, and to make them operational. The continuous interaction of institutions and organizations (or 'micro-institutions') specifically designed to embed them in the actual running of economies is a key characteristic of institutional change.

We now turn to this organizational dimension.

Part III
Organizational Change and Public Procurement Reforms: The Role of Micro-Institutions

> Political institutions will be stable only if they are supported by organizations with an interest in their perpetuation. Therefore, an essential part of political economic reforms is the creation of such an organization.
>
> Douglass C. North (1992a: 3)[1]

So far we have examined public procurement reforms in the context of the forces that push towards change and the institutional environment that provides support or creates barriers to these changes. To sum up, we have been mainly concerned with the institutional dimension in which reforms are embedded. In what follows, we switch our attention to 'micro-institutional' arrangements, or the specific organizations created to support and implement institutional changes. In North's quote, he points out that political institutions will be stable only if they are supported by organizations with an interest in their perpetuation. We take this view as our point of departure and focus on the organizational changes that accompany institutional reforms.

More specifically, public procurement is a way to organize transactions between public authorities and operators (who can be public or private) through a form of contract. Such contracts are embedded in institutionally defined rules and are implemented through specific arrangements. Indeed, there are many different possibilities for organizing and monitoring these transactions. It can be done through a bureau. It can be done through a central tender board which specializes in this task. It can be done through an autonomous public agency. We identify as 'micro-institutions' those arrangements that are at the interface between the institutionally embedded rules framing the organization of procurement, and the way operators act and respond to these rules.

---

[1] Douglass C. North (1992), 'The New Institutional Economics and Development.' Published in *The American Economist* (Spring): 36 (1) 3–6 under the title 'Institutions and Economic Theory'.

In the following chapters we pay special attention to a specific category of such 'micro-institutions', namely administrative entities that we group under the generic term of 'procurement regulatory authorities', to which procurement oversight and regulatory functions are delegated. In other words, we explore in greater depth a category of organizations, or 'mechanisms of governance' in Williamson's terminology, which were developed especially to provide support to institutional reforms and to make changes effective.

Our analysis remains aligned with North's (1971, 2005) classical distinction between institutions and organizations. However, we enrich his approach by pointing out the existence of an intermediate category of players that structure the interface between the general institutions defining the rules of the game and the actual entities (public or private) that operate within these rules. There is little in the economic literature on these bureaucratic organizations as essential support to institutional reform, and there is almost nothing on the status and role of public procurement organizations in sub-Saharan Africa. Although administrative agency design has been a source of considerable scholarly attention in developed countries, mainly if not exclusively in relation with the so-called deregulation movement and the role of regulatory agencies in that process,[2] it has received little attention in the context of public procurement reform. Yet at the time reforms were initiated in SSA, sixteen countries out of the forty-seven that were engaged in procurement reforms had created procurement regulatory authorities (PRA) or similar entities, to which oversight and regulatory procurement functions were delegated.

In what follows, we examine the nature and role of the PRAs to address two key questions: What has shaped these new organizational solutions? And why have some countries decided to embrace them while others rejected them?

---

[2] See Laffont (2005).

8

A Theoretical Framework to Interpret Organizational Changes

Institutional change leads to the creation of new rules that need to be supported either by existing organizations which may need to be reshaped, or by building new ones where none had existed before. In the case of public procurement, the institutional reforms that emerged in sub-Saharan Africa in the beginning of this century were accompanied by a substantial reorganization of the governance mechanisms that dealt with procurement. In the attempt to understand these changes, we rely on some key concepts underlying the sequence that goes from institutional change to the creation of new organizational arrangements. We summarize this sequence as follows:

Institutional changes
↓
Changes in //creation of new rules of the game
↓
Changes in //creation of micro-institutions
to provide support to the new rules
↓
Among the different possible types of micro-institutions,
key role of public agencies operating as modes of governance (i.e. organizations)
↓
Design of agencies depends on the institutional environment
↓
Advantages and consequences of the delegation to new modes of governance depend on the political and economic transaction costs

This chapter lays out the general framework we have developed to capture these different phases in the sequencing of events and their interactions, while Chapters 9 and 10 focus on the last two steps. However, let us emphasize that the sequence is a logical one, not necessarily the actual order that reforms systematically follow. For our framework we rely on the existing literature on *institutional endowments* and *organizational arrangements*, with particular attention given to the unifying concepts of *political* and *economic transaction costs*.[1] However, we extend these analytical tools to include the contributions that have highlighted the consequences of delegation (e.g. Moe 1989; Aghion and Tirole 1997; Lupia and McCubbins 2000). We do so in order to understand better why governments have chosen to delegate public procurement functions to oversight bodies, and what the advantages and consequences of this choice are.

Section 8.1 reviews some key concepts and presents a short summary of the alternative modes of organization that can be implemented to monitor public procurement. Section 8.2 builds on the literature on a specific mode of organization, i.e. public agencies which we interpret as 'micro-institutions', to better delineate what is expected from this type of organization. Section 8.3 outlines how this analytical framework is used in the next two chapters to explain the emergence of the new mode of organization in public procurement, the procurement regulatory authorities (PRA), as well as the reasons why so many countries did not follow this path. Our analysis adopts a transaction cost perspective, with special attention to political transaction costs, and it introduces elements from the literature on delegation.

8.1 Key Concepts: A Reminder and an Extension

As already discussed, our framework is derived from the distinction between institutional environment, which is about the rules of the game, and institutional arrangements (or organizations, also identified as the 'mechanisms of governance' in Williamson 1996), which are the players of the game. With respect to institutional arrangements, we introduce a distinction between the intermediate structures—that is, the special entities created specifically by public authorities to implement new rules or reforms, or to be precise in our case, the public procurement reforms—and the organizations (be they public or private) which operate within the rules defined at the level of the institutional environment and implemented through these intermediate arrangements. We call these interface entities 'micro-institutions'.

Our analysis of these micro-institutions and their institutional embeddedness is based mainly on NIE, because we find this approach particularly relevant for examining the complex articulation between the institutional environment (the polity, judiciary, laws of contract, and property) and the players of the game. Williamson (2000) summarizes these interactions and

---

[1] See, among others, North (1990b); Levy and Spiller (1994); Ménard (1995); Williamson (2000); and Ménard and Shirley (2005/2008).

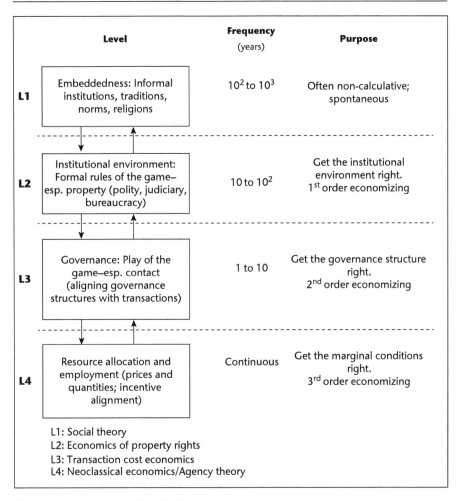

Figure 8.1 Economics of institutions
Source: Williamson (2000: 197).

the different time-scope characterizing the associated levels of analysis as follows (Figure 8.1).

With respect to the theoretical framework underlying this figure, our analysis is almost exclusively concerned with level 2 and level 3 and their interactions. Having examined the forces at work in the institutional environment and the changes that dealt mostly with level 2 (see Part II), we now turn to the examination of the forms of governance that public authorities have implemented to support production and exchange in public procurement, which refers mostly to level 3.

In order to avoid confusion, since many of the concepts at stake are not fully standardized, we start with a short summary of the key concepts to be used later on, and an indication of their relation with some of the concepts already introduced.

8.1.1 From Institutions to Organizations through Micro-Institutions

In his seminal book from 1990, North contrasts institutions and organizations by defining the latter as follows (1990b: 5):

> ...an organization is a group of individuals bound by some common purpose to achieve objectives. Organizations include political bodies (political parties, regulatory agencies), economic bodies (firms, trade unions), social bodies (churches, clubs), and educational bodies (schools, universities). The term 'institution' refers to the rules of the game, whereas 'organization' refers to players of the game.

Building on this approach, Ménard (1995) goes further to articulate the respective contributions of Williamson and North in more detail. He does so by contrasting markets and organizations (or 'hierarchies'), viewed on the one hand as the key modes of governance, and on the other as embedded in institutions, according to three main categories: (i) foundations, which identify the principles that provide the consistency of each specific organizational structure as well as consistency among institutions; (ii) modes of coordination, which identify the specific devices associated to the implementation of rules and actions framing the different types of transactions (economic transactions for markets and organizations; political transactions in the case of institutions); and (iii) *raison d'être*, which captures the central goals and functions, generally unintentional, underlying the logic that sustains each type of arrangement. Box 8.1 summarizes some of these traits.

Institutions, however, do not interact with markets and hierarchical organizations on a flat field; they operate as an overarching entity, within which transactions are made through alternative arrangements: markets, integrated organizations, and inter-firm agreements (also identified as 'hybrid' arrangements, which were not considered extensively at the time Box 8.1 was published).

8.1.2 Extensions of the Initial Model

Indeed, recent developments in the economic literature on organizations have introduced substantial changes to the streamlined view given in Box 8.1.[2] First, it is increasingly acknowledged that transactions are not necessarily

---

[2] The neglect of 'hybrids' partially reflects the state-of-the-art direction in organization theory until quite recently. For an analysis of hybrid arrangements, see Ménard (2013) and more generally, Gibbons and Roberts (2012) for recent developments in organization theory.

Box 8.1 DIFFERENTIATION BETWEEN INSTITUTIONS AND KEY MODES OF ORGANIZATION

Foundations	Modes of coordination	*Raison d'être*
Institutions		
Stable, universal, and impersonal set of rules that frame actions and behaviour	Tradition, customs, laws, regulations (political transaction costs)	Definition, implementation, and enforcement of the rules of the game
Markets		
Non-cooperative arrangements supporting transactions (require substitutability, repetition, and reversibility).	(Monetary) prices determined through competition (economic transaction costs)	Transfer of property rights, with access to substitutes
Organizations		
Formal voluntary agreements to process transactions through deliberate coordination	Conscious governance based on hierarchy (operating through fiat in last resort) (economic transaction costs)	Combination of specific assets monitored through collective action to face uncertainty and/or complexity

Source: Adapted from Ménard (1995: 174).

---

processed through markets or integrated/unified organizations: there is a whole array of arrangements, often identified as 'hybrids', which provide alternative organizational solutions. Modes of organization therefore designate much more than the polar cases of markets and (integrated) hierarchies, and the related trade-off initially pointed out by Williamson (1975).

Second, and more important for our purpose, the interactions between institutions and these alternative modes of organization are far more complex than is suggested by Box 8.1. Most of the time, these interactions are 'mediated' by intermediary arrangements, the 'micro-institutions', within which general rules are interpreted and translated into specific guidelines, and monitored.

Both issues are important for our understanding of PRAs. Indeed, these 'mechanisms of governance' are at the interface between public authorities and operators (public or private) in charge of delivering goods, works, and services to the government. Depending on the implementation of general rules defined by these PRAs, operators can be subjected to different rules (e.g. market bids, regulations preventing mergers and acquisitions, etc.) and to constraints on their mode of organization (from arm's-length outsourcing to integrated monopoly).

This is to say that: (i) there are alternative ways to organize transactions between public authorities and private entities—similarly to those prevailing in business-to-business arrangements—that extend far beyond the polar cases of markets and hierarchies (or formally integrated organizations)

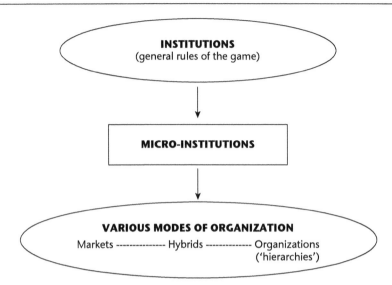

Figure 8.2 General interactions
Source: Authors.

defined in Box 8.1; (ii) these different modes usually interact with rules defined at the general institutional level through mediating arrangements or 'micro-institutions' specifically designed to implement and monitor more or less formal agreements between the operators actually in charge of delivering goods, works, and services under public procurement agreements, and the public authorities that decide which goods and services should be delivered under the general rules framing procurement. Figure 8.2 summarizes our view.

8.2 A Specific Example of Micro-Institutions: Public Agencies

A major difficulty in understanding the nature and role of the arrangements responsible for public procurement is that analysts as well as decisionmakers often mix the functions of the 'micro-institutions' in charge of the actual implementation of the rules defined at the general institutional level, with the functions of the specific organizational arrangements (or, to make it short, 'organizations') in charge of actually delivering expected goods and services (e.g. private operators, consortia, alternative forms of public–private partnerships, public utilities).

Among the various types of 'micro-institutions' (they can be bureaus, local agencies, etc.), public agencies illustrate this difficulty well and thus deserve special status. On the one hand, they share most of the properties and traits of formal organizations (typically those we find in firms); on the other, they differ from standard organizations in that they operate as extensions of the institutions in which they are deeply embedded, operating as the organizational arm in charge of implementing and monitoring the 'rules of the game'. This ambiguity has been well captured in some principal–agent analyses of regulatory agencies (Estache and Martimort 2000). New institutional economics also provides insights into this complex relationship through a comparative assessment of these interface arrangements that play a particularly important role in regulated sectors.[3]

8.2.1 Strengths and Weaknesses of a Public Agency: An Extended Transaction Cost Approach

In an analysis that partially overlaps with, and responds to, Hart et al. (1997), Williamson (1999) applies the transaction cost reasoning to the analysis of public bureaucracies, which he considers as constituting a part of the different modes of organizations, and concludes that there is room for efficiency in public bureaucracy. The underlying assumption is that each mode of organization or governance mechanism (markets, hybrids, firms, public bureaus) is well suited for a specific purpose and poorly suited for others (Williamson 1999: 307). Focusing on foreign affairs, he explains why foreign affairs transactions are not privatized and shows that the attributes of those transactions, the hazards that foreign affairs face, and the related important concerns with respect to human assets and probity make the public bureau best suited to monitor those attributes. Public administration of foreign affairs enjoys a comparative advantage over private arrangements or other modes of governance: low-powered incentives, convoluted bureaucratic procedures, employment security, leadership of the agency, and the career staff are all economizing considerations.

This transaction cost approach, initially developed to comparatively assess the costs and benefits of alternative modes of economic organizations, has been extended to analyse the efficiency of politics. North (1990a: 355) suggests complementing the economic concept of transaction costs with that of political transaction costs, in order to better assess the performance of polities as well as of economies over time. He argues that 'institutions are not necessarily or even usually created to be socially efficient; rather they, or at least the formal rules, are created to serve the interests of those with bargaining power to create new rules' (North 1994: 360–1). He goes further, arguing that 'high

---

[3] See Spiller (2009) and, more generally, several contributions in Ménard and Ghertman (2009).

transaction cost issues gravitate to the polity' (North 1994: 372), because 'political markets are far more prone to inefficiency' (North 1994: 362).

In our framework, we would argue that in monitoring procurement transactions between public authorities and operators, micro-institutions typically mix economic transaction costs with political ones. Embedded in those micro-institutions are the costs that occur in implementing the rules of the games and that are subjected to political pressures as well as to inherent bureaucratic inefficiencies. These costs partially differ from the costs associated with general institutions (e.g. the costs of running a political system or judiciary system) as well as the costs supported by business organizations (as well as non-profit organizations in that respect) operating within the rules of the game (e.g. the costs of dealing with the public bureaucracy).

8.2.2 The Consequences of Delegation to a Public Agency

The delegation theory, through its analysis of public agencies, can help to understand and delineate better these costs and the roles of these interface arrangements. Indeed, several authors, particularly political scientists, have studied the consequences of delegation thoroughly in the context of the relationships between public authorities and entities in charge of implementing and monitoring their decisions. Although they do so in a different context and theoretical framework from the one we develop, we argue that the 'delegation theory' throws light on the nature and costs of what we identify as 'micro-institutions'. Table 8.1 refers to some key contributions in this field.[4]

Lupia and McCubbins (1994a) outline the issues at stake in a government's delegation of the more or less extended domain of decisions to a public

Table 8.1 Authors contributing to the analysis of delegation with respect to public authorities

Authors	Consequences of delegation
Fiorina (1982)	– Political escape
McCubbins (1985); Wood (1989); Kiewiet and McCubbins (1991)	– Risks of slippage, of loss of control over agenda
McCubbins (1985); Moe (1989)	– Inertia
Aghion and Tirole (1997)	– Participation with risk of loss of control
Lupia and McCubbins (1999)	– Transfer of expertise
Gormley and Balla (2004)	– Transfer of expertise and control

Source: Authors.

[4] In a sense, the analysis of delegation goes back to the analysis of bureaucracies by Niskanen (1971). Our list focuses on contributions that explicitly refer to a theory intended to explore delegation issues in the context of the relationship between public authorities and agencies.

bureau or an agency. On the one hand, delegation can yield benefits for the government, as it will bring expertise (the expertise argument), but on the other, it can be detrimental if delegation is used against the government (the abdication and agenda control arguments). The following quote (Lupia and McCubbins 1994c: 96) summarizes this ambiguity well:

> The potential advantage of delegation to the bureaucracy is that bureaucrats may have the expertise that legislators desire. As a result, legislators may be able to rely on the bureaucracy to formulate policies that they themselves would have formulated if they had spent the time and resources necessary to acquire the bureaucracy's level of expertise. The potential drawback of delegation is that a bureaucrat who possesses both expertise and policymaking authority can also take actions that make legislators worse off than if they had never delegated. In this case, the act of delegation is equivalent to abdication, wherein the will of the people, as expressed by the people's elected representatives, neither constrains nor motivates the formulation of public policy.

The underlying model is based on a game theoretic approach in which delegation defines and delineates a game between a principal (Congress and its members) and an agent (a bureaucratic agency). Delegation occurs when the principal assigns the responsibility to take certain types of actions to the agent. Two key issues emerge in that context: *control over the agenda* and the extent of agency *expertise*.

AGENCY EXPERTISE

One important determinant of delegation and its consequences is the extent of *agency* expertise (Gormley and Balla 2004). To capture this effect, Lupia and McCubbins (1994c) consider two non-overlapping cases. In the first case, the agent has no specific expertise about the policy choice (i.e. the principal and the agent have the same information), which means that the legislative principal is as able as the bureaucratic agent to distinguish proposals that are beneficial (for the principal) from proposals that are deleterious. The consequences of delegation in this case are that the principal may be better off because he can transfer decisions without the risk of getting distorted or biased information from the agent. In modern parlance, there are no problems of observability or of verifiability, so that an optimal contract can be implemented. In the second case, the agent has the expertise that the principal lacks (i.e. the principal is relatively uninformed about the consequences of accepting the agent's proposal). If the principal believes that the agent is likely to make a proposal that is better for him (the principal) than the status quo, then he should accept the offer. Otherwise, he should stick with the status quo. The consequences of delegation are then beneficial for the principal only when the agent prefers policies similar to those preferred by the principal. Conversely, if the agent prefers policies different from those favoured by the principal but the principal believes otherwise, the principal may accept a proposal that should be rejected. The consequences of delegation in the case of agency expertise, then, may be that the outcome is worse for the principal than the existing policy. Designing adequate screening procedures for the proposals made by the agent then becomes crucial.

AGENDA CONTROL

One important aspect in that respect is the capacity of the principal (the public authorities) to control the agenda of the agent to which he delegates. Bendor et al. (2001) determine two models of delegation in the case of agenda control. In the first case, the principal explicitly decides whether or not to give the agent or agency the authority to take action without requiring the agent to report back first. There is also a second type of delegation in which the agent gathers certain kinds of information and makes proposals to the principal, without having the authority to take action if the principal does not consent. Again, the choice of the most adequate form of delegation depends on the distribution of information between the principal and the agent.

There are numerous problems resulting from delegation that these analyses help to understand. Examining these problems goes beyond the scope of this chapter and, indeed, this book. However, a key lesson of this literature with respect to our purpose is that asymmetric information is a major problem in all forms of delegation.

8.3 Application to the Case of Procurement Regulatory Authorities: An Overview

A paradox of the specific public agencies (the procurement regulatory authorities or PRAs) that we intend to analyse in relation to public procurement reforms is that although contributing to information asymmetry, they were also created to overcome this difficulty in their role as intermediaries between policymakers deciding which goods and services should be delivered, and operators getting the contract(s) to deliver these goods and services.

Procurement regulatory authorities (PRAs)[5] are administrative entities that are part of the executive branch, with varying degrees of autonomy. We consider these entities as 'micro-institutions' in that they are both an extension of the government, in charge of tailoring the general rules of the

---

[5] Once more we insist that we analyse the PRAs using a common denominator (without focusing on the particularities of some PRAs) as well as a generic term (without consideration of the different names that almost identical agencies can have in some countries of our sample).

game for more specific purposes and supervising their implementation, and distinct public organizations with their own structure, role, and rules that differ from those of the general institutions framing them as well as from those of the organizations (private or public) in charge of delivering goods and services under procurement. We focus on PRAs because of their importance in public procurement reforms in SSA and also because they are quite typical of the 'micro-institutions' that operate at the interface of institutions and organizations.

Indeed, a PRA is responsible for the formulation of procurement policy and the implementation and monitoring of effective public procurement reform, thereby fostering good governance, transparency, efficiency, and economy in public procurement operations. As we will see in more detail in the next chapter, procurement regulatory agencies were created because of the weak institutional environment and as second-best alternatives, partially in response to the asymmetric information problems mentioned previously. However, this delegation of procurement matters to a public agency is not without economic and political transaction costs for the government.

8.3.1 Reasons for the Emergence of a New Mode of Governance

Procurement regulatory agencies came into existence as an alternative organizational arrangement to overcome institutional weaknesses. As we already pointed out (Chapter 5, section 5.2), Levy and Spiller (1994: 205–6), building on a long tradition and on the more recent contributions from North, propose taking five major components of institutional endowment into account in evaluating the chances of success (or failure) of reform. They are: (i) the country's legislative and executive institutions; (ii) the country's judicial institutions; (iii) customs and other informal but broadly accepted norms; (iv) the character of the contending social interests within a society and the balance between them, including the role of ideology; (v) the administrative capabilities of the nation. They implemented this framework through the analysis of a specific case—that of the relationship between institutional endowments and regulatory incentives in the reform of the telecommunication industry in five countries.

An important lesson from that study in our perspective is the emphasis they put on the conditions that build credibility in a context of reforms. First, they propose a distinction between those countries that have domestic institutions capable of credibility and that can prevent arbitrary administrative action, and those that do not. The existence of an independent judiciary with a reputation for impartiality and whose decisions are enforced is a necessary condition for making commitments credible. The second distinction is between countries whose electoral, legislative, and executive institutions are structured in such a way that it enables them to achieve credible commitments via legislation, and those countries that can best achieve credible commitments by embedding their regulatory systems in the operating licences of private companies. The third distinction is between countries that require specific, substantive rules to achieve credibility, and countries that can use flexible regulatory processes and still restrain arbitrary action.

The fourth and final distinction which directly connects to the issue at stake in this chapter is between countries that have strong administrative capabilities and those that do not. Countries with strong administrative capabilities may have to settle for less efficient rules in order for their regulatory system to work. Although Levy and Spiller do not attach as much importance to administrative capabilities as to the political system or the judiciary, their analysis has the important merit of not only mentioning the role of the bureaucracy, but also to depart from the traditional critique of bureaucracy and to emphasize that this role can be essential to the success of reforms. In our view this is a key issue in successful reform of public procurement: the ability of the nation's professionals to handle complex regulatory processes in a relatively efficacious manner, without triggering excessive disputes and litigation and without feeding corruption.

Table 8.2 summarizes our view on the relationship between the weaknesses among the components of the institutional environment and the incentive to create a new mode of governance in the reform process.

In a more detailed exploration of telecommunication reforms, Levy and Spiller (1996) go further and demonstrate that the key to undertaking reform lies not just in introducing change, but also in introducing changes that are consistent with a country's institutional endowment, so that second- and

Table 8.2 Relationship between the institutional endowment and the creation of a new mode of governance in public procurement

Five elements of institutional endowment	The conditions of the institutional endowment applicable to procurement organizations	Mode of governance
1 Legislative and executive institutions of a country	Weak enforcement and measurement mechanisms	Emergence of new modes of governance (the procurement regulatory agencies) to overcome nation's weak institutional endowment
2 Judicial institutions of a country	Weak judicial system making changes in governance structures hardly credible and sustainable	
3 Customs and informal norms of a country	Weak understanding of public procurement rules and no culture of competitive process	
4 Character of the contending social interests	Weak understanding of possible benefits of reforms	
5 Administrative capabilities	Weak administrative capabilities	

Source: Authors.

third-best solutions might survive better than the theoretically most optimal setting. However, they say very little about the organizational arrangements required to make rules effective, which is an essential piece of the reform puzzle which could work in one institutional environment but not in the other. In our view this is precisely the role and contribution of the PRAs, the agencies on which we are focusing. They emerged and, in several cases, developed successfully as tools for at least partially filling the gap between poor institutional endowment and the requirements to make reforms credible. In that role, PRAs had to build their credibility on delegation.

8.3.2 Transaction Costs in the Delegation Process

In addition to understanding the ex-ante reasons that could explain the emergence of this new mode of governance, we also need to understand the advantages and drawbacks of such arrangements, as they can be evaluated ex-post. Procurement regulatory authorities emerged in certain countries because they were viewed as a positive response to the prevailing weaknesses in institutional environment; however, in other countries faced with similar problems, PRAs or similar agencies were not created or never became operational.

Our interpretation of this phenomenon is that it stems from the combination of economics and political transaction costs, likely with prevalence of the latter. As is well established by transaction costs economics, different modes of organizing transactions have different costs, depending on the attributes of these transactions.[6] Delegating procurement functions to a new administrative entity involves such economic transaction costs. However, because of the nature of delegation when the relationship is between public authorities and more or less independent agencies, as is the case with PRAs, there are also important political costs involved. Costs and benefits of the delegation of public procurement functions to an administrative body have a specific content which differentiates it from delegation in private organizations, mainly because of the potential interference of policymakers who ultimately have some control over the institutional framework in which PRAs are embedded, making political transaction costs particularly significant. Chapter 10 comes back to this issue in more detail.

8.4 Conclusion

This chapter has reviewed the key concepts, some of which were already introduced in Parts I and II, and proposed extensions for better understanding

---

[6] For a survey of the achievements of transaction costs in that respect, see Shelanski and Klein (1995), Klein (2005/2008), and Ménard (2013).

the creation of new arrangements at the interface between institutions defining the rules of the game and organizations operating within these rules to deliver goods, works, and services in the context of public procurement. We developed this framework with reference to the new institutional economics and the delegation theory, with special attention at the empirical level to the creation of specific entities operating at this interface in the context of public procurement reforms in SSA.

The key issue we emphasize is that reforms and their success or failure depend not only on changes in the institutional environment and their adequate fit to a country's institutional endowment, but also on the building of appropriate organizational arrangements to implement and monitor these reforms. Because of the requirements and the complex articulation of these dimensions, second- and third-best solutions, although relatively inefficient, might survive better in a given institutional context than what is considered to constitute the optimal solution.

Through a short review of some main contributions on delegation, we also point to two other key issues in the decision to delegate to a bureaucracy: building expertise and controlling the reform agenda. These two aspects are a significant part of the political transaction costs that amplify the economic transaction costs associated with the development of organizations in charge of implementing and monitoring the rules of the game.

The combination of these two approaches, new institutional economics on the one hand and the delegation theory on the other, opens the way to a more profound analysis of a specific type of public agency: the procurement regulatory agency (or similar arrangements). More generally, it is our view that far from being antagonistic, they mutually enrich our understanding of the interactions between institutions and organizations.

9

Micro-Institutions as a Response to Weak Institutional Endowment: The Procurement Regulatory Authorities

As was explicated through our theoretical framework, the central hypothesis of our analysis of public procurement reform is that the constraints entrenched in the existing institutional environment led to the emergence of a new mode of governance, the procurement regulatory agencies (PRAs). As rightly emphasized by North (1990b: 4):

> Organizations will be designed to further the objectives of their creators. They will be created as a function, not simply of institutional constraints, but also other constraints (e.g., technology, income, and preferences). Like institutions, organizations provide a structure to human interaction. Indeed when we examine the costs that arise as a consequence of the institutional framework, we see they are a result, not only of that framework, but also of the organizations that have developed in consequence of that framework.

In that respect, PRAs (or similar agencies with different names) share some properties of business organizations, but they also differ on central characteristics. Indeed, these arrangements are at the frontier between the institutions responsible for the formulation of procurement policy, particularly the polity, and organizations in charge of implementing and monitoring effective public procurement reforms, thereby fostering good governance, transparency, efficiency, and economy in public procurement operations. This ambivalence is reflected in the status of PRAs as administrative entities which are part of the executive branch, yet remain relatively autonomous.

Created to overcome inefficient procurement systems, to oversee government spending, and to lessen the possibility of rent-seeking and corruption, PRAs have been—and still are—viewed as key instruments to foster good governance by limiting the discretion of procurement officers, increasing transparency in procurement operations, monitoring compliance to procedures, and increasing public investment productivity through competition and improved efficiency.

Because of these ambitious goals, designing and implementing PRAs is a complex process which requires a long incubation period and time for actual implementation. Although public agencies[1] monitoring regulated operations related to securities, waste disposal, water supply, provision of electricity, etc. have received a lot of scholarly interest, particularly in developed countries, very little attention has been given to the design of the administrative agency within public procurement and the reasons for their creation, and even less so when it comes to SSA countries.[2]

However, the movement towards creating such entities has been quite significant in this region. By the beginning of this century, sixteen countries in SSA had created procurement regulatory agencies (or their equivalent) with the goal of improving how public procurement is handled at both central and decentralized levels. Through a careful examination of this development, we show that the weak political systems in which the existing modes of governance (e.g. central tender boards, CTBs) were embedded, the limited role of courts to enforce compliance, and the lack of adequate human capital to effectively measure and monitor procurement activities, have been the main incentives to the emergence of these new arrangements.

The forms these arrangements took reflect a fragile equilibrium between the interests of policymakers, international donors, operators (local and/ or international) involved in public procurement, and pressure from civil societies. We argue that these new 'micro-institutions' represent a 'second-best' option for countries with limited administrative capacity, inadequate judicial systems, and weak formal mechanisms to enforce rules and monitor compliances. Our analysis is based on extensive interviews by one of the authors[3] with representatives from the Ministries of Finance in SSA or their equivalent as part of World Bank missions on the preparation of procurement reports. We also took advantage of available World Bank reports and discussions with Bank specialists in public procurement, and the detailed case studies on three countries (Botswana, Tanzania, and Uganda).

---

[1] These agencies are, for instance, Environmental Protection Agencies, Securities and Exchange Commissions, Water Agencies, Energy Regulators, or their equivalent.

[2] An exception is the recent book by Quinot and Arrowsmith (2013), which examines regulations and regulatory authorities from a legal perspective in nine SSA countries.

[3] Christine Léon de Mariz.

9.1 Social Interests and Administrative Capabilities: The Need to Replace Central Tender Boards

Procurement regulatory agencies were not created *ex nihilo*. As with most organizational innovation in the public sector, they sought to improve the existing system in the face of changing social interests, often apparent as political changes, and weak administrative capabilities.

More specifically, many of our sample countries have set up PRAs as a measure to move away from the central tender boards (CTBs), the existing mode of governance that oversees and approves large contracts, to a more decentralized approach where procurement entities become accountable and subject to independent audits. PRAs, therefore, are mainly the result of the restructuring of existing organizations that were viewed as inefficient. The increasing awareness of inefficiency issues mirrors the change in societal preferences in several SSA countries, as exemplified by the emergence of anti-corruption initiatives, the developing interest in new public management tools, and a renewed perception of the adverse consequences of scarce administrative capabilities.

9.1.1 The Central Tender Boards

Since the 1980s, and even earlier for some, many countries in sub-Saharan Africa introduced centralized procurement boards, often known as central tender boards (CTBs), for organizing the contractual delivery of goods, services, and works to government institutions and other public bodies. These boards, such as the Mauritius Central Tender Board or the National Tender Board in Rwanda, typically supervise and approve the contract award process when contracts are above a certain threshold.[4] Generally, a CTB establishes the appropriate tender procedures and ensures compliance with tender guidelines and notices; invites tenders locally or internationally; receives, opens, examines, and evaluates tenders; and approves the award of related contracts.

These boards differ from other mechanisms of governance established to deal with public procurement. Box 9.1 explains the difference between CTBs and centralized purchasing agencies and executing agencies. The major difference is that CTBs are responsible for the approval of major procurement contracts, whereas the executing agencies or centralized purchasing agencies have more limited responsibilities, mainly procuring goods and services or purchasing them directly for some or all public bureaus and similar agencies.

---

[4] This threshold usually corresponds to a legally determined value. Contracts above this amount must be allocated according to formal procurement procedures.

Box 9.1 COMPARING CENTRAL TENDER BOARDS WITH CENTRALIZED PURCHASING ENTITIES OR EXECUTING AGENCIES

A CTB differs from a central purchasing agency (such as the *Bureau National d'Etudes Techniques et de Dévelopement* (BNETD) in Côte d'Ivoire). A central purchasing agency operates as an agent responsible for procuring goods and services for public administration and public agencies. The creation of such an entity relies on the assumption that centralized procurement can produce economies of scale through bulk purchases, better information, capacity, and transparency (OECD 2000). However, its role is limited to purchasing activities, while the task of CTBs is to endorse or clear proposed contracts awards.

A CTB also differs from *executing agencies* in that it reviews and endorses contract awards submitted by executing agencies.

In some countries, governments set up parallel external independent contract *management agencies* to which they delegate contract administration. These agencies (for example, *Agence d' Execution des Travaux d'Intérêt Public* (AGETIP) in Senegal or *Bureau Central de Coordination* (BCECO) in the Democratic Republic of Congo) act as procurement agents, responsible for devising design and bidding documents, awarding contracts, and managing/supervising contracts. For example, in Senegal the government delegates the execution of works to the AGETIP for small and medium-size labour-based public works. Donors have channelled a growing share of external funding for infrastructure development in sub-Saharan countries through these agencies.

Source: Authors.

One important element that fostered the creation of the new organization modes (PRAs) in the procurement reform process was the change in social interests and norms and values that pushed for better performance, more accountability, and transparency, making the existence of CTBs questionable. CTBs fell under close scrutiny because they came to be viewed as the cause of bureaucratic delays and bottlenecks to efficient procurement. The centralized system of contract awarding of these entities became controversial because the approval needed from the CTBs induced delays and because in many cases, these delays were perceived as part of corruption schemes. With the growing volume of contracts, the workloads of the CTBs became too demanding, which favoured lack of transparency, and replacing them was eventually deemed necessary.

This is evident in the following three country cases. The description of the functions performed by the CTBs in Botswana, Uganda, and Tanzania provides a concrete overview of the difficulties encountered by public authorities at the time reforms were implemented. Table 9.1 provides a short summary of the extensive analyses conducted with regard to CTBs in these three countries. These reports quite frequently mention issues such as poor performance, lack of training and motivation, lack of authority, and bottlenecks. This situation was not specific to these three countries; CPARs showed

Table 9.1 Some key issues faced by the CTBs in Botswana, Tanzania, and Uganda

Country	Description of issues related to the CTB	Source
Botswana	Composed of part-time members who were not procurement professionals; no training policy and no budget for developing procurement skills; morale low and professional standards weak; growing perception in the contract community that award decisions were being manipulated to favour certain parties.	Lionjanga (2003)
Tanzania	Authority of CTB eroded by ad hoc arrangements in different sectors; CTB was handling procurement processes of minimal value; lack of consistency and malpractices.	Nkinga (2003)
Uganda	Disparate (in that the district governments were not covered); outdated procurement regulations and procedures; suspicion of corruption.	Agaba (2003)

Source: Authors' compilation.

that Cameroon, Guinea, and Madagascar, among others, also faced similar issues.

Lionjanga (2003) provides a relatively detailed review of the situation in Botswana, explaining why the CTB was inefficient and why a procurement regulatory agency was viewed as a remedy to these inefficiencies. According to this author, the Botswana's CTB was composed of part-time members who were not procurement professionals, who had not had appropriate training, and who could not count on adequate funding to develop their procurement skills. The lack of training and recognition of status as official procurement agent contributed to low morale among the staff. Poor performance and a perception of corruption became increasing concerns. Lionjanga (2003: 7) summarizes the situation as follows:

> The absence of a professional procurement stream in the public service, an appropriate certification system for entry and promotion and a training policy to prepare cadres for a career in procurement management were all discernible weaknesses in the system at a time when procurement management had become increasingly professional in response to the complex demands of the market place. As a result, motivational levels were low and professional standards suffered. There was also a growing perception in the contracting community arising out of delayed award decisions by the Board, that award decisions were being manipulated to favour certain parties. Happily, in the majority of cases these allegations proved unfounded.

In this context, the creation of a PRA was considered a potential solution, although a second-best one because it could not overcome all these inefficiencies by itself, particularly the weak human capabilities. Note that the procurement regulatory agency is not a restructured CTB, but a regulatory body put in place to accompany the decentralization of procurement decisions to contracting authorities at the sector level.

The situation in Tanzania did not differ substantially, although it confronted some additional problems. A detailed report submitted by Nkinga (2003) highlights issues very similar to those faced by the governments of Botswana and Uganda. In Tanzania, the CTB processed tenders for the ministries and government departments, with several major exceptions, which made the procurement system even more complex and opaque.[5] There were bottlenecks as well, but also a lack of consistency in the manner in which different contracts were handled. As noted by Nkinga (2003: 10):

> The authority of the central tender board was eroded by ad hoc arrangements in different sectors (e.g., works, health, education and local government authorities), levels of authority were far too low and the central tender board was handling far too low value work, there was no regulatory body to enforce the legal framework, regulations, rules and procedures...

Lastly, in Uganda, the CTB was the main overseer of the public procurement process and derived its authority from the Tender Board Regulations of 1977 established under the Public Finance Act, Cap. 149. Formally, this entity was established to regulate and control (i) the purchase or sale of government stores and equipment, and (ii) the awarding of government contracts for goods, services, and works (Agaba 2003). The Board was also responsible for approving purchases above the threshold of one million shillings for goods and two million shillings for works and services, these purchases being submitted by procuring entities. This centralized organizational structure, however, made it increasingly difficult to deal satisfactorily with the growing number of transactions as well as the scale and technical complexity of procurement activities. Moreover, the Board was no longer able to fulfil procurement tasks adequately, since the Board's mandate did not cover the district governments. As a consequence, major bureaucratic delays, combined with the lack of coordination, continued to plague the system. According to Agaba (2003: 7–8):

> ... malpractice and unethical conduct also saddled the system. There was a high incidence of vested interests, interference and insider dealings. There were occasional cases of retroactive approvals of contract awards. [...] The central tender board, which oversaw the procurement process in the country, had a set of disparate (in the sense that the district governments were not covered) and outdated procurement regulations and procedures.

In sum, the existing CTBs in these three countries as well as in several others were perceived as inefficient and an increasing source of tension among

---

[5] These exceptions concerned Urban and District Authorities, Ministry of Education and Culture, educational institutions, para-state enterprises, Ministry of Defence and National Service, and Medical Stores Departments.

decisionmakers, while their credibility in the society became increasingly negative, feeding into forces that pushed towards a change in the way the procurement system was organized. However, to shift away from this inefficient mode of governance that involved important entrenched interests, countries had to find alternative structural solutions that would be acceptable to policymakers, public agents, and the civil society. Countries had to accept second-best solutions to avoid creating a situation with few winners and too many losers, a situation that would involve the risk of failure because of the weak administrative capabilities of SSA countries. Abolishing CTBs and creating procurement regulatory agencies was viewed as such a solution, although in many instances previous review mechanisms for large contracts were maintained.

9.1.2 A Procurement Regulatory Agency as the Second-Best Solution

Procurement regulatory agencies (or their equivalent) were thus created in response to the deficiencies of CTBs, which caused delays in awarding decisions due mainly to malpractice and vested interests, weak administrative capabilities, too low value procurement thresholds, increasing procurement transaction volumes, and the scale and technical complexity of procurement activities. It also mirrored the new demand for more transparency and accountability.

However, to avoid creating a potentially explosive situation in which losers would largely outnumber the winners, thus generating important political risks, reformers and their international advisers adopted a strategy aimed at a smooth transfer from the CTB by increasing the contract review threshold and by giving the new entity an oversight role. Hence, PRAs were established as a second-best solution designed to move away from the current inefficient situation while accommodating those who stood to lose from the outcome of the reform. As a consequence, the objective was not to completely dismantle the CTB, but to build up its capacity and to change the implicit and explicit agreements about its role and jurisdiction. For example, the new mode of governance would have a role in policymaking with respect to procurement. The reform in Uganda illustrates this point well: the old CTB was transformed into an oversight agency with policy functions, described as follows (Agaba 2003: 8):

> The task force proposed that a national procurement policy unit (NPPU) be established and that the CTB be restructured to perform all the functions of the NPPU set forth below. The tender awarding functions hitherto undertaken by CTB should be taken over by the new Ministry Contracts Committees. Thus the restructured CTB would be a policy body with specific functions of monitoring

the public procurement system through other entities...The Ministry, based on the task force recommendations, submitted in November 1999 a Cabinet Document seeking the approval of the Cabinet Minister to proceed with the creation of a procurement reform implementation unit (PRIU) in the Ministry and to task it with their implementation of the task force recommendations. This was approved in January 2000.

A similar strategy was adopted in Botswana in 2001. In this case, the jurisdiction of the newly created PRA was limited to policy recommendations, making its responsibilities substantially different from the old CTB: while the latter was involved in the award process for major contracts and the purchase of large volumes of goods, the PRA would conduct tenders only for its own needs and have an advisory role with regard to policy, while the responsibility for the procurement aspects of contract awards would be distributed to line ministries and district administrations through the establishment of tender committees.

These differences between procurement regulatory agencies and CTBs are important and should not be viewed as purely semantic; the jurisdiction of the PRA differs largely from that of the CTB, in that it is much less centralized with respect to actual procurement transactions. This is very well illustrated by the case of Botswana. The government of Botswana, through the Public Procurement and Asset Disposal Act (No.10 of 2001), established a new organizational structure with responsibilities that Lionjanga (2003: 19) describes as follows:

> The Public Procurement & Asset Disposal Board (PPADB) is responsible for the setting of policies, principles, rules and methods of procurement, and the monitoring of and reporting of compliance to Parliament, as well as assigning the procurement and disposal responsibilities to line ministries and district administrations through the establishment of ministerial and district administration tender committees. This is in contrast to the situation, which existed hitherto, where procurement and asset disposal decisions were concentrated in the central tender board.

Enforcement would be improved through capacity-building activities (i.e. public procurement training) and through the audits this new micro-institution would conduct and which could then be transferred to different overarching institutions (supreme audit institutions or parliament).[6] This shift paved the way for the decentralization of some of the work previously undertaken by the CTB. Line ministries and district administrations established tender committees which were granted adjudication and decisionmaking powers within given financial ceilings and within the confines of adequate reporting

---

[6] Enforcement mechanisms are further explored in section 9.3.

and monitoring arrangements by the public procurement and asset disposal board (PPADB). These measures, through decentralization and improvements in transparency, were aimed at speeding up the procurement cycle.

Another instructive illustration is provided by Madagascar, where the objective was to move away from the old CTB by progressively increasing the threshold for public procurement review and by enlarging its scope of work. The restructured CTB would therefore be renamed and take the form of an oversight entity; it would not participate in the review of public procurement processes except for high-value contracts. The resulting external and internal definition and allocation of procedures and responsibilities for processing and controlling public procurement is quite complex, the inevitable consequence of a more decentralized system. Figure 9.1 summarizes the different functions and the entities responsible for public procurement control and monitoring.

These examples illustrate well the complexity of institutional changes when they require modifications not only in the formal rules of the game, but

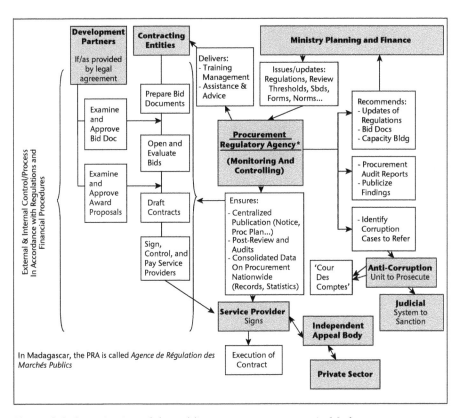

Figure 9.1 Organization of the public procurement system in Madagascar

also to the organizational arrangements in charge of calibrating and implementing the new rules. These arrangements need to take into account not only the economic costs, but also the political transaction costs associated with the changes in the balance among interest groups.

9.2 Improving Measurement and Enforcement

The recognition that existing organizations were not performing adequately and that reform would require dealing with contending social interests as well as with administrative capabilities was not limited to the case studies mentioned previously. The same forces and constraints were at work in the other SSA countries and pushed towards the emergence of a new mode of governance. However, reforms also faced other challenges, emanating from institutional endowments going beyond vested interests and limited capabilities, namely weak legislative and executive institutions and a weak judiciary branch. In the next section we focus on weaknesses in the oversight mechanisms that could otherwise have provided support to the polity in enforcing procurement reforms. After this we come back to the issue of weak judiciary.

9.2.1 The Oversight Environment

In addition to solving the problems inherited from the CTBs, procurement regulatory agencies also sought to strengthen the weak legislative systems embodied in inadequate oversight mechanisms, and to improve measurement and enforcement in public procurement. In that respect, the PRA can be seen as a micro-institution complementing the executive entities responsible for monitoring and enforcing contracts as well as the traditional audit entities.

There are several possible entities playing this role. For instance, the Supreme Audit Chamber (also known as the *Cour des Comptes* or *Tribunal de Contas*) is often the entity responsible for controlling public funds and the legal aspects of public procurement. Box 9.2 summarizes some key characteristics of the main types of audit institutions, representing three different institutional traditions.

PRAs were considered to constitute an adequate solution for addressing the deficiencies of the oversight systems in controlling public procurement processes in countries using the Napoleonic system (francophone and lusophone SSA countries) as well as the Westminster system (anglophone SSA countries). These deficiencies and the related issues are summarized in Table 9.2. Among the most significant problems are the lack of an adequate legal framework to

---

Box 9.2 THE DIFFERENT TYPES OF AUDIT INSTITUTIONS

In the Napoleonic system, the supreme audit institution—also called the *Cour des Comptes* (court of accounts)—has both judicial and administrative authority and is independent of the legislative and executive branches. The institution is making judgments on government compliance with laws and regulations as well as ensuring that public funds are well spent. In principle, the *Cour des Comptes* audits every government body, including ministries, departments, and agencies; commercial and industrial entities under the purview of ministries; and social security bodies. This model is used in the Latin countries of Europe (France, Italy, Portugal, Spain, and others), Turkey, and most Latin American and francophone African countries.

In the Westminster system, used in most Commonwealth countries (Australia, Canada, India, the United Kingdom, and many Caribbean, Pacific, and Sub-Saharan African countries), the office of the *auditor general* is an independent body that reports to parliament. Made up of professional auditors and technical experts, the office submits periodic reports on the financial statements and operations of government entities—but with less emphasis on legal compliance than in the Napoleonic system. The office serves no judicial function, but, when warranted, its findings may be passed to legal authorities for further action.

The *board system*, prevalent in Asia, is similar to the Westminster model in that it is independent of the executive and helps parliament perform oversight. Indonesia, Japan, and the Republic of Korea, for example, have an audit board composed of an audit commission (the decisionmaking body) and a general executive bureau (the executive organ). The president of the board is the de facto auditor general. The board's primary mandate is to analyse government spending and revenue, and report its findings to parliament.

Source: Compilation by authors based on World Bank (2001b).

Table 9.2 Issues related to the absence of adequate oversight mechanisms

Issues	Risks	Tasks for procurement regulatory agency
Lack of modern legal framework	Juridical vacuum	Modernize law and regulations
Lack of training	– Tasks are performed differently – No compliance with rules	Improve capacity-building
Lack of data	No information on activities	Improve data collection
Lack of audits	No checks on operations	Carry out audits
Lack of quick mechanism for monitoring complaints	No complaints Lack of competition	Establish quicker system for registering and monitoring complaints

Source: Authors.

legitimize and support oversight mechanisms, sub-standard or non-existent training for staff, paucity of audits, unavailability of data, and the absence of a complaints mechanism. A PRA could address these problems, helping to close the gap between the objectives of the government and those of the procuring agencies. One of its main tasks would be to monitor and enforce the regulations of public procurement arrangements, thereby changing the incentives of public procurement officers and their relationship to the executive.

9.2.2 Different Approaches to Improving Measurement and Enforcement

There are different ways to reach these goals. For example, it can be done by offering advice to contracting entities, providing procurement information, managing procurement statistics databases, reporting on procurement to other government agencies, developing and supporting the implementation of initiatives for improvements in the public procurement system, and providing documents and implementing tools to support training and capacity development of enforcement staff.

In line with the need to take into account vested interests so as to lower political transaction costs and make reform possible, PRAs were conceived and installed to complement activities usually performed by supreme audit institutions and internal audit entities as well as by executive entities. Hence the idea to endow PRAs with the mandate to conduct audits and be responsible for data collecting and reporting on the quality of procurement.

Conducting audits and collecting statistical information are aimed to improve screening. The probability of being audited and penalized creates incentive for agents to monitor contracts adequately, and reduces the risk of dishonesty and fraud. Statistics and data collection is an indirect way of controlling agents. Data collection, however, is only possible for contracts exceeding a certain threshold. More direct ways of controlling agents are possible through audits and training programmes. Audits provide the means to extract information on current procurement procedures. Training ensures that relevant officers are knowledgeable about procurement practices and thus capable of enforcing rules and regulations.

9.3 Weak Judicial Institutions: Procurement Regulatory Agencies as a 'Second-Best' Alternative

One essential element of institutional endowment is a country's judicial institutions and its capacity to register and monitor complaints and to have judgments enforced. Judicial institutions comprise not only the constitutions, laws, and rules framing their activities, but also formal mechanisms for appointing judges and determining the internal structure of the judiciary, and for impartially resolving disputes among private parties or between private parties and the state (Hadfield 2005/2008: chap. 8).

In sub-Saharan Africa, formal mechanisms for impartially resolving disputes between private parties and the state were weak and basically not used in practice. Enforcement mechanisms could not be secured by existing judicial institutions, as these lacked the expertise and resources to carry out procurement audits. Firms would not go to court to resolve disputes with the state because the judicial system was unable to offer a ruling in a timely manner and, in most countries of our sample, because of continuing political interference associated with the fear of unfair treatment in future procurement endeavours. As a consequence, firms either would not work for the state or would integrate this in their bids as a commercial risk, or would rely on corruption to solve problems.

In this context, PRAs were devised as an alternative to public judicial ordering, with the role of third-party enforcement, responsible for evaluating and enforcing the terms of a contract so that offending parties had to compensate the injured party. They would therefore be considered as a 'second-best' alternative with a partial role as judicial institutions.

9.3.1 Protest and Appeals Mechanisms to Complement the Judicial Action

In the prevailing procurement systems, parties (private or public) were unable to bring their cases to a third party (e.g. court) or had difficulties in doing so. As a result, enforcing contracts translated into high transaction costs because contractual issues had to be resolved through discretionary agreements or even illegal strategies. Deficient courts were supplemented or even substituted by other public orderings to effectively protect the parties against opportunistic behaviour.

According to Glaeser et al. (2001: 855) and Shleifer (2005), there is some advantage in having public regulators or similar entities curb disorder and establish the conditions under which regulatory enforcement is an attractive alternative to judicial enforcement, because 'unlike judges, public regulators can be experts and are motivated to pursue social objectives in specific areas. They can be provided with incentives to enforce social policy and can, in principle, be more difficult to subvert than the disinterested judges'. Furthermore, public regulation is generally faster and cheaper than the court.

In the case of SSA, the theory was that public ordering could partially be taken over by the PRAs. For example, in Kenya, public procurement law opened the possibility for the bidders themselves to monitor the procedure of the procuring entities and to subsequently lodge protests. Usually, protests and appeals are undertaken if the value of procurement exceeds a certain amount.

In a well-run system, suppliers and contractors with legal grievances are able to take action at three levels: (i) lodge protests to the procuring entity;

(ii) submit appeals, i.e. suppliers can apply to the PRA for settling disputes through an appeals mechanism; and (iii) complain to the court.

Filing a protest can be done for various reasons. It is usually related to infringements regarding equal treatment, fair competition, and transparency in the award process mechanism. For instance, the contracting entity may have failed to define the criteria, other than the price, used to evaluate bids or to clearly identify the applied method. Or, the contracting entity may have failed to disseminate information on the selected bid or the evaluated and/or rejected bids, or may have deviated from the specifications identified in the selection criteria. Third, the contracting entity may have modified the evaluation criteria after the submission deadline. Marshall et al. (1993: 40) analyse the protest mechanisms applied in connection with a federal purchase of automated data processing and telecommunication equipment in the United States. They show that the protest mechanism helps 'to alleviate potential problems (that is, overly restrictive minimum specifications, biased evaluation criteria, inappropriate exclusion of potentially bidding firms, and assessments by the procurement officer that are inconsistent with the stated criteria) by allowing losing firms to act as private attorney generals'.

These protest mechanisms, however, might be difficult to implement in the context of legal, political, cultural, and economic circumstances existing in a given country. Among the many factors that could prevent the implementation or the actual usage of a protest mechanism we can include weak political integrity characterized by favouritism or corruption, limited technical expertise in public procurement for establishing independent and robust mechanisms for protest, and the lack of will, time, or money from the private sector to challenge government decisionmakers that might make them worse off in the long run, especially when the number of bidders is small.

In practice, where protest mechanisms exist and work reasonably well—as was the expectation of the reforms introducing PRAs—the plaintiff or the injured supplier/contractor submits a written protest to the procuring entity justifying why his legal interests have been violated. Once a protest is filed, the procuring entity cannot proceed with the contract in question.[7] After resolution or rejection of the protest, the interested supplier or contractor may file an appeal with the PRA, where an independent arbitration panel[8] composed of several members examines the case. The arbiters can uphold or reject the appeal. If an appeal is upheld, the arbiters may order the execution

---

[7] In reality, this happens only in countries where complaints can suspend the contract award decision. However, the preferred solution in most agreements is that a decision has to be rendered within a maximum number of days (usually twenty) whether or not the complaint is founded. If so, then the contract award can be suspended.

[8] For instance, a *Comité de Règlement des Differends*.

Box 9.3 THE POSITIVE ROLE OF APPEALS MECHANISMS

The appeal mechanism as a complement to judicial action has been used for a long time by other countries outside sub-Saharan Africa. Because PRAs are newly created entities in the African region and little information is available on their performance, it is interesting to examine how they function in other countries in different regions.

Eastern Europe, although at another stage of development, offers an interesting illustration of how an appeal mechanism may function. For example, since the fall of the communist regime, Poland has been dealing with the weaknesses of its judiciary and procurement systems. In 1995 an appeal mechanism was set up, based on an arbitration model, with a crucial role played by the Council for Public Procurement, which is a consultative and advisory body of the public procurement office (PPO), which has some similarities with the PRAs.

When a protest is filed, a panel of three arbiters selected from a list of arbiters maintained by the Chairman of the PPO reviews the appeal within fourteen days. One arbiter is selected by the supplier or contractor who has filed the appeal, one by the procuring entity, and one by the Chairman of the Office. Verdicts of arbitration panels may be appealed in regional courts (through the process of judicial review). Observers are present at the workings of tender committees in case of contracts of substantial value (ten million euros for public works; five million euros for supplies and services). The Table herewith presents the number of appeals lodged with the Polish Public Procurement Office from 1995 to 1999, the period when public procurement reforms were being discussed in SSA. A comparison with recent data shows the increasing role of appeals as a way to regulate public procurement.

However, it should be noted that these figures do not provide any details on the percentage and relative value of procurement that these might represent, so that interpretation must be cautious. Nevertheless, the increasing number of appeals provides an indication of the significance of having mechanisms of appeal.

Year	No. of appeals
1995	348
1996	837
1997	1,005
1998	1,195
1999*	1,327 *
2008	1,539
2009	1,653
2010	2,992
2011	2,789

Note: * Data for 1999 illustrate well the role of the appeals mechanism: out of the 1,327 appeals filed that year, 57 per cent concerned public works, 24 per cent goods, and 19 per cent services; 387 appeals were found to be justified: the average period for a trial was eleven days.

Source: *Report of the Office of Public Procurement*, Poland. Available at: www.uzp.gov.pl

or repetition of the relevant procedure, or may invalidate it, although they generally only offer an opinion without issuing a final decision with respect to the contract award.

Should the supplier or contractor not accept the verdict of the arbitration panel, he can in theory complain to the court, but this is almost never done because of the length of time involved and because of the complainant's concern of being shunned in future procurement contracts. If a complaint is upheld, the court can reverse the verdict, and rule on the merits of the case. If the appeal is rejected or there are grounds for discontinuation of the proceedings, the court can reverse the verdict and reject the appeal or discontinue the proceedings.

The role of procurement regulatory agencies as an appeals mechanism is important for another reason: it provides an indirect way of ascertaining whether the procurement officer has acted improperly and thus it works towards achieving greater transparency, efficiency, and accountability (see Box 9.3 for an illustration in a different institutional environment). Indeed, by exercising their right to complain, bidders provide additional information to the PRA. The resolution of conflicts between bidders and executing agencies would therefore play a central role in the collection of information. As Schooner (2002) points out, this procedure also improves the quality of supervision at no or very small cost to the government.

However, the creation of a bid protest system that embodies speed and efficiency is complicated, and takes time to evolve into a significant mechanism. This is well illustrated by the case of Kenya. The Kenyan procurement regulatory agency, known as the *Public Procurement Directorate*, was created as part of the Ministry of Finance and Planning through the Exchequer and Audit Act in 2001. The *Public Procurement Complaints Review and Appeal Board* was created in March 2001 to deal with complaints regarding procurement decisions. A year after its creation, the Board had examined only forty-three cases, of which twenty-one were annulled with the procuring entities instructed to re-tender, seven were cancelled and re-awarded, and thirteen were dismissed for lack of substance. In 2005 the Board was merged into the Administrative Review Board, a new micro-institution, and it now examines between fifty and sixty cases a year, still a relatively low number.

9.4 Conclusion

In this chapter we have shown that weak institutional endowment explains the search for and the subsequent arrival of the new mode of public procurement governance in SSA. We argued that this weak institutional environment within public procurement was embedded in the existing inadequate mode of governance (the CTBs), the limited role of the courts in enforcing and monitoring compliance, and low human capital to effectively monitor or evaluate procurement contracts. Of course, these factors alone do not fully explain the interest in establishing the new micro-institution, the procurement regulatory agency (or similar arrangements): international donor pressure and emerging demands from civil society also played an important role.

We also argued that these new organizational arrangements were created as second-best options. This was the case because of weak administrative capacity, lack of an adequate judicial system, and imperfect formal mechanisms to enforce and measure contracts in the countries under review. The best option would have meant a system founded on the existing, functioning institutions and judicial and executive organizations within an environment where public procurement is handled by the executing entities without any intervention from a central entity or political interference. But low country capacity and a weak judicial and executive environment largely account for the reasons why PRAs became an attractive solution.

This situation raises another issue: since all sub-Saharan countries in our sample confronted the same weaknesses, although with varying intensity, what explains the fact that some countries chose to delegate public procurement functions to oversight bodies, through the creation of these PRAs, while others did not, preferring instead to maintain the status quo? We now turn to this question.

10

To Delegate or Not to Delegate: The Advantages and Limits of Micro-Institutions

In the previous chapter, we argued that weak institutional endowment led to the delegation of procurement functions to an oversight entity in several sub-Saharan African countries.[1] These oversight entities can be viewed as 'micro-institutions' that operate as the organizational arm of existing institutions, with varying degrees of autonomy and resources. Taking the procurement regulatory agency (PRA) as an example of these entities, we now examine the reasons why some countries have chosen to delegate public procurement functions to an oversight entity, the PRA, while others have not taken this route. These PRAs, on the one hand, are part of the executive branch and are responsible for overseeing public procurement by government entities, project implementation units, statutory bodies, government agencies, and local government authorities. On the other hand, they often enjoy a significant degree of autonomy, with the executive delegating an important role to them in the allocation of resources determined by public procurement.

However, delegation raises important questions. Mathew McCubbins (2005/2008: 140) summarizes well the issue at stake with entities like PRAs:

> There are two driving forces behind legislative organization. One is the need to delegate authority in order to allocate resources in effective and electorally-beneficial ways, which involve the classic tradeoff inherent in delegation of any kind: giving the agent enough power to do what needs to be done, while simultaneously limiting the agent's ability to act in mischievous ways. The other is the need to structure this delegation such that it mirrors external political forces.

---

[1] Sixteen such entities were formally created before the end of 2004, although not all were operational. Details on their creation are provided in Chapter 4.

What are the advantages of such a delegation from the government's perspective? And what are the limits to this choice, obstacles that could help understand why several countries rejected this solution? To examine these questions, we draw on the delegation literature as well as on that branch of the new institutional economics which is predominantly concerned with governance issues. Our analysis is qualitative and is based on World Bank reports to which one of the co-authors actively contributed.[2] These reports are the CPARs (country procurement assessment reviews); in-depth case studies for Botswana, Uganda, and Tanzania were also used. The analysis also draws on interviews with World Bank procurement specialists.

Section 10.1, focusing on the presentation of PRAs, sets out the various organization models (or governance structures) that conduct procurement operations. These PRAs operate as the organizational arm in charge of protecting compliance with the rules of the game: as such, they are micro-institutions at the interface between the institutions which secures their legitimacy and the organizations they have to oversee, and at the same time they operate as organizations in their own right. Section 10.2 examines the advantages that accrue to a government through the creation of such a new mode of organization. One major argument supporting the creation of a PRA is the expertise element: improving the competence of specialized staff will reduce uncertainty and lower transaction costs. Another argument, and without a doubt the most powerful, is a political one. The dilemma is as follows: countries may decide to create such an organization as a response to national and international political pressures, but this in turn may be very costly politically, as it could work to the disadvantage of some elite groups. As section 10.3 shows, delegating to a PRA can be costly, while the benefits can be limited, since the efficiency of a PRA depends mainly on available resources and the prevailing institutional environment.

10.1 Alternative Modes of Governance in Public Procurement

To understand why a government will choose to delegate certain procurement functions to a relatively autonomous administrative entity necessitates the analysis of three main dimensions:

---

[2] Christine Léon de Mariz. Also Bernard Abeillé was and remains very actively involved in public procurement in Africa. See Abeillé (2011).

- the types of *transactions* that need to be carried out;
- the *governance structures* that can carry out these transactions and the responsibilities that define their jurisdiction[3], and;
- the different *transaction-cost economizing* factors that are embedded in the process.

In Chapter 3 we analysed the complexity of public procurement transactions, emphasizing that the ex-ante characteristics and ex-post conditions which in principle should be taken into account in drawing up a contract are actually the source of uncertainty and open the door to opportunistic behaviour. In this section, we focus on the second dimension, i.e. the different structures for governing these complicated transactions.

A government can choose between two main options. First, it can decide not to delegate procurement oversight to a new organization, but rather to maintain the status quo by monitoring the agencies dealing with public procurement itself. It will therefore rely on existing governance mechanisms, typically a public procurement unit (e.g. a central tender board, CTB) or a department of the administration. Conversely, it can decide to delegate procurement oversight to a newly created organizational entity, typically a procurement regulatory agency. Ideally, a government would analyse the advantages and drawbacks of delegation and, based on these factors, decide whether or not to delegate. Table 10.1 summarizes the different functions delegated to the different types of organizations, depending on the degree of centralization in their governance.

More precisely, public procurement functions can be carried out by different governmental organizations. Each ministry or spending agency could have its own procurement unit which would issue its own procurement rules and regulations. Public procurement can also be carried out by executing entities and a CTB, an entity that would approve the contract award process when the contract amount exceeds a certain threshold. As was examined in the previous chapter, many SSA countries in the 1980s implemented these centralized procurement boards. Generally, a CTB establishes the appropriate tender procedures and ensures compliance with tender documents and notices; invites tenders locally or internationally; receives, opens, examines, and evaluates tenders; and approves the award of such contracts. Hence, CTBs are responsible for approval of the awarding of major contracts for government institutions and other public bodies, whereas the executing agencies or centralized purchasing agencies are responsible for the actual procurement of goods and services. The CTBs may also perform some oversight functions.

---

[3] E.g. do they have regulatory functions? Do they play a quasi-judicial role?

Table 10.1 Different modalities of governance in public procurement

Function	Modalities of governance
Public procurement unit or department	
To carry out the procurement process	Fully decentralized to the executing agencies (ministries or local level)
Procurement directorate	
Responsible for the clearance of procurement awards above a certain threshold, without procurement award authority	Partially centralized (administrative entity part of the executive branch)
Central Tender Board (CTB)	
Carry out the procurement process in lieu of the executive agencies	Fully centralized into one entity
Procurement Regulatory Agency (PRA)	
Responsible for policy formulation, the oversight of procurement contracts, and eventually the handling of complaints	Partially centralized (administrative entity part of the executive branch) with possibility of significant transfer of responsibilities, making it a relatively autonomous entity operating at the interface between government, civil society, and the private sector.*

* Some PRAs are tripartite (with representatives of public authorities, private sector, and civil society).

Source: Authors.

A procurement regulatory authority is an alternative modality of governance. As already noted in Chapter 9, a PRA is an entity responsible for the formulation of procurement policy and the implementation and monitoring of effective public procurement reform. The main role of a PRA is to foster good governance by limiting the discretion of procurement officers, increasing transparency in procurement operations, monitoring compliance with procedures, and increasing public investment productivity through competition and better efficiency in the process.

Procurement regulatory authorities, or their equivalent with different names (e.g. 'lead procurement body', *'agence de regulation des marchés publics'*, 'directorate', etc.), were implemented in several countries in the context of public procurement reforms during the first decade of this century. Table 10.2 presents the countries that created variations of PRAs through laws, regulations, or decrees during the initial reform period. But making these bodies operational was extremely difficult. Although the process had been initiated years before, only ten out of the sixteen legally established bodies were operational at the end of 2004, while the other six still lacked complementary regulations and financing to start functioning. A decade later, most of the PRAs created in the initial period were finally operational, although with very unequal performance or autonomy (Abeillé 2011).

In practice, the structure of procurement regulatory authorities varies among countries: we find agencies, directorates, offices, regulatory entities,

Table 10.2 Procurement regulatory authorities (PRAs) in sub-Saharan Africa

	Country	PRA created through laws or regulations	Date of creation (year)	PRA operational in:	
				2004	2012
1	Benin	***	2004		***
2	Botswana	***	2002	***	***
3	Cameroon	***	2001	***	***
4	Chad	***	2004	***	***
5	Ethiopia	***	2004	***	***
6	Gambia	***	2003	***	***
7	Ghana	***	2003	***	***
8	Kenya	***	2001	***	***
9	Madagascar	***	2004		***
10	Malawi	***	2004		***
11	Niger	***	2004		***
12	Nigeria	***	2003		***
13	Sierra Leone	***	2004		***
14	South Africa	***	2003	***	***
15	Tanzania	***	2004	***	***
16	Uganda	***	2003	***	***
	Total (out of 47) countries in SSA	16		10	16

*Note:*** This indicates 'yes'.

Source: Authors' own compilation.

or independent bodies, and they have different roles and levels of competence. However, despite their diversity, they share certain common characteristics. They all are administrative entities responsible for overseeing public
procurement entities of the government, project implementation units, statutory bodies, government agencies, local government authorities, and public
enterprises. They can be either cabinet departments or independent agencies
designed to operate with relative autonomy, independent from the executive branch. While agencies, regulatory entities, and independent entities
are relatively familiar forms, encompassing some authority to make recommendations, issue regulations, or even give orders and impose sanctions, this
is less obvious for directorates. A directorate is a group of individuals chosen to govern the affairs of procurement, or they can be offices, which are
executive agencies that advise the head of government or the president on
procurement-related issues.

Several examples illustrate this diversity, which in some cases is largely
nominal. In Cameroon, the procurement agency was called the *Agence de
Régulation des Marchés Publics*, created by Decree No. 2001/048 in 2001. The
'Public Procurement Directorate' in Kenya was created in 2001 and is a government agency which serves as the central organ for policy formulation,

implementation, human resource development, and oversight of the public procurement process. Botswana's 'Public Procurement and Asset Disposal Board' (PPADB) was established through an Act of Parliament in 2002. Gambia's 'Public Procurement Authority' (GPPA) was established in 2003, Ethiopia's 'Public Procurement Board' and Sierra Leone's 'National Public Procurement Authority' in 2004.

These PRAs share some characteristics with standard regulatory agencies,[4] although they also differ from the typical 'regulatory bodies' found in the energy or telecom sectors, for example. Guasch and Spiller (1999) classify regulatory bodies according to the type of regulation they oversee: economic, social, or process regulation. A procurement regulatory authority would correspond to the third category, in that it is meant to be an organization that regulates procurement procedures. However, contrary to regulation in the energy sector, it does not intervene in matters relating to price or quantity of goods or services produced. In addition, a PRA is not concerned with social considerations, contrary to the regulatory entities for the environment or public health. Lastly and most importantly, PRAs differ from existing fully fledged regulatory bodies in that they do not focus exclusively on firms. Their main task is to increase capacity within the administration, and improve regulation and control in order to improve the management of the public procurement system.

It is worth noting that the authority of PRAs differs among countries. They may have more or less extended functions, and varying degrees of financial autonomy. But all face similar limitations. First, they lack the power to make administrative decisions. Second, their regulatory functions are limited in that they cannot organize procurement by establishing rules; they draft rules but cannot enact them (this authority belongs to the prime minister, the president, or parliament). Lastly, although in principle they should only offer advice and recommendations, they are frequently involved in action to sanction or debar persons or firms for non-compliance or violations to the procurement principles or the rules. In that respect, PRAs are administrative agencies that differ from standard regulatory agencies: strictly speaking, they do not have full 'regulatory' functions. In other words, they are

---

[4] A regulatory agency refers to an administrative body that implements, interprets, or prescribes law or policy, and sets forth through regulations the standards by which people and groups are governed for certain types of actions. It also describes the organization, procedure, or practice requirements of any administrative body. These regulations have the full force of law and establish mandatory stipulations. However, as an administrative body, a regulatory body remains subjected to the rules defined by the regulation under which it operates. These regulations are usually promulgated by the executive branch (the various cabinets, offices, and departments) and reviewed by the legislative branch. In principle, at least in a democratic regime, regulations cannot be circumvented, except by a court of law.

'micro-institutions' with an ambiguous status, depending on the level of delegation embodied in their relation with the government.

10.2 Assessing the Possible Benefits of Delegation to a Procurement Regulatory Authority from a Government's Perspective: The Transaction-Cost Economizing Factors

We now turn to the examination of the benefits believed to be generated by the creation of these micro-institutions. In the decision to delegate specific functions to a PRA, a government and/or international organization expects to gain in terms of transparency, efficiency, value for money, and accountability in procurement operations. Government also expects economic, political, and diplomatic benefits from the delegation, thanks to a better alignment between this new mode of governance and future transactions. Indeed, if one ignores the costs of the new arrangement—such as those related to the transition and its operations, which are not necessarily measurable in monetary terms—a government would always benefit. However, taking these costs as well as the political costs into account may change the picture. In what follows, we examine the possible benefits of delegating procurement transactions to a new public agency based on a consideration of some of the economizing (10.2.1) and political (10.2.2) factors related to transaction costs. The next section will explore the costs and limitations to delegation.

10.2.1 Expertise as a Way to Reduce Uncertainty

To be attractive, the benefits generated by delegation must outweigh its costs. Therefore, a necessary condition for a government to choose to delegate is the expectation of net gains. A key argument put forward in the literature is that delegating to a specialized entity would yield benefits in terms of expertise (Lupia and McCubbins 1994c, 2000; see our Chapter 8, section 8.2.2). Increased proficiency would reduce uncertainty, providing motivation to the government as well as to private parties involved to reform procurement systems.[5]

Procurement regulatory authorities were and remain viewed as a major factor in that respect. Concentrating capabilities in one governmental body rather than spreading them over multiple executing agencies and making this body responsible for monitoring procurement activities, developing and enforcing regulations sanctioned by the legislative process, and educating

---

[5] The transaction cost literature considers uncertainty to be one of the key variables—in addition to frequency and asset specificity—determining transaction costs (see Williamson 1985: 56).

citizens through the transparency of upheld decisions would foster the development of expertise. Consequently, countries recognizing the advantages of proficiency would be inclined to delegate procurement functions to a specialized entity, and by the same token partially resolve some of its controversies.

As we have already emphasized (see Chapters 3 and 5), part of the uncertainty related to procurement transactions comes from their complexity. McCubbins notes as early in 1985 (p. 722) that 'the creation of administrative agencies is primarily in response to the technical complexity of modern society'.[6] With delegation, a government could expect to economize on the time and resources devoted to procurement as well as improve measurement and enforcement in the transaction process. As Lupia and McCubbins (1994c: 97) emphasize, for a government the potential advantage of delegating to bureaucracy is that:

> ...bureaucrats may have expertise that legislators desire. As a result, legislators may be able to rely on the bureaucracy to formulate policies that they themselves would have formulated if they had the time and resources necessary to acquire the bureaucracy's level of expertise.

Delegation to experts would have a positive impact on the efficiency of procurement operations by reducing the government's costs to acquire and directly apply the needed proficiency on its own, assuming that it could do so, or to coordinate the expertise spread among numerous ministries and departments.

Let us look a bit more closely into this black box of expertise to examine some of the key sources fostering the positive expectations that have been linked to the PRAs.

First, by delegating to a well-defined entity, governments could expect to improve the legal and regulatory procurement framework as well as procurement practices. This would have an impact on transparency, and establishing better-defined 'rules of the game', particularly if these were aligned with international standards, could improve value for money and accountability through the provision of control mechanisms, oversight, and the means to impose sanctions. In practice, the main function of PRAs in sub-Saharan Africa was focused on establishing or improving formal rules. It was to design or improve procurement legislation as well as devise and implement the associated set of regulations and procedures (typically, standard bidding documents), particularly in countries where no procurement legislation existed, was outdated, or needed major improvement. A significant number of these procurement laws are based on the 1994 United Nations Commission on International Trade Law (UNCITRAL) model. This 'model', designed to assist

---

[6] See also Ripley and Franklin (1991).

states[7] to reform and modernize their laws on procurement, mainly encompasses procedures for achieving competition, transparency, fairness, and objectivity in the procurement process, thereby increasing economy and efficiency. Thus, the model establishes the minimum criteria that good procurement legislation should meet. Although partially inspired by this model, there is some deviation in the model used by the World Bank in SSA countries. A specificity of the 2002 World Bank Draft Model Public Procurement Law Applicable to Administrative Law Countries is the strong emphasis on the transparency and predictability of procurement procedures (Verdeaux 2005).[8]

Second, governments had expected delegation to increase human capital through training programmes prepared by the oversight entity for procurement officers. A national survey conducted by consultants in Angola in 2002 found that 54.2 per cent of the procurement officers in different ministries and at the provincial level were not aware of the existence of the main decree regulating public procurement in the country. Capacity-building programmes would be prepared by PRAs, which could be expected to have an impact on the performance of these procedure officials. Typically, this role would encompass the preparation of procurement-capacity programmes to increase the level of awareness and compliance of the relevant officials. It would also make procurement officers more knowledgeable about the best practices, while increased ethics training would curb corruption and advance accountability. By enhancing capacity in public procurement, PRAs would help reduce transaction costs resulting from mismanagement and/or corruption. These advantages would be complemented by the benefits derived from data collection and analysis that delegation would promote; indeed, data collection and analysis could divulge information on the doings of the procurement officers, enable having an overview of the transparency of procurement and practices used, and facilitate the development of benchmarks across executing agencies.

Third, delegation could help to improve conflict resolution. Some countries have created appeals mechanisms in order to speed up the complaints process and to circumvent the need to go to court. This possibility reduces costs related to delays in the decisionmaking process, increases the efficiency

---

[7] The UNCITRAL model is not a legally binding document and countries therefore are not required to implement it fully.

[8] This model also makes a sharp distinction between services and consultancies. Other sources include guidelines from such international organizations as the African Development Bank (AfDB) or the World Trade Organization's Government Procurement Agreement (GPA) of January 1996, which sought to reinforce rules guaranteeing fair and non-discriminatory conditions of international competition.

of procurement operations, and contributes to an increased value for money and lower corruption (bidders can lodge complaints or signal misconduct).

Expertise can therefore be considered an important cost-economizing factor, as it would contribute to reducing the uncertainty resulting from the complexity of public procurement transactions. Centralizing public procurement experts within a public agency enables the government to have a better overall perspective of the procurement contracts being carried out by the different agencies, enabling it to monitor transactions, or at times, realize economies of scale. If procurement operations are performed by spending agencies without the supervision of an oversight body, procurements tend to be of lower quality because not all agencies can be procurement-proficient. This argument is particularly relevant in countries with poor procurement capacity and where checks and balances are either poor or do not function at all. Again, PRAs could provide the necessary expertise.

In sum, PRAs were created with the assumption that they could address the complexity of procurement issues through better information, better monitoring functions, and improved capabilities. The functions and characteristics of the procurement regulatory agencies reflect this expectation; at the time of their formal inception, the emphasis was put on aspects linked to expertise, e.g. capacity-building activities, drafting laws and regulations, and so forth. Figure 10.1, based on numerous interviews with government officials, summarizes the main dimensions that expertise is expected to generate.

In practice, the PRAs have tackled these different dimensions, albeit with varying determination. During the period under review, the primary task of the PRAs was to draft new rules and regulations, and to conduct some training. In this context, enforcement mechanisms were not touched. According to the depth of institutional change identified and analysed in

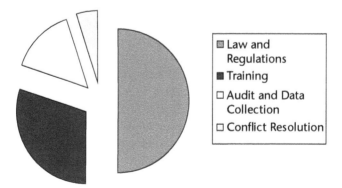

Figure 10.1 Main dimensions of expertise

Sources: Authors' estimates based on interviews with government and World Bank procurement specialists.

Part II, procurement regulatory authorities in SSA are still at the first level, that is, striving for changes in the formal rules of the game while postponing informal rules and enforcement mechanisms to a later stage. Graduating to the second level would imply that the PRAs become responsible for participating in audits, gathering data, and, for some of them, solving conflicts, i.e. a task that touches upon enforcement mechanisms.[9] Governments were (and often remain) reluctant to provide PRAs with sufficient resources to conduct audits, as this could expose a government to the risk of uncovering its inadequate compliance with the new formal rules. During the period under review, virtually no country in our sample reached this level, which raises doubts about the sustainability of the reform process.

10.2.2 Political Escapism Combined with International Pressure

In addition to the potential economic benefits derived from reduced transaction costs, the balance between political benefits and costs is certainly a powerful factor in explaining the lukewarm interest in setting up PRAs. Indeed, in addition to the benefit of expertise and the various economies expected to arise from the development of capabilities, there are arguably two other dimensions, essential if not even more important than the economic arguments. One is the 'political escape': politicians use PRAs as an umbrella so as not to have to confront or deal with pressure related to bad procurement practices. The second is international pressure, particularly from donors stipulating reform as a condition for loans and support. These two dimensions are a substantial factor in explaining why some SSA countries have set up procurement regulatory agencies.

Indeed, delegation may also trigger benefits to the government from a political point of view. As already emphasized by Fiorina (1982: 35), 'Delegation is a result of efforts on the part of legislators to escape the costs, political and otherwise, of regulating directly'. The delegation of procurement oversight functions to a public agency would mean that complaints would be addressed to the public agency, not the government, therefore lowering its reputational risk. Similarly, in cases of non-transparency or corruption, the attention of the civil society would tend to focus on the agency in charge. Therefore, countries with fragile political leadership could be among the first to adopt delegation. Also, a newly elected government with an important reform agenda could take advantage of its initial support and use it to introduce new agencies, delegating decisionmaking authority to them in order to consolidate its own legitimacy and to use them as an umbrella for reforms

---

[9] In many instances, government entities are not motivated to allocate sufficient resources that would allow PRAs to conduct audits that could point out their misconduct!

that might produce numerous losers. For instance, it has been observed that prior to election, governments tend not to make substantial changes, preferring to launch major procurement reforms after elections, as is well illustrated by the case of Senegal at the time of re-election of former President Wade.

In addition and more importantly, the government can expect to reduce international pressure through delegation. As was seen in Part I, public procurement was a part of the broader economic reforms that were launched during the late 1990s in the context of fiscal constraints and high debt levels in sub-Saharan Africa. Creating a PRA and delegating it significant power could be viewed as a 'signal' to international organizations and the donor community that the country was making an effort to increase transparency and efficiency in its procurement system. However, it must be acknowledged that in many cases, the initiative was not purely endogenous. As was already substantiated in Chapter 3, setting up these bodies and organizing delegation were often the conditions for receiving budget support or debt relief. This could explain why some bodies were created through the legislation of the country but never became operational: countries would aim to comply with international requirements, but would refrain from putting adequate structures and resources in place to implement the law. This situation might have been exacerbated by the fact that international organizations use visible benchmarks such as the enactment of laws and/or decrees, so that reforms often extended to formal institutions only.

More specifically, in many cases the government's decision to delegate procurement oversight to a procurement regulatory authority resulted from pressure from the IMF, the World Bank, and other international organizations and donors. Countries needing foreign aid assistance were strongly motivated to comply and to create these micro-institutions as the new mode of governance for public procurement. Even when the creation of such a monitoring apparatus was not a requirement, some governments were nevertheless inclined to push for its creation to show that they are addressing public procurement issues. Similarly, the setting up of anti-corruption agencies can be attributed to the same motives: in forming these agencies, the country would 'notify' civil society and the international community that it was dealing with corruption. The importance of this reputational factor should not be underestimated: it was a decisive factor in the delegation of important decisions to relatively independent agencies.

These elements can be interpreted as an attempt by government to deal with political transaction costs, with its internal opposition or even its own constituencies, but also with the international community. In that respect, delegation can be understood as a way to lower political transaction costs as well as to economize on costs the government would incur if it were to monitor procurement directly through different bureaus or departments.

10.3 Constraints to Delegating Public Procurement Functions

Delegation can also bring adverse transaction costs. There are limitations and challenges related to delegating public procurement functions to PRAs. These can also induce costs: the physical and capital costs required to set up an autonomous agency; the development of an additional bureaucracy; slippage and inertia of the administrative agency; risks of collusion; and the consequences for the government of uncovered malpractices. If the costs, or even one cost item, outweigh the benefits, a country will likely choose not to delegate and to maintain the status quo. We start with a review of the different costs involved, and then turn to the limitations that might come from the disproportionate expectations with respect to the resources available, particularly human capital.

10.3.1 Drawbacks of Delegation

There are many reasons why a country might decide against delegating strategic public procurement decisions. First, transparency, efficiency, accountability, reduced corruption, and value for money in procurement operations may not be a substantial concern for a country, a situation particularly prevalent in authoritarian regimes. Second, some countries have no interest in improving these elements because procurement issues are not a priority. Third, some countries may recognize the benefits of delegation, but may consider the consequences to be economically or politically too costly. Many of the factors opposing delegation emanate from a mix of economics and politics: political economy is at stake here.

TRANSPARENCY AND REVELATION COSTS
An important factor, and the potential source of significant political risk, is the question of 'revelation'. This constitutes an important drawback for SSA countries because delegation can cause problems by bringing to light the government's wrongdoings. For the government, the political transaction cost of increased transparency may become a formidable obstacle to the creation of an administrative agency that could uncover its misconduct. As Evenett (2000) observes, the impetus for reform is undermined when losers from the reform, which might include government, form a small circle, often well organized, while beneficiaries are in large number, most of the time dispersed—a problem so well illustrated by reforms of public utilities.[10] The cost

---

[10] Reforms of urban water systems provide numerous examples (see Savedoff and Spiller 1999 and Shirley 2002).

of transparency could be high for a government that has reaped benefits from an opaque procurement framework. The costs could also be high for certain individuals or groups with vested interests, seeking to maintain or control an existing system or activity from which they derive private gain. In these cases, the political transaction outlay is particularly high if these individuals or groups are constituencies that support the government, taking advantage of the existing procurement system. These vested interests may represent a powerful force opposing the creation or fully fledged operational capacity of a PRA. In the same vein, public procurement is often an area where civil servants can extract high private benefits. Frequently it is a source of financing for political parties, and the costs of exposure from increased transparency may simply therefore be too high and politically too risky compared to the derived benefits.

AGENCY SHIRKING AND SLIPPAGE

Agency slippage or shirking is another issue which may help to explain the reluctance of some countries to establish a new body to deal with public procurement. Lupia and McCubbins (1994c: 92) identify the risks associated to what they call the 'equivalent of abdication' in delegation:

> The potential drawback of delegation is that a bureaucrat who possesses both expertise and policy-making authority can also take actions that make legislators worse off than if they had never delegated. In this case, the act of delegation is equivalent to abdication, wherein the will of the people, as expressed by the people's elected representatives, neither constrains nor motivates the formulation of public policy. (emphasis added)

More specifically, through delegation a government risks losing control of the administrative agency's decisions because the agency can pursue a course of action that is contrary to the preferences of the government. This form of agency drift is known as 'agency slippage'. The administrative agency also can be inefficient, leading to inertia, often a form of 'shirking', where the agent deliberately pursues self-interested objectives, fully aware that they differ from those of the principal. These two forms of agency drifts have an impact on the efficiency of public procurement and could exacerbate other factors such as corruption. Kiewiet and McCubbins (1991: 49) emphasize that:

> There is almost always some conflict between the interests of those who delegate authority and the agents to whom they delegate it. Agents behave opportunistically, pursuing their own interest subject only to the constraints imposed by their relationship with the principal.

Aghion and Tirole (1997: 27) similarly note that if, on the one hand, 'delegation will facilitate the agent's participation...and foster his incentive to acquire relevant information…on the other hand delegation involves a costly loss of control for the principal'.

Different structural arrangements have been developed to deal with these issues, proposing control mechanisms embedded in the design of the institutional framework. This is because the government, along with parliament, has several alternative institutional settings for a PRA. For example, it can be established as a board, or a commission, or a department within a ministry. Already the selection of the type of organization signals the degree of independence the government will grant its PRA. The regulatory mandate of the agency—that is, the domain of potential regulatory issues or problems that the entity may address—can also limit its role. Moreover, a regulatory act could delineate the legal tools or instruments that the administrative agency can use to implement the rules of the game, thus tightly controlling its domain of action. Lastly, the procedures that the agency must follow to promulgate a ruling may be embedded in the act and impose restrictions on its potential functions.

In other words, there are different degrees of delegation, depending on the constraints imposed by the structural arrangement on the substantive discretion of the administrative entity and on the channels it opens for decisionmaking within the administration (McCubbins 2005/2008). In that respect, Bendor et al. (2001) distinguish two possible types of delegation: one in which public authorities explicitly give the power to a subordinate to take action without obligation to report back,[11] and one in which the agency can only gather certain kinds of information and/or make proposals to the governing authority which then decides the action to be undertaken. Delegation in the case of PRAs is often a mix of the two. Typically, besides gathering information, PRAs—as administrative entities for public procurement—prepare and review related legislation and regulations, deal with capacity-building issues in procurement, carry out research, participate in audits, and coordinate the appeals process. Generally PRAs are in charge of collecting data on procurement practices and reporting their findings to a governing authority.

However, in our sample countries, the role of procurement regulatory authorities has remained limited. Far from being a form of 'abdication' as defined by McCubbins, they have no regulatory functions and remain ultimately under the control of the executive. This reduces the risks of agency 'shirking' and 'slippage', but also limits their autonomy and credibility.

---

[11] An important issue in this case is whether the decisions are revocable or not.

10.3.2 Bureaucratization, Politicization

Besides the risks mentioned previously, other obstacles to forming PRAs or to delegating significant power to them exist, especially in countries with few checks and balances. Heavy structures might be too expensive to maintain and are perceived as useless, encouraging politicians to refrain from setting up such agencies or even from dismantling existing entities. Increased bureaucratization, with its attendant costs and the increase in corruption that it could promote, may also be a concern, particularly if a government is under international pressure to reform and reduce public expenses. There is also the risk of collusion, which might make the government cautious with respect to delegation. Collusion linked to corruption could occur between the administrative agency and the executing procurement agencies, which in turn could affect the outcomes expected by the government from delegation. This may also give the incentive for the government to intervene with increased politicization of the agency. As a result, a procurement regulatory authority could, in certain countries, only worsen existing problems: bringing an additional bureaucratic layer, greater possibilities for corruption, and making the economic as well as political costs of collusion between this entity and the executing agencies too high for the government.

10.3.3 Financial Costs and Funding

It is now generally acknowledged that in order for an agency to be proficient and to escape the risk of political manipulation, it should have financial autonomy. This implies that it has well-defined resources that are stable over time and that escape interference from the government. On the other hand, this autonomy also raises the issue that delegation needs to mirror the prevailing political forces, particularly in a democratic regime: experts can be expected to be subjected to some oversight and, in the last resort, submitted to decisions from representatives democratically elected.

Financial autonomy also raises the issue of the costs, encompassing both physical and human costs, which might be dissuasive in the creation of a PRA or for making the investments that would make it fully operational. There are salaries and capital expenditures related to the running of a PRA. In addition to operational expenses, there are costs involved in enabling the agency to conduct its own activities (such as audits, collection of data, and training), which depend on the functions allocated to the entity. On the one hand, there might be economies of scope: the more responsibilities a procurement regulatory agency has, the less costly it becomes, thanks to the increased capacity created within the body. Extensive responsibilities, on the other hand, necessitate the existence of qualified human capital which may not be available, or available only at very high costs. This trade-off could partially explain why the functions assigned to PRAs and their numbers vary so significantly among countries. It also helps to understand why financial costs could be another reason for not delegating.[12]

In that context, which is typical in many SSA countries, delegation might not be the appropriate strategy. The question of adequate funding and staffing provided by the executive branch can be a decisive factor in many countries in creating a PRA. As Donahue (1989) points out, bureaucracies are like machines: they are costly to build and keep in operation, and are prone to break down if neglected. Let us give an example concerning audits. In order to improve transparency and efficiency, some countries, e.g. Madagascar, Niger, and Sierra Leone, enacted procurement laws that not only created PRAs, but also planned regular audits. Audit technology is meant to detect fraudulent reporting and to allow for reprimand once a false report is detected. However, this concept implies a standing commitment with the auditing agencies. Regular audits, on the other hand, can be done only at a cost and with the availability of experts (often including international professionals) at very high costs. As a consequence, regularity is not respected: the principal is unlikely to carry out audits regularly, and the efficient agent might 'anticipate this and may start acting untruthfully' (Laffont and Martimort 2002).

10.3.4 Over-Optimistic Expectations?

Many PRAs, although endowed with legal status, never became fully operational and face difficulties moving in that direction. This is due to the different factors mentioned previously (politicization, bureaucratization, and to a lesser extent agency-shirking and slippage), but is also due to their inadequate funding and staffing shortages which challenge their credibility. Indeed, aligning these micro-institutions with the transactions they are required to monitor calls for substantial administrative capability that is rarely available in the countries of our sample.

The analysis of the emergence of procurement regulatory agencies must be done in the context of weak human assets and scarce resources. The implementation of the PRAs could disrupt the established status quo and challenge the existence of rents shared by different groups, which would generate powerful opposition and fuel administrative resistance all the way to sabotage. As laid out by North et al. (2009) in their analysis of violence and limited access orders, a dominant coalition might adopt institutions (in our case, proposed by international organizations or bilateral donors) without fundamentally

---

[12] Unfortunately, to our knowledge there is no extensive study on the costs of creating and maintaining (efficient) procurement regulatory agencies.

changing the way society operates. The economic and political costs may then exceed the expected benefits by far.

Another problem may arise from the allocation of too many functions and responsibilities to PRAs. The well-intentioned motivation of making the entity credible, for example, can be detrimental to its success in the context of limited administrative capabilities. Many existing organizations in SSA countries illustrate the point: numerous agencies, statistics departments, or even directorates cannot fulfil their mission because of a lack of qualified staff and funding. Consequently they become empty shells. Analysing the role of ethics offices, Tanzi (1998) argues that 'to be effective, [they] must have independence from the political establishment, ample resources, and personnel of the highest integrity. They must also have the power to enforce penalties or, at least, have others, including the judiciary, enforce the penalties'. This is quite a demand in countries with a shortage of qualified human resources and very limited funding.

10.4 Conclusion

In sum, perhaps too much was expected from the creation of procurement regulatory authorities. These micro-institutions alone cannot solve all the issues related to public procurement systems and to institutional weaknesses. Without an adequate institutional environment to guide player behaviour towards transparency and efficiency, building new organizations may end up as additional layers of bureaucracy and increased rent-seeking behaviour.

In this chapter we have taken note of some factors rooted in economic and political transaction costs that could account for the uneven implementation of relatively independent procurement regulatory authorities in SSA. With reference to the delegation theory, we have drawn attention to the expectations, thanks to these entities, regarding the improvements in procurement proficiency. But we also noted an even more compelling factor for setting up PRAs: internal political pressure, particularly with regard to corruption, and international pressure. SSA countries had to signal their willingness to conform to the expectations of civil society that had become increasingly concerned with inefficiency and corruption in public procurement. Countries also needed to be able to point to improvement in the public finance sphere in order to gain access to credits and grants from the international community.

However, the creation of an oversight body presented significant risks and challenges from the perspective of the government, particularly if this entity was well endowed with human capabilities and funding. These risks partially account for the fact that some PRAs are still not operational and that several countries did not implement them. This reluctance among political

Identification of costs and benefits		Resulting mode of governance
Costs	**Benefits**	**• If costs > Benefits** Status quo, i.e. keep central tender board and/or ministries/agencies handle the procurement processes **• If costs = Benefits** a. Status quo, i.e. increase the thresholds for review and the scope of work b. PRA: change the role of the central tender board so that it becomes an oversight agency **• If costs < Benefits** PRAs created as a new mode of governance
• Countries not interested in reforming procurement systems • Financial costs of delegation • Costs of revelation of government practices • Abdication of policymaking authority • Agency slippage or shirking	• Expertise of the staff • Reduction of uncertainty and transaction costs • Comply with international pressure for best practice • Increased transparency, efficiency, and accountability • Limitation of the discretion of the procurement officers • Increase the efficiency of public spending	

Figure 10.2 Cost-benefit analysis of delegation: a summary
Source: Authors.

decisionmakers may also have been fuelled by or found a pretext of risk in the politicization, bureaucratization, agency-shirking and agency-slippage, and lack of adequate human resources that could be associated to delegation. Although difficult to measure, the resulting transaction costs (economic as well as political) could have been a dissuasive factor in many cases, which could explain the limited number of procurement regulatory agencies and the difficulties faced from the very start. Nevertheless, almost a decade after their creation, most PRAs in our sample countries have made significant progress in becoming more operational, yet almost all are still striving to gain financial independence, so as to operate without political interference and build credibility (Abeillé 2011; see also Quinot and Arrowsmith 2013, particularly introduction and chap. 12). In that respect, they are still struggling with the limits and challenges outlined in this chapter, as summarized in Figure 10.2.

General Conclusions

In the context of increasingly tight financial constraints, reforming public procurement has become an important priority in economic and business circles as well as among policymakers. This is evidenced by the growing concerns among donors, governments, civil society, professional organizations, the private sector, and the general public with respect to procurement systems, often understood as part of the much-needed reform of the government. This book contributes to the analyses of the institutional factors and organizational requirements that are intertwined in the reform process. Through a review of important reforms introduced in sub-Saharan Africa since the late 1990s, it draws lessons from the success and failures of these real-life experiments.

Our book relies on a theoretical framework derived mainly, although not exclusively, from the new institutional economics. Indeed, we consider this approach particularly appropriate for shedding new light on the two inter-related dimensions involved in all public procurement reforms (and more generally, in all public sector reforms)—the institutional environment, which determines the 'rules of the games' that guide individual as well as collective behaviour in the process of reform; and the specific micro-institutions that develop and, in many cases, implement the guidelines rooted in these rules, and structure the interaction between public authorities and operators in delivering the goods and services articulated under procurement agreements. Exploring this interaction and its impact on the governance of public procurement and its reform is at the core of this book.

What We Have Learned

Our analysis, nourished by the rich experience of procurement reforms in SSA since the late 1990s, has emphasized the complex netting of endogenous and exogenous factors that induces fundamental changes in the relative preference of decision-makers, pushing them towards public procurement reforms.

These factors of change, however, faced formidable obstacles. Vested interests opposed changes in the formal rules of the game, pushing political transaction costs upward. At a more micro level, distortions in the definition, implementation, and enforcement of the new laws and regulations often derailed or even paralyzed the process that reforms intended to initiate. Gaps developed, and in many cases deepened, between formal changes, the micro-institutions responsible for their implementation, and informal behaviour of the parties involved, all of which increased economic transaction costs.

Indeed, one main lesson of our careful examination of the experiences in twenty-eight SSA countries shows that the flaws and drawbacks in the reform of procurement generally resulted from the overly zealous focus on changing formal rules while neglecting informal and enforcement mechanisms. Restructure of the formal rules is, of course, an essential part of the reform process. It sends important signals to the parties involved and sets the foundations and principles; and in most countries of our sample, changes in legislation were non-negligible. However, as our progress index shows, actual implementation of the new rules was very slow and ended in substantial discrepancies, largely because of the 'benign neglect' of informal components such as conventions, norms of behaviour, and self-imposed codes of conduct, not to mention the effect of administrative traditions and corruption.

Our analysis, based on the World Bank database[1] developed during the initial phase of reforms in the countries under review and cross-checked against other databases, interviews, and available documents, reveals the role of specific institutional elements as the most significant factors to explain progress or stagnation in the design and implementation of procurement reforms. These include: the degree of freedom that allows criticism to be voiced, the quality of the bureaucracy, the perception of the degree of corruption, and the level and type of foreign aid.

In addition to this institutional dimension, the collected information complements our on-the-ground experience and singles out the key role played by the existence (or non-existence) of adequate transmission mechanisms between formal rules and individual behaviour in making reforms operational. We labelled these mechanisms as 'micro-institutions'. Indeed, an important factor of success in several of our sample countries seems to have been the switch to new modes of governance for implementing and monitoring reforms. More specifically, based on the data collected from the sixteen countries that established procurement regulatory agencies or their equivalent in the initial period of reform, we show that the previous arrangements (namely central tender boards or similar micro-institutions) failed because of poor or ineffective human capital and the often counterproductive role of

---

[1] Two co-authors of this volume contributed to the development of the World Bank database. The data not submitted to confidentiality as well as a methodological note providing indications about tentative econometric tests are available from the authors.

courts. A new mode of governance to which more responsibilities would be delegated was viewed as a way to move away from the flawed institutional arrangements, to build expertise, to reduce uncertainty, and to lower transaction costs generated by procurement responsibilities spread over numerous entities and ministries. Clustering responsibilities in a well-identified entity was also believed to help curb corruption by facilitating more transparency through the interaction with civil society and international organizations and donors. On the other hand, such a heavy reliance on a single entity was perceived to be a 'second-best' solution, an alternative to failing institutions, albeit with some drawbacks. The risk of creating a corrupted super-entity, and the economic and political transaction costs of adopting this new mode of governance may explain why several countries did not endorse this solution, or did so reluctantly.

Only empirically based knowledge can provide the information needed to assess the resulting trade-off between costs and benefits. Although the collected data and information are limited, they indicate important short- and medium-term gaps between the reform design and the outcome. But, over the long run some progress was made in most SSA countries under review, particularly those that have implemented this new mode of governance, as has happened in other regions where similar reforms were adopted (see Abeillé 2011). The forces at work in the first generation of reforms, particularly the demand for greater transparency, integrity, and value for money, became important drivers of progress and the impetus for the second generation of reforms.

Nevertheless, lax enforcement, lack of incentives to induce behavioural changes, and political obstacles kept national procurement systems under-performing in comparison to expectations. The gap between expectations based on diagnosis and action plans and tangible outcomes has been and continues to be significant in SSA as well as in other non-African countries. Part of the problem clearly emanates from the political economy of reform.

Despite recognition that reforms require supporters and political commitment, there has been insufficient focus on the forces that could promote this momentum, manage the formally adopted reforms, or develop capabilities with respect to procurement. For instance, procurement has rarely been included in projects dealing with judiciary or political system reforms. Similarly, training programmes for lawyers, engineers, businessmen, or bureaucrats have rarely been included as an integral part of public sector reforms. Changing the prevailing approach, with its strong focus on formal reform, and paying more attention to the alignment between institutional changes, human capabilities, and reforms under consideration should be high on the agenda for second-generation procurement reforms. Creating micro-institutions that are endowed with adequate human and financial capacities, and are socially accountable so as to improve compliance and empower civil society to expect results, should become an essential component of future reforms.[2]

Looking Forward

This book provides insights for moving in this direction. Through an in-depth analysis of the forces and limits affecting the first-generation public procurement reforms in SSA, the book attempts to shed light on the drivers and obstacles to the process of institutional changes. As North (2008: 29) notes:

> We are just beginning systematically to explore the process of economic change. Our laboratory is not only our history but particularly what we are learning in the ongoing efforts to improve the performance of third world and transition economies. We have made some progress but we still have a long way to go.

The main lessons from the analysis of public procurement reforms that indicate the direction for future research can be summarized under five headings.[3]

(1) *Political economy is central for understanding the success and failure of reform.* In addition to formal changes that can be introduced through laws and regulations, it is essential to capture the equilibrium of political forces because political commitment is a key driver of reform and its outcome. Political forces can be the engine in making reform operational, as illustrated by the case of Rwanda, or the barrier to the performance of an otherwise formal, well-established procurement system, as illustrated by the case of Cameroon.

(2) *Lack or absence of coordination is a major obstacle to successful reforms.* Insufficient coordination among the development partner organizations and within the countries themselves is a serious obstacle to the adoption and, above all, to the implementation of reform. A key question then becomes: what mode of organization, and with what specific characteristics, would fit in well with the changes in the rules of the game in order to create the much-needed synergies?

(3) *Reforming civil service is a central component* in creating the much-needed supportive environment for successful procurement reform. Indeed, an important lesson from our analysis is the key role played by the

---

[2] These dimensions are becoming a part of the agenda of decisionmakers, as illustrated by the Declaration of May 2011, in Cusco, by the OECD/DAC Task Force on Procurement.

[3] See World Bank (2012). One of the authors (Bernard Abeillé) wrote this report.

existence and the integrity of human capability. Hence, an important field of research concerns the character and content of civil service reform, e.g. professionalization, retention policies, adequate incentives, so as to ensure that procurement staff perform as expected and to address the issue of staff turnover. Many implementation and enforcement problems still remain unresolved because of inefficient and demoralized civil servants in the countries reviewed in this book. At the same time, realistic goals must be assigned to such reforms.

(4) *Training and managing adequate human resources still ranks too low on the agenda of reformers.* One of the greatest challenges in SSA and, more generally, in the developing as well as the so-called 'emerging' economies is to ensure that human resource functions in each procurement entity are provided with a clear framework and standards for: (i) the entry-level qualification requirements; (ii) a competitive selection method; (iii) the appropriateness of remuneration; (iv) the provision of a career path; and (v) the dissemination and enforcement of these standards. These are central aspects in creating positive incentives for better civil service performance. Unfortunately, these have often been absent from training programmes, or ignored in the structure in which procurement staff operated.

(5) *The 'benign neglect' of implementation and enforcement issues leads to important flaws and weaknesses.* Finding ways to better align micro-institutions with the 'new' rules of the game is a key issue for decisionmakers and an important domain of investigation. Scholars, development agency consultants, and reforming governments have so far emphasized ex-ante conditions: modifying formal rules (e.g. adopting new regulations), designing sophisticated contracts, and so forth. Going forward into second-generation reforms will require focusing on enforcement and oversight control systems and their efficiency through a better understanding of: (i) the government's internal audit devices; (ii) the parliamentarian oversight committee(s); (iii) the micro-institutions' role in implementing and monitoring the rules of the game; and (iv) judicial bodies enforcing the legal framework for procurement and settling disputes when they are referred to court.

From a Positive to a Normative Perspective

Our analysis has been oriented essentially towards identifying and understanding the drivers of public procurement reform and pinpointing the factors that could explain the success or failure in the sample countries.

However, as our summary suggests, there are also lessons for policymakers and for development agencies. Among these lessons, we would emphasize three major requisites, which go beyond the change to formal rules:

(1) *Increase financial and human resources devoted to capacity-building* in order to create or increase the human capital indispensable for the implementation and enforcement of reform;

(2) *Promote coordination between the actors* involved in public procurement reform, and do so through specific measures with a focus on building efficient and accountable public procurement systems;

(3) *Promote benchmarking through the adoption of tools and the implementation of devices* that will allow measuring and assessing quality and results in a comparative way, in order to enable governments to monitor ongoing performance reliably.

In sum, procurement reform should pay increasing attention to the conditions affecting implementation and enforcement. This reorientation requires not only more emphasis on building the skills of public agents, but also reinforcing: (i) political commitment; (ii) civil service reforms; (iii) judicial systems; and (iv) private sector and civil society organizations. It also requires taking serious account of informal rules and behaviour, which are the main obstacles to improved performance of national procurement systems. Unfortunately, this is an area where development partners have little leverage. In addition, it entails measures that need time to be implemented, which is not the most popular approach among economists, consultants, and development partners.

Adequate procurement systems require not only well-designed procedures and regulations, but also well-functioning organizations in charge of, and with the capacity to implement, the rules of the game. Reaching this goal was and still is challenging. Recent compilations of the ratings of procurement systems, also for the sample countries in this book, allow comparisons to be made of their development from 2001 until 2011.[4] This comparison shows that there has been progress as well as drawbacks in public procurement reform, which is in line with our analysis. In particular, countries that had made significant progress in the initial reform period are now rated as those with 'moderate procurement risks'; on the other hand, countries that have experienced political turbulence and lack of security, but also those experiencing political interference or weak control and enforcement systems, are

---

[4] See Abeillé/World Bank (2011, 2012). The 2012 report summarizes the ratings for the countries in our sample for 2011. For a more qualitative analysis for a subset of countries in our sample, see Quinot and Arrowsmith (2013).

not progressing well, regardless of the fact that they might have put in place satisfactory formal legal and institutional frameworks.

These recent observations confirm the main point made in this book. On the one hand, there is a close relationship between the quality of institutional endowment and successful institutional change. On the other hand, it is quite clear that the links between the intentions of the reformers, the output in terms of formal rules, and the consequences for the economy at large depend substantially on the development of organizational arrangements that can implement the new rules and build adequate human capabilities. This lesson is in line with what we have learned from the analyses of other reforms, e.g. reforms in infrastructure such as water systems, energy, transportation, etc.[5] Going deeper into the analysis and understanding of these linkages would certainly help to spark the interest of governments and citizens in the reform of public procurement, which remains a major issue in so many countries worldwide.

[5] Good illustrations can be found in Savedoff and Spiller (1999), Shirley (2002), and Finger and Kunneke (2011), among others.

Annex

A.1 Pillars and their main indicators (2001–4)

Pillar I: Legal framework and regulations
Indicator 1. Procurement Law complies with applicable obligation.
Indicator 2. Availability of supporting regulation and documentation.

Pillar II: Procurement procedures
Indicator 3. Mainstreaming procedures into public financial management.
Indicator 4. Functional regulatory body at the Centre.
Indicator 5. Existence of institutional development capacity.

Pillar III: Procurement capacity
Indicator 6. Efficient procurement operations and practice.
Indicator 7. Functionality of public procurement market.

Pillar IV: Independency of fiduciary control
Indicator 8. Effective control and audit systems.
Indicator 9. Efficiency of appeals mechanism.

Pillar V: Effectiveness of anti-corruption measures
Indicator 10. Ethics and anti-corruption measures.

Source: Bernard Abeillé, Presentation to Fiduciary Week, World Bank, Washington DC, 8–11 March 2004.

A.2 Pillars and their main indicators (after 2005)[a]

Pillar I: Legislative and regulatory framework
Indicator 1. Public procurement legislative and regulatory framework achieves the agreed standards and complies with applicable obligations
Indicator 2. Existence of implementing regulations and documentation.

Pillar II: Institutional framework and management capacity
Indicator 3. The public procurement system is mainstreamed and well integrated into the public sector governance system.
Indicator 4. The country has a functional normative/regulatory body.
Indicator 5. Existence of institutional development capacity.

Pillar III: Procurement operations and market practices
Indicator 6. The country's procurement operations and practices are efficient.
Indicator 7. Functionality of the public procurement market.
Indicator 8. Existence of contract administration and dispute resolution provisions.

Pillar IV: Integrity and transparency of the public procurement system
Indicator 9. The country has effective control and audit systems.
Indicator 10. Efficiency of appeals mechanism.
Indicator 11. Degree of access to information.
Indicator 12. The country has ethics and anti-corruption measures in place.

[a] 2005 was a year of transition. In the reform of the index that followed OECD–World Bank meetings in 2004–5, pillars were reduced from 5 to 4, with some changes in the main indicators, and more substantial ones in subindicators and sub-subindicators.

Source: OECD (2010c).

References

Abed, George T., 1999. 'The Changing Role of the State.' Paper presented at the Joint African Development Bank/International Monetary Fund/World Bank Inaugural Seminar on 'Capacity Building, Governance, and Economic Reform in Africa', Abidjan, Cote d'Ivoire, 2–3 November 1999.

Abeillé, Bernard, 2003. 'Overview of Procurement Reforms in Africa.' Presentation made at the Joint WTO–World Bank Regional Workshop on Procurement Reforms and Transparency in Public Procurement for Anglophone Countries, 14–17 January 2003, Dar Es Salaam. Available at <http://www.wto.org/english/tratop_e/gproc_e/wkshop_tanz_jan03/wkshop_tanz_jan03_e.htm>.

Abeillé, Bernard, 2011. 'Last 10 years on capacity building in public procurement.' Paper prepared at the request of the Operations Policy and Country Services for the World Bank Board. Washington, DC: World Bank.

Abeillé, Bernard, 2012. 'Country Procurement Risk Assessments: achievements, and Bank's contribution to improvements.' Report to the World Bank, Africa Region (AFTPC), February. 35 pages. Available from the authors.

Acemoglu, Daron and James A. Robinson, 2012. *Why Nations Fail. The Origins of Power, Prosperity and Poverty*. New York: Crown Publishers (Random House).

Acemoglu, Daron, Simon Johnson, and James A. Robinson, 2001. 'The Colonial Origins of Comparative Development: An Empirical Investigation.' *American Economic Review*, 91: 1369–401.

Agaba, Edgar, 2003. 'Reformed Central Tender Board and Uganda Procurement Reforms. Issues and Challenges.' Paper presented at the Joint WTO–World Bank Regional Workshop on Procurement Reforms and Transparency in Public Procurement for Anglophone African countries, 14–17 January, Dar Es Salaam, Tanzania.

Agaba, Edgar and Nigel Shipman, 2009. 'Procurement Systems in Uganda'. In *International Handbook of Public Procurement*. Edited by K. V. Thai. Auerbach Publications, Chapter 18: 393–406.

Aghion, Philippe and Jean Tirole, 1997. 'Formal and Real Authority in Organizations.' *Journal of Political Economy* 105(1): 1–29.

Alchian, Armen A., 1965. 'Some Economics of Property Rights'. *Il Politico*, 30(4): 816–19. Reprinted in A. A. Alchian, *Economic Forces at Work*. Indianapolis: Liberty Press, 1977.

Araujo, Armando, 2002. 'CPAR Memorandum.' The World Bank: Washington, DC. Available at <http://web.worldbank.org/WBSITE/EXTERNAL/PROJECTS/PROCURE

MENT/0,,contentMDK:20105519~menuPK:84283~pagePK:84269~piPK:60001558~
theSitePK:84266,00.html>.

Arndt, Christiane, and Charles Oman, 2006. 'The Uses and Abuses of Governance
Indicators.' Paris: OECD. Available at <http://www.oecd.org/document/25/0,2340
,en_2649_33935_37081881_1_1_1_1,00.html>.

Arrow, Kenneth, 1963. 'Research in Management Controls: A Critical Synthesis.'
In *Management Controls: New Directions in Basic Research*, edited by. C. Bonini, R.
Jaediche, and H. Wagner, pp. 317–27. New York: McGraw-Hill.

Arrowsmith, Sue, 1998. 'Towards a Multilateral Agreement on Transparency in
Government Procurement.' *International and Comparative Law Quarterly*, 47
(October): 793–816.

Arrowsmith, Sue, Steen Treumer, Jens Fejo, and Lili Jiang, 2010. *Public Procurement
Regulation: An Introduction*. Asia Link and EuropAid, University of Nottingham.
Available at <http://www.nottingham.ac.uk/pprg/documentsarchive/
asialinkmaterials/publicprocurementregulationintroduction.pdf>.

Bajari, Patrick and Steven Tadelis, 2001. 'Incentives versus Transaction
Costs: A Theory of Procurement Contracts.' *RAND Journal of Economics*, 32(3),
Autumn: 387–407.

Bajari, P., R. McMillan, and Steven Tadelis, 2009. 'Auctions versus Negotiations in
Procurement: An Empirical Analysis.' *Journal of Law, Economics, and Organization*,
25: 372–99.

Banerjee, Niloy, Leonel Valdiva, and Mildred Mkandla, 2002. 'Is the Development
Industry Ready for Change?' *Development Policy Journal #2*. UNDP December: 131–
60, <http://www.capacity.undp.org/focus/BDP_Policy_Journal_Vol_2.pdf>.

Bates, Robert, 1987. *Essays on the Political Economy of Rural Africa*. Berkeley: University
of California Press.

Bates, Robert, 1989. *Beyond the Miracle of the Market: The Political Economy of Agrarian
Development in Rural Kenya*. Cambridge: Cambridge University Press.

Bendor, Jonathan, Ami Glazer, and Thomas Hammond, 2001. 'Theories of
Delegation.' *Annual Review of Political Science*, 4 (June): 235–69.

Bouley, Dominique, J. Fournel, and Luc Leruth, 2002. 'How do Treasury Systems
Operate in sub-Saharan Africa?' *IMF Working Paper* WP/02/58 (March). Washington,
DC: IMF.

Brookings Institution–World Bank Africa Region, 2009. 'Procurement Systems in
sub-Saharan African Countries. Hindering or Helping Improve Public Spending.
Lessons from the World Bank's 2000 to 2008 Country Procurement Assessment
Reports.'

Coase, Ronald H., 1960. 'The Problem of Social Costs.' *Journal of Law and Economics*, 3
(October): 1–44.

Coase, Ronald H., 1984. 'The New Institutional Economics.' *Journal of Institutional
and Theoretical Economics*, 140 (March): 229–31.

Coase, Ronald H., 1998. 'New Institutional Economics.' *American Economic Review*,
88(2): 72–4.

Commission of the European Communities, 1998. *Public Procurement in the European
Union*. # 143, 11 March.

Compte Olivier, Ariane Lambert-Mogiliansky, and Thierry Verdier. 1999. 'Corruption and Competition in Public Market Auctions.' Paper presented at the 9th International Anti-Corruption Conference, Durban, South Africa, 10–15 October.

Compte Olivier, Ariane Lambert-Mogiliansky, and Thierry Verdier, 2005. 'Corruption and Competition in Procurement Auctions.' *RAND Journal of Economics*, 36, 1–15.

Côte d'Ivoire, 2010. Direction Générale du Budget et des Finances, Direction des Marchés Publics de Côte d'Ivoire. Available at <http://www.dmp.finances.gouv. ci/Consultations/Statistiques/2010/Evolution_des_march_s/Statistique_annuelle/ index.html>.

Cox, Gary, Mathew McCubbins, and Mikitaka Masuyama, 2000. 'Agenda Power in the Japanese House of Representatives.' *Japanese Journal of Political Science*, 1: 1–22.

Danielson, Anders, Paul Hoebink, and Benedict Mongula, 2002. 'Are Donors Ready for Change?' *UNDP Development Policy Journal*, 2 (December): 161–78.

Davis, Lance, and Douglass C. North, 1971. *Institutional Change and American Economic Growth*. Cambridge: Cambridge University Press.

Della Porta, Donatella, and Alberto Vanucci, 1999. *Corrupt Exchanges, Actors, Resources and Mechanisms of Political Corruption*. New York: de Gruyter.

Domberger, Simon, Shirley Meadowcroft, and David Thompson, 1987. 'The Impact of Competitive Tendering on Costs of Hospital Domestic Services.' *Fiscal Studies*, 8: 39–54.

Domberger, Simon, and Stephen Rimmer, 1994. 'Competitive Tendering and Contracting in the Public Sector: A Survey.' *International Journal of the Economics of Business*, 1: 439–53.

Domberger, Simon, and Christine Hall, eds, 1995. *The Contracting Casebook: Competitive Tendering in Action*. Canberra: AGPS Press.

Domberger, Simon, Christine Hall, and Eric Ah Lik Li, 1995. 'The Determinants of Price and Quality in Competitively Tendered Contracts.' *The Economic Journal*, 105: 1454–70.

Donahue, John D., 1989. *The Privatization Decision. Public Ends, Private Means*. New York: Basic Books.

Easterly, William, 2006. *The White Man's Burden: Why the West's Efforts to Aid the Rest Have Done So Much Ill and So Little Good*. Oxford, New York: Oxford University Press.

Easterly, William, and Ross Levine, 2003. 'Tropics, Germs, and Crops: How Endowments Influence Economic Development.' *Journal of Monetary Economics*, 50: 3–40.

Ekphenkio, Sam A., 2003. 'Public Procurement Reforms: The Nigerian Experience.' Paper presented at the Joint WTO–World Bank Regional Workshop on Procurement Reforms and Transparency in Public Procurement for Anglophone Countries, 14–17 January 2003, Dar Es Salaam, Tanzania.

Engermann, Stanley L., Stephen H. Harber, and Kenneth L. Sokoloff, 2000. 'Inequality, Institutions and Differential Paths of Growth Among New World Economies.' In *Institutions, Contracts and Organizations*, edited by C. Ménard. Cheltenham and Northampton: Edward Elgar Publishing, pp. 108–35.

References

Estache Antonio, and David Martimort, 2000. 'Transaction Costs, Politics, Regulatory Institutions and Regulatory Outcomes.' In Luigi Manzetti (ed.), *Regulatory Policy in Latin America*. University of Miami: North–South Press Center, pp. 49–82.

Evenett, Simon J, 2000. 'Capital Controls: Theory, Evidence and Policy Advice: Review Article.' *International Finance*, 3(3): 471–86.

Evenett, Simon, 2002. 'Multilateral Disciplines and Government Procurement.' In Philip, Bernard, M. Hoekman, and Aaditya Matto (eds), *Development, Trade and the WTO*. Geneva: World Trade Organization, pp. 417–27.

Evenett, Simon J., 2002. 'The WTO Government Procurement Agreement: An Assessment of Current Research and Options for Reforms.' Working Paper, World Bank Conference, Cairo, May 2002.

Evenett, Simon, and Bernard Hoekman, 1999. 'Government Procurement: How does Discrimination Matter?' Working Paper. Washington, DC: World Bank.

Evenett, Simon, and Bernard Hoekman, 2000. 'Notes on the Interaction of Corruption and Discrimination in Government Procurement.' Mimeo.

Evenett, Simon, and Bernard Hoekman, 2004. 'International Cooperation and the Reform of Public Procurement Policies.' London: *CEPR Discussion Paper No. 4663*.

Evenett, Simon, and Bernard Hoekman, 2005. 'Government Procurement: Market Access, Transparency, and Multilateral Trade Rules.' *European Journal of Political Economy*, 21, Elsevier, (March): 163–83.

Finger, Matthias and Rolf Kunneke (eds), 2011. *International Handbook of Network Industries: The Liberalization of Infrastructures*. Cheltenham: Edward Elgar Publishing.

Fiorina, Morris P., 1982. 'Legislator Uncertainty, Legislative Control, and the Delegation of Legislative Power.' *The Journal of Law, Economics and Organization*. <http://jleo.oxfordjournals.org/cgi/pdf_extract/2/1/33>.

Freedom House <http://www.freedomhouse.org/report-types/freedom-world#.UwTLDmCYbmI>.

Furubotn, Eirik, and Rudolf Richter, 2005. *Institutions and Economic Theory: The Contribution of the New Institutional Economics*, 2nd edn. Ann Arbor: University of Michigan Press.

Gibbons, Robert, and John Roberts (eds), 2012. *Handbook of Organizational Economics*. Princeton: Princeton University Press.

Glaeser, Edward L., and Andrei Shleifer, 2001. 'The Rise of the Regulatory State.' *HIER Discussion Paper* No. 1934. <http://ssrn.com/abstract=290287>.

Glaeser, Edward, Simon Johnson, and Andrei Shleifer, 2001. 'Coase Versus the Coasians.' *Quarterly Journal of Economics*, 116 (3): pp. 853–99.

Gormley, William T., and Steven J. Balla, 2004. *Accountability and Performance*. Washington, DC: CQ Press.

Greif, Avner, 1993. 'Contract Enforceability and Economic Institutions in Early Trade: The Maghribi Traders.' *American Economic Review*, 83 (3): 525–47.

Guasch, José Luis, 2004. *Granting and Renegotiating Infrastructure Concessions. Doing it Right*. Washington, DC: World Bank Development Institutions.

Guasch, José Luis, and Pablo Spiller, 1999. *Managing the Regulatory Process: Design, Concepts, Issues, and the Latin America and Caribbean Story*. Washington, DC: World Bank.

Guasch, José Luis and Pablo Spiller, 1999. 'The Design of Concession-type Classifications: Competitive Reserve of Goods and Services to Government by the Private Sector in Developing Countries.' In José Luis Guasch and Pablo Spiller (eds), *Managing the Regulatory Process: Designs, Concepts, Issues, and the Latin America and Caribbean Story*. Washington, DC: World Bank, pp. 171–7.

Gurgur, Tugrul, and Anwar Shah, 2005. 'Localization and Corruption: Panacea or Pandora's Box?' *World Bank Policy Research Working Paper* 3486, Washington, DC: The World Bank.

Hadfield, Gillian K., 2005/2008. 'The Many Legal Institutions that Support Contractual Commitments.' In Claude Menard and Mary Shirley (eds), *Handbook of New Institutional Economics*. Berlin: Springer, pp. 175–204.

Hart, Oliver, Andrei Shleifer, and Robert W. Vishny, 1997. 'The Proper Scope of Government: Theory and Application to Prisons.' *The Quarterly Journal of Economics*, 112 (Nov.): 1127–61.

Hoekman, Bernard, 1998. 'Using International Institutions to Improve Public Procurement.' *World Bank Research Observer*, 13: 249–69.

Hoekman, Bernard, and Petros C. Mavroidis, 1995. 'The World Trade Organization's Agreement on Government Procurement. Expanding Disciplines, Declining Membership?' *Policy Research Working Paper*. Washington, DC: World Bank.

Hunja, Robert, 1998. 'The UNCITRAL Model Law on Procurement of Goods, Construction and Services and its Impact on Procurement Reform.' In Sue Arrowsmith and A. Davies (eds), *Public Procurement: Global Revolution*. London: Kluwer Law International, pp. 97–109.

Hunja, Robert, 2003. 'Obstacles to Public Procurement Reform in Developing Countries.' In Sue Arrowsmith and Martin Trybus (eds), *Public Procurement: The Continuing Revolution*. London: Kluwer Law International, pp. 13–22.

IMF, Statistical Appendix. <http://www.imf.org/external/pubs>.

International Country Risk Guide, ICRG. 2013. <http://www.prsgroup.com/CountryData.aspx>.

Jensen, Kirsten Ejlskov, 2004. 'Procurement Reforms in Developed and Developing Countries.' Keynote speech at International Public Procurement conference, 21–23 October 2004, Fort Lauderdale.

Jutting, Johannes, 2003. 'Institutions and Development: A Critical Review.' OECD, Working Paper no. 210. Dev (Doc) 08.

Jutting, Johannes, and Indra de Soysa, (n.d.). 'Informal Institutions and Development: Think Local, Act Global?' The OECD Development Center and the Development Assistance Committee-Network on Governance (GOVNET).

Kabbaj, Omar, 1999. 'Capacity Building, Governance, and Economic Reform in Africa.' Paper presented at the Joint African Development Bank/International Monetary Fund/The World Bank Inaugural Seminar on Capacity Building, Governance, and Economic Reform in Africa, 2–3 November 1999, Abidjan, Côte d'Ivoire..

Karangizi, Stephen, 2003. 'Regional Procurement Reform Initiative.' Paper presented at the Joint WTO–World Bank Regional Workshop on Procurement Reforms and Transparency in Public Procurement for Anglophone African countries, 14–17 January, Dar Es Salaam, Tanzania.

Kaufmann, Daniel, Aart Kraay, and Pablo Zoido-Lobaton, 1999. 'Governance matters.' Policy Research Working Paper Series 2196, The World Bank.

Kaufmann, Daniel, Aart Kraay, and Pablo Zoido-Lobaton, 2002. 'Governance Matters II. Updated Indicators for 2000/01.' Washington, DC: World Bank, Development Bank Research Group and World Bank Institute, Governance, Regulation and Finance Division.

Kaufmann, Daniel, Aart Kraay, and Massimo Mastruzzi, 2006. 'The Worldwide Governance Indicators Project: Answering the Critics.' The World Bank, September 2006.

Kelman, Steven L., 2002. 'Contracting.' Chapter 9 in Lester M. Salamon (ed.), *The Tools of Government: A Guide to the New Governance*. Oxford: Oxford University Press, pp. 282–318.

Kelman, Steven L., 2004. 'Changing Big Government Organizations: Easier than Meets the Eye?' Ash Institute for Democratic Governance and Innovation, Cambridge: Harvard University.

Kiewiet, Roderick D., and Mathew D. McCubbins, 1991. *The Logic of Delegation*. Chicago: The University of Chicago Press.

Klein, Peter, 2005/2008. 'The Make-or-Buy Decisions: Lessons from Empirical Studies.' In Claude Menard and Mary Shirley (eds), *Handbook of New Institutional Economics*. Berlin: Springer, pp. 435–64.

Klitgaard, Robert, 1988. *Controlling Corruption*. Berkeley: University of California Press.

Klitgaard, Robert, 1998. 'International Cooperation against Corruption.' *Finance & Development*, 35 (1) (March): 3–6.

Knack, Stephen, and Philip Keefer, 1995. 'Institutions and Economic Performance: Cross-Country Tests Using Alternative Institutional Measures.' *Economics and Politics*, 7 (3): 207–27.

Kunneke, Rolf, John Groenewegen, and Jean-François Auger (eds), 2009. *The Governance of Network Industries: Institutions, technology and policy in reregulated infrastructures*. Cheltenham: Edward Elgar.

Laffont, Jean-Jacques, 2005. *Regulation and Development*. Cambridge: Cambridge University Press.

Laffont, Jean-Jacques, and David Martimort, 2002. *The Theory of Incentives: The Principal–Agent Model*. Princeton: Princeton University Press.

Laffont, Jean-Jacques, and Jean Tirole, 1993. *A Theory of Incentives in Procurement and Regulation*. Cambridge: MIT Press, p. 661.

Lecat, Jean-Jacques, and Alfonso Sanchez, 2008. 'Improving the Quality of Public Spending in Sub-Saharan African Countries: Lessons from the World Bank 2000 to 2008 Country Procurement Assessment Reports.' Washington, DC: Brookings Institution.

Levy, Brian, and Pablo T. Spiller, 1994. 'The Institutional Foundations of Regulatory Commitment: A Comparative Analysis of Telecommunications Regulation.' *The Journal of Law, Economics and Organization*, 10: 201–46.

Levy, Brian, and Pablo Spiller, 1996. *Regulations, Institutions and Commitments. A Comparative Analysis of Telecommunications Regulation*. Cambridge: Cambridge University Press.

Libecap, Gary, 2005/2008. 'State Regulation of Open-access, Common-pool Resources.' In Claude Menard and Mary Shirley (eds), *Handbook of New Institutional Economics*. Berlin: Springer, pp. 545–72.

Lindbeck, Assar, 1998. *Swedish Lessons for Post-Socialist Countries*. Stockholm: University of Stockholm Institute for International Economic Studies. <http://www.iies.su.se/2.6594/publications/seminar-papers>.

Lionjanga, Armando V., 2003. 'Procurement Reforms in Botswana.' Paper presented at the Joint WTO–World Bank Regional Workshop on Procurement Reforms and Transparency in Public Procurement for Anglophone African Countries, 14–17 January, Dar Es Salaam, Tanzania.

Lupia, Arthur, and Mathew McCubbins, 1994a. 'Designing Bureaucratic Accountability'. *Law and Contemporary Problems*, 57: 91–126.

Lupia, Arthur, and Mathew McCubbins, 1994b. 'Who Controls? Information and the Structure of Legislative Decision Making.' *Legislative Studies Quarterly*, XIX, 3, (August): 361–84.

Lupia, Arthur, and Mathew McCubbins, 1994c. 'Learning from Oversight: Fire-Alarms and Police-Patrols Reconstructed.' *Journal of Law, Economics, & Organization*, 10 (April): 96–126.

Lupia, Arthur, and Mathew D. McCubbins, 1999. 'Representation of Abdication? How Citizens Use Institutions to Help Delegation Succeed.' *European Journal of Political Research*, 37: 291–307.

Lupia, Arthur, and Mathew D. McCubbins, 2000. 'When is Delegation Abdication? How Citizens Use Institutions to Make Their Agents Accountable.' *European Journal of Political Research*, 37: 291–307.

Manning, Richard, 2003. 'Development Committee Meeting: Statement.' Sixty-eighth meeting of the Development Committee (Joint Ministerial Committee of the Boards of Governors of the World Bank and the IMF on the Transfer of Real Resources to Developing Countries), OECD Development Assistance Committee (DAC), Dubai meeting (September).

Marshall, Robert C., M. J. Meurer, and J. F. Richard, 1993. 'Incentive-Based Procurement Oversight by Protest.' In *Incentives in Procurement Contracting*, edited by J. Leitzel and J. Tirole. Boulder: Westview Press pp. 39–57.

Mauro, P., 1998. 'Corruption and the Composition of Government Expenditure.' *Journal of Public Economics*, 69: 263–79.

McAfee, R. Preston, and John McMillan, 1989. 'Government Procurement and International Trade.' *Journal of International Economics*, 26: 291–308.

McCubbins, Mathew, 1985. 'The Legislative Design of Regulatory Structure.' *American Journal of Political Science*, 29(4): 721–48.

McCubbins, Mathew, 2005/2008. 'Legislative Process and the Mirroring Principle.' In Claude Menard and Mary Shirley (eds), *Handbook of New Institutional Economics*. Berlin: Springer, pp. 123–48.

McCubbins, Mathew D., and Thomas Schwartz, 1984. 'Congressional Oversight Overlooked: Police Patrols versus Fire Alarms.' *American Journal of Political Science*, 28 (194) (February): 195–79.

McCubbins, Mathew D., and D. Rodrick Kiewiet, 1991. *The Logic of Delegation–Congressional Parties and the Appropriation Process*. Chicago: University of Chicago Press.

Ménard, Claude, 1995. 'Markets as Institutions versus Organizations as Markets? Disentangling some Fundamental Concepts.' *Journal of Economic Behaviour and Organization*, 28: 161–82.

Ménard, Claude, 1996. 'Why Organizations Matter. A Journey Away From the Fairy Tale.' *Atlantic Economic Journal*, 24 (December 1996): 281–300.

Ménard, Claude, 1997. *Transaction Cost Economics – Recent Development*. Brookfield: Edward Elgar.

Ménard, Claude, 2001. 'Methodological Issues in New Institutional Economics.' *Journal of Economic Methodology*, 8 (1): 85–92.

Ménard, Claude, 2004. *L'économie des organisations*. Paris: La Découverte.

Ménard, Claude, 2005. 'A New Institutional Approach to Organization.' In C. Ménard and M. Shirley (eds), *Handbook of New Institutional Economics*. Boston–New York: Springer, pp. 281–318.

Ménard Claude, 2009. 'Why to Reform Infrastructures and with what Institutional Arrangements? The Case of Public–Private Partnerships in Water Supply.' In R. W. Kunneke, J. Groenewegen, and J. F. Augier (eds), *The Governance of Network Industries. Institutions, Technology and Policy in Reregulated Infrastructures*. Cheltenham: Edward Elgar Publishing, pp. 25–45.

Ménard, Claude, 2013. 'Hybrid Modes of Organization. Alliances, Joint Ventures, Networks, and Other "Strange" Animals.' In R. Gibbons and J. Roberts (eds), *The Handbook of Organizational Economics*. Princeton: Princeton University Press, pp. 1066–108.

Ménard, Claude and Michel Ghertman, 2009. *Regulation, Deregulation, Reregulation. Institutional Perspectives*. Cheltenham: Edward Elgar Publishing.

Ménard, Claude and Jean-Michel Oudot, 2009. 'L'évaluation préalable dans les contrats de partenariat.' *Revue Française d'Administration Publique*, 130, Summer: 349–64.

Ménard, Claude, and Mary M. Shirley (eds), 2005/2008. *Handbook of New Institutional Economics*. Boston: Springer.

Ménard, Claude and Egizio Valceschini, 2005. 'New Institutions for Governing the Agri-food Industry.' *European Review of Agricultural Economics*, 32(3): 421–40.

Milne, Robin, and Magnus McGee, 2005. 'Compulsory Competitive Tendering in the NHS: a New Look at Some Old Estimates.' *Fiscal Studies*, 13 (March): 96–111.

Moe, Terry M., 1989. 'The Politics of Bureaucratic Structure.' In John E. Chubb and Paul E. Peterson (eds), *Can the Government Govern?* Washington, DC: Brookings Institution pp. 267–329.

Mogilianski, Ariane, 1994. *Corruption in Procurement: the Economics of Regulatory Blackmail*. Research Paper in Economics, Department of Economics, University of Stockholm, (5 May).

Nee, Victor and Richard Sweedberg, 2005/2008. 'Economic Sociology and the New Institutional Economics.' In *Handbook of New Institutional Economics*, edited by C. Ménard and M. Shirley. Boston: Springer, pp. 789–818.

Niskanen, William A., 1971. *Bureaucracy and Representative Government*. Chicago: Aldine-Atherton, Inc.

Nkinga, N. S. D., 2003. 'Public Procurement Reform, the Tanzanian Experience.' Paper presented by the Secretary of the Central Tender Board (Ministry of Finance) at the Government Procurement workshop, Dar Es Salaam, Tanzania, 14–17 January 2003.

North, Douglass C., 1971. 'Institutional Change and Economic Growth.' *The Journal of Economic History*, (1), The Tasks of Economic History (March): 118–25.

North, Douglass C., 1981. *Structure and Change in Economic History*. New York: Norton and Co.

North, Douglass C., 1984. 'Government and the Cost of Exchange in History.' *Journal of Economic History*, XLIV(2) (June), pp. 255–64.

North, Douglass C., 1989. 'Institutional Change and Economic History.' *Journal of Institutional and Theoretical Economics (JITE)*, 145: 238–45.

North, Douglass C., 1990a. 'A Transaction Cost Theory of Politics.' *Journal of Theoretical Politics*, 2: 355–67.

North, Douglass C., 1990b. *Institutions, Institutional Change and Economic Performance*. Cambridge: Cambridge University Press.

North, Douglass C., 1991a. 'Towards a Theory of Institutional Change.' *Quarterly Review of Economics and Business*, 31 (Winter): 3–11.

North, Douglass C., 1991b. 'Institutions.' *Journal of Economic Perspectives*, 5 (Winter): 97–112.

North, Douglass C., 1992a. 'The New Institutional Economics and Development.' Published in *The American Economist* (Spring): 3–6 under the title 'Institutions and Economic Theory'.

North, Douglass C., 1992b. 'Transaction Costs, Institutions, and Economic Performance.' International Center for Economic Growth.

North, Douglass C., 1993. 'Economic Performance through Time.' Nobel Prize in Economics lecture. Reprint in *American Economic Review*, 84 (June): 359–68.

North, Douglass C., 1994. 'Economic Performance through Time.' *The American Economic Review*, 3 (June), 84: 359–68.

North, Douglass C., 2005. *Understanding the Process of Economic Change*. Princeton: Princeton University Press.

North, Douglass, 2005/2008. 'Institutions and the Performance of Economies Over Time.' In C. Ménard and M. Shirley (eds), *The Handbook of New Institutional Economics*. Berlin: Springer, chap. 1: 21–30.

North, Douglass C., and Barry Weingast, 2000. 'Introduction: Institutional Analysis and Economic History.' *The Journal of Economic History*, 60 (June): 414–17.

North, Douglass C., John Wallis, and Barry Weingast, 2009. *Violence and Social Orders. A Conceptual Framework for Interpreting Recorded Human History*. Cambridge: Cambridge University Press.

Obiri, Luke, 2003. 'Public Procurement Reform Strategy: Kenya Experience.' Paper presented at the Joint WTO–World Bank Regional Workshop on Procurement Reforms and Transparency in Public Procurement for Anglophone African Countries, Dar Es Salaam, 14–17 January.

Odhiambo, Walter, and Paul Kamau, 2003. 'Public Procurement: Lessons from Kenya, Tanzania and Uganda.' *Working Paper No. 208*. OECD: March 2003. <http://www. oecd.org/countries/tanzania/2503452.pdf>.

OECD, 1997. 'Public Procurement.' *SIGMA Papers: No. 3*, Paris: SIGMA/OECD. <http://www.sigmaweb.org>.

OECD, 1999. 'Competition Policy and Procurement Markets.' Directorate for Financial, Fiscal and Enterprise Affairs. Committee on Competition Law and Policy. May 1999. Paris: OECD.

OECD, 2000. 'Centralized and Decentralized Public Procurement.' *SIGMA Papers*, Paris: SIGMA/OECD.

OECD, 2002. 'The relationship between Regional Trade Agreements and Multilateral Trading System: Government Procurement.' Trade Directorate: Trade Committee, Paris.

OECD/DAC, 2003a. *Harmonising Donor Practices for Effective Aid Delivery*. Guidelines and Reference Series. Good Practice Papers. (March) <http://www.oecd.org/ development/effectiveness/20896122.pdf>.

OECD, 2003b. 'Transparency in Government Procurement: The Benefits of Efficient Governance and Orientations for Achieving It.' Working Party of the Trade Committee (May). Paris: OECD.

OECD/World Bank 2005. *Harmonising Donor Practices for Effective Aid Delivery. Vol. 3: Strengthening Procurement Practices in Developing Countries*. DAC Guidelines and Reference Series. Paris: OECD. <http://www.oecd.org/development/ effectiveness/34336126.pdf>.

OECD, 2009. *Principles for Integrity in Public Procurement*. Paris: OECD. <http://www. oecd.org/gov/ethics/oecdprinciplesforintegrityinpublicprocurement.htm>.

OECD, 2010. *Collusion and Corruption in Public Procurement*. Policy roundtable (15 October).

OECD, 2013. *Government at a Glance 2013: Procurement Data*. OECD Meeting of Leading Practitioners on Public Procurement, 11–12 February 2013, Paris: OECD.

Ostrom, Elinor, 2005/2008. 'Doing Institutional Analysis: Digging Deeper than Markets and Hierarchies.' In Claude Menard and Mary Shirley (eds), *Handbook of New Institutional Economics*. Berlin: Springer, pp. 849–66.

Pande, Rohini, and Christopher Udry, 2005. 'Institutions and Development: A View from Below.' Economic Growth Center, Yale University. Center discussion paper 928. <http://www.econ.yale.edu/~egcenter/>.

Philp, Mark, 2002. 'Why do systems produce corruption?' In *Tackling Corruption and Establishing Standards in Public Life*, Conference Report of British Council held at Corpus Christi College in Oxford, UK.

Pope, Jeremy, 2000. *Confronting Corruption: The Elements of a National Integrity System*. Transparency International Source Book 2000. Berlin: Germany.

Quinot, Geo, 2013. 'Promotion of social policy through public procurement in Africa.' In Geo Quinot and Sue Arrowsmith (eds), *Public Procurement Regulation in Africa*. Cambridge: Cambridge University Press, pp. 370–403.

Quinot, Geo, and Sue Arrowsmith, 2013. *Public Procurement Regulation in Africa*. Cambridge: Cambridge University Press.

Rege, V., 2001. 'Transparency in Government Procurement: Issues of Concern and Interest to Developing Countries.' *Journal of World Trade*, 35: 489–515.

Ripley, Randall B., and Grace A. Franklin, 1991. *Congress, the Bureaucracy, and Public Policy*. Belmont: Brooks.

Rodrik, Dany (2002). 'Trade Policy Reform as Institutional Reform.' In B. M. Hoekman, P. English, and A. Mattoo (eds), *Development, Trade, and the WTO: A Handbook*. Washington, DC: World Bank pp. 3–11.

Rodrik, Dani, 2004. 'Getting Institutions Right.' Working paper: Harvard University Paper (April).

Rodrik, Dani, Arvind Subramanian, and Francesco Trebbi, 2004. 'Institutions Rule: The Primacy of Institutions over Geography and Integration in Economic Development.' *Journal of Economic Growth*, 9: 131–65.

Rose-Ackerman, Susan, 1978. *Corruption: A Study in Political Economy*. New York: Academic Press.

Rose-Ackerman, Susan, 1999. *Corruption and Government: Causes, Consequences, and Reform*. Cambridge: Cambridge University Press.

Rose-Ackerman, Susan, 2001. 'Political Corruption and Democratic Structure.' In Arvind K. Jain (ed.), *The Political Economy of Corruption*. London and New York: Routledge, pp. 35–62.

Rose-Ackerman, Susan (ed.), 2007. *International Handbook on the Economics of Corruption*. Cheltenham-Northampton: Edward Elgar.

Sachs, Jeffrey, 2003. *Human Development Report 2003: Millennium Development Goals: A Compact Among Nations to End Human Poverty* (guest contributing editor). UNDP: New York.

Sanchez, Alfonso, and Jean-Jacques Lecat, 2008. *Improving the Quality of Public Spending in sub-Saharan African Countries. Lessons from the World Bank's 2000 to 2008 Country Procurement Assessment Reports*. Brookings Institution/World Bank.

Savedoff, William D., and Pablo T. Spiller (eds), 1999. *Spilled Water: Institutional Commitment in the Provision of Water Services*. Washington, DC: Inter-American Development Bank.

Schooner, Steven, 2002. 'Desiderata: Objectives for a System of Government Contract Law.' *Public Law and Legal Theory, Working Paper No. 37*.

Shelanski, Howard, and Peter Klein, 1995. 'Empirical Research in Transaction Cost Economics: A Survey and Assessment.' *Journal of Law, Economics and Organization*, 11(2): 335–61.

Shepsle, Kenneth, and Barry Weingast, 1995. 'Positive Theories of Congressional Institutions.' In K. Shepsle and B. Weingast (eds), *Positive Theories of Congressional Institutions*. Ann Arbor: University of Michigan, pp. 5–35.

Shirley, Mary (ed.), 2002. *Thirsting for Efficiency. The Economics and Politics of Urban Water System Reform*. Amsterdam, London and New York: Elsevier Science, Pergamon.

Shirley, Mary, 2003. 'What does Institutional Economics tell us about Development?' Paper presented at ISNIE, 2003, Budapest, Hungary.

Shirley, Mary, 2005/2008. 'Institutions and Development.' In C. Ménard and M. Shirley (eds),, *Handbook of New Institutional Economics*. Berlin–New York: Springer pp. 611–39.

References

Shirley, Mary, 2008. *Institutions and Development.* Cheltenham: Edward Elgar.

Shirley, Mary and Claude Ménard, 2002. 'Cities Awash: Reforming Water Supply in Developing Countries.' In M. Shirley (ed.), *Thirsting for Efficiency: The Economics and Politics of Urban Water Reforms.* Amsterdam: Elsevier-Pergamon, pp. 1–42.

Shleifer, Andrei, 2005. 'Understanding Regulation.' *European Financial Management,* 11: 439–45.

Shleifer, Andrei, and Robert Vishny, 1993. 'Corruption.' *The Quarterly Journal of Economics,* MIT Press 108 (August): 599–617.

Soreide, Tina, 2002. *Corruption in Public Procurement. Causes, Consequences and Cures.* Report 2002: 1. CMI Chr Michelsen Institute Reports. Bergen: Norway.

Soreide, Tina, and Susan Rose-Ackerman, 2012. 'Introduction.' In *International Handbook on the Economics of Corruption,* Vol. 2. Cheltenham: Edward Elgar Publishing pp. xiv–xxxviii.

Spiller, Pablo, 2009. 'An Institutional Theory of Public Contracts: Regulatory Implications.' In Michel Ghertman and Claude Ménard (eds), *Regulation, Deregulation, Re-regulation: Institutional Perspectives.* Cheltenham: Edward Elgar Publishing pp. 45–66.

Stock, Elisabeth, and Jan de Veen, 1996. 'Labor-based Methods for Road Works in Africa.' *World Bank Working Paper.* Washington, DC: World Bank.

Strombom, Donald, 1998. 'Corruption in Procurement.' USIA, *Economic Perspectives* (November) <http://usinfo.state.gov/journals/ites/1198/ijee/strombom.htm>.

Tanzi, Vito, 1995. 'Corruption, Arm's-Length Relationships, and Markets.' In Gianluca Fiorentini and Sam Peltzman (eds), *The Economics of Organized Crime.* Cambridge, MA: Cambridge University Press, pp. 161–80.

Tanzi, Vito, 1997. 'Corruption in the Public Finances.' Paper presented at the 8th International Anti-Corruption Conference, Lima, Peru, 7–12 September 1997.

Tanzi, Vito, 1998. 'Corruption around the World. Causes, Consequences, Scope, and Cures.' *IMF Staff Papers* 45 (December).

Tanzi, Vito, 1999. 'Governance, Corruption, and Public Finance: An Overview.' In S. Schiavo-Campo (ed.),*Governance, Corruption and Public Financial Management.* Asian Development Bank, pp. 1–17.

Tanzi, Vito, and Hamid Davoodi, 1997. 'Corruption, Public Investment and Growth.' Washington, DC: IMF. Paper presented at the 53rd Congress of the International Institute of Public Finance, Kyoto, Japan, 25–28 August 1997.

Tanzi, Vito, and Hamid Davoodi, 2002. 'Corruption, Public Investment and Growth.' In George T. Abed and Sanjeev (eds), *Governance, Corruption, and Economic Performance.* Washington, DC: International Monetary Fund, pp. 280–99.

Tirole, Jean, 1994. 'The Internal Organization of Government.' *Oxford Economic Papers,* 46: 1–29.

Trionfetti, Federico, 1997. 'Public Expenditure and Economic Geography.' *Annales d'Économie et de Statistique,* 47: 101–20.

Trionfetti, Frederico, 2000. 'Discriminatory Public Procurement and International Trade.' *The World Economy,* 23(1): 57–76.

UNCITRAL, 1994. Model Law on Procurement of Goods, Construction and Services. <http://www.uncitral.org/pdf/english/texts/procurem/ml-procurement/ml-procure.pdf>. ⁓

UNCITRAL, 2011. Model Law on Procurement of Goods, Construction and Services. United Nations Commission on International Trade Law (UNCITRAL) first version 1994. <http://www.uncitral.org/pdf/english/texts/procurem/ml-procurement/ml-procure.pdf>.

UNDP, 2003. *Human Development Report 2003: Millennium Development Goals: A Compact Among Nations to End Human Poverty*. New York: UNDP.

Urra, Francisco Javier, 2007. 'Assessing Corruption. An analytical review of corruption measurement and its problems: Perception, Error and Utility.' Georgetown University. Working Paper (May).

Verdeaux, Jean-Jacques, 2005. 'Procurement Reform in sub-Saharan Africa.' *International Government Contractor*, 2: 3–8.

Watermeyer, Ron, 2004. Project Synthesis Report: Unpacking Transparency in Government Procurement – rethinking WTO Government Procurement Agreements. *CUTS International*.

Wei, Shang-Jin, 1997. 'Gradualism versus Big Bang: Speed and Sustainability of Reforms.' *Canadian Journal of Economics*, 30(4b): 1234–47.

Wei, Shang-Jin, 2000. 'Local Corruption and Global Capital Flows.' *Brookings Papers on Economic Activity*, 2000(2): 303–54.

West, William F., 1997. 'Searching for a Theory of Bureaucratic Structure.' *Journal of Public Administration Research and Theory*, J-PART 7(October): 591–613.

Williamson, Oliver E., 1971. 'The Vertical Integration of Production: Market Failure Considerations.' *American Economic Review*, 61(May): 112–23.

Williamson, Oliver, 1975. *Markets and Hierarchies: Analysis and Antitrust Implications*. New York: Free Press.

Williamson, Oliver E., 1985. *The Economic Institutions of Capitalism*. New York: Free Press.

Williamson, Oliver E., 1994. 'Institutions and Economic Organization: The Government Perspective.' *Annual Bank Conference on Development Economics* (April).

Williamson, Oliver E., 1996. *The Mechanisms of Governance*. New York: Oxford University Press.

Williamson, Oliver E., 1999. 'Public and Private Bureaucracies: A Transaction Cost Economics Perspective.' *Journal of Law, Economics, and Organization*, 15(Spring): 306–42.

Williamson, Oliver E., 2000. 'The New Institutional Economics: Taking Stock, Looking Ahead.' *Journal of Economic Literature*, 38(3): 595–613.

Wittig, Wayne A., 1999. 'Building Value through Procurement: A Focus on Africa.' Paper presented at the International Anti-Corruption Conference in Durban, South Africa, 10–15 October 1999.

Wood, Dab B., 1989. 'Principal–Agent Models of Political Control of Bureaucracy.' *American Political Science Review*, 83(3): 970–8.

Wood, Dab B., and Richard W. Waterman, 1994. *Bureaucratic Dynamics. The Role of Bureaucracy in a Democracy*. Boulder: Westview Press.

World Bank, 2000. 'Utilization of Project Implementation Units (PIUs).' World Bank Operations Evaluation Department. Washington, DC, 2000. <http://lnweb18. worldbank.org/oed/oeddoclib.nsf/DocUNIDViewForJavaSearch/ADF4B0AD4AE0BB 25852569BA006E34B4?opendocument>.

World Bank, 2002. *Ethiopia*: CPAR. Washington, DC: World Bank.

World Bank, 2002–4. *Country Procurement Assessment Reports* (CPARs) on Ghana 2004, Ethiopia 2002, Malawi 2004, Uganda 2004, Guinea 2002. Washington, DC: World Bank.

World Bank, 2002, last revised 2011. *Country Procurement Assessment Report – Instructions.* <web.worldbank.org/WBSITE/EXTERNAL/PROJECTS/PROCUREMENT/ 0,,pagePK:84271~theSitePK:84266,00.html>

World Bank, 2004. *Guidelines. Procurement under IBRD Loans and IDA credits.* Washington, DC: World Bank. <http://siteresources.worldbank.org/ INTPROCUREMENT/Resources/ProcGuid-05-04-ev1.pdf>.

World Bank, 2005. *Expanding the Use of Country Systems in Bank-Supported Operations: Issues and Proposals.* Operations Policy and Country Services, 4 March 2005. Washington, DC: World Bank.

World Bank, 2011a. *Uganda: Note of the Regional Procurement Manager Office on 'Thresholds for Procurement Methods'.* Washington, DC: World Bank.

World Bank, 2011b. 'Last 10 years Capacity Building in Public Procurement.' 21 November 2011. Washington, DC: World Bank.

World Bank, 2012. International Bank for Reconstruction and Development, Articles of Agreement. Washington, DC. Last revised: June 2012. <http://siteresources. worldbank.org/EXTABOUTUS/Resources/IBRDArticlesOfAgreement_links.pdf>.

World Bank, 2013. *International Debt Statistics* (IDS). <http://data.worlbank.org>.

World Bank Guidelines, 2010. *Procurement Under IBRD Loans and IDA Credits.* May 2010. Washington, DC: World Bank.

World Bank International Development Association, Articles of Agreements. <http:// www.worldbank.org/ida/articles-agreement/IDA-articles-of-agreement.pdf>.

Websites to find additional bibliographical information on government procurement:
<http://www.cuts-international.org/biblio-tgp.htm>.
<http://www.ppl.nl/hugo/wtobibliographygovproc.htm>.

Author Index

Subject Index